NATIONAL

SCIENCE

EDUCATION

STANDARDS

observe

Interact

Change Learn

NATIONAL ACADEMY PRESS

WASHINGTON, DC

NATIONAL ACADEMY PRESS • 2101 Constitution Avenue, NW • Washington, DC 20418

NOTICE: The project that is the subject of this report was approved by the Governing Board of the National Research Council, whose members are drawn from the councils of the National Academy of Sciences, the National Academy of Engineering, and the Institute of Medicine. The members of the committee responsible for the report were chosen for their special competences and with regard for appropriate balance.

This report has been reviewed by a group other than the authors according to procedures approved by the Report Review Committee consisting of members of the National Academy of Sciences, the National Academy of Engineering, and the Institute of Medicine.

The National Research Council was organized by the National Academy of Sciences in 1916 to associate the broad community of science and technology with the Academy's purposes of furthering knowledge and advising the federal government. Functioning in accordance with general policies determined by the Academy, the Council has become the principal operating agency of both the National Academy of Sciences and the National Academy of Engineering in providing services to the government, the public, and the scientific and engineering communities. The Council is administered jointly by both Academies and the Institute of Medicine. Dr. Bruce Alberts and Dr. Harold Liebowitz are chairman and vice chairman, respectively, of the National Research Council.

The study was supported by the National Science Foundation, the U.S. Department of Education, the National Aeronautics and Space Administration, the National Institutes of Health, and a National Academy of Sciences president's discretionary fund provided by the Volvo North American Corporation, The Ettinger Foundation, Inc., and the Eugene McDermott Foundation.

Thirteenth Printing, October 2008

Library of Congress Cataloging-in-Publication Data

National Science Education Standards.
    p.   cm.
   "National Research Council."
   Includes bibliographical references and index.
   ISBN 0-309-05326-9
   1. Science—Study and Teaching—Standards—United States.
 I. National Research Council (U.S.).
 Q183.3.A1N364 1996
 507.1'0973—dc20   95-45778
                                     CIP

National Science Education Standards is available for sale from the National Academy Press, 2101 Constitution Avenue, NW, Box 285, Washington, DC 20055. Call 800-624-6242 or 202-334-3313 (in the Washington metropolitan area).

Cover by Grafik, Inc., Alexandria, Virginia.

Acknowledgments

The *National Science Education Standards* are the product of the efforts of many individuals and groups. We want to acknowledge

The National Committee on Science Education Standards and Assessment

The Chair's Advisory Committee

The Executive Editorial Committee

The Content Working Group

The Teaching Working Group

The Assessment Working Group

The Focus Groups

The National Review Groups

The many individuals who have served as consultants to the project

All who have diligently reviewed the drafts

The National Science Education Standards Development Team

    Angelo Collins, Director

    Rodger Bybee, Chair, Content Working Group

    Karen Worth, Chair, Teaching Working Group

    Audrey Champagne, Chair, Assessment Working Group

    Harold Pratt, Senior Program Officer

The National Research Council Staff

    Donna M. Gerardi, Special Assistant for New Initiatives

    Patrice Legro, Senior Program Officer

    Lee R. Paulson, Managing Editor

    Douglas K. Sprunger, Senior Project Assistant

    Suzanne White, Senior Project Assistant

    Tina M. Winters, Editorial Assistant

See Appendix for members of the above groups.

Major funding for this project was provided by the National Science Foundation, the U.S. Department of Education, the National Aeronautics and Space Administration, the National Institutes of Health, and a National Academy of Sciences president's discretionary fund provided by the Volvo North American Corporation, The Ettinger Foundation, Inc., and the Eugene McDermott Foundation.

National Science Education Standards is available for sale from the National Academy Press, 2101 Constitution Avenue, NW, Box 285, Washington, DC 20055. Call 800-624-6242 or 202-334-3313 (in the Washington metropolitan area).

observe

explore

encourage

understand

Contents

The world looks so different after learning science.

For example, trees are made of air, primarily. When they are burned, they go back to air, and in the flaming heat is released the flaming heat of the sun which was bound in to convert the air into tree. [A]nd in the ash is the small remnant of the part which did not come from air, that came from the solid earth, instead.

These are beautiful things, and the content of science is wonderfully full of them. They are very inspiring, and they can be used to inspire others.

Richard Feynman

Call to Action

This nation has established as a goal that all students should achieve scientific literacy. The *National Science Education Standards* are designed to enable the nation to achieve that goal. They spell out a vision of science education that will make scientific literacy for all a reality in the 21st century. They point toward a destination and provide a roadmap for how to get there.

All of us have a stake, as individuals and as a society, in scientific literacy. An understanding of science makes it possible for everyone to share in the richness and excitement of comprehending the natural world. Scientific literacy enables people to use scientific principles and processes in making personal decisions and to participate in discussions of scientific issues that affect society. A sound grounding in science strengthens many of the skills that people use every day, like solving problems creatively, thinking critically, working cooperatively in teams, using technology effectively, and valuing life-long learning. And the economic productivity of our society is tightly linked to the scientific and technological skills of our work force.

Many types of individuals will play a critical role in improving science education: teachers; science supervisors; curriculum developers; publishers; those who work in museums, zoos, and science centers; science educators; scientists and engineers across the nation; school administrators; school board members; parents; members of business and industry; and legislators and other public officials.

Individuals from all of these groups were involved in the development of the *National Science Education Standards*, and now all must act together in the national interest. Achieving scientific literacy will take time because the *Standards* call for dramatic changes throughout school systems. They emphasize a new way of teaching and learning about science that reflects how science itself is done, emphasizing inquiry as a way of achieving knowledge and understanding about the world. They also invoke changes in what students are taught, in how their performance is assessed, in how teachers are educated and keep pace, and in the relationship between schools and the rest of the community—including the nation's scientists and engineers. The *Standards* make acquiring scientific knowledge, understanding, and abilities a central aspect of education, just as science has become a central aspect of our society.

The *National Science Education Standards* are premised on a conviction that all students deserve and must have the opportunity to become scientifically literate. The *Standards* look toward a future in which all Americans, familiar with basic scientific ideas and processes, can have fuller and more productive lives. This is a vision of great hope and optimism for America, one that can act as a powerful unifying force in our society. We are excited and hopeful about the difference that the *Standards* will make in the lives of individuals and the vitality of the nation.

Richard Klausner, Chairman
National Committee on Science Education
Standards and Assessment

Bruce Alberts, President
National Academy of Sciences

observe

learn

Change

Interact

Children on the
Einstein statue at the
National Academy
of Sciences
in Washington, DC,
remind us that there is
no more important task
before us as a nation.

National Science Education Standards: An Overview

In a world filled with the products of scientific inquiry, scientific literacy has become a necessity for everyone. Everyone needs to use scientific information to make choices that arise every day. Everyone needs to be able to engage intelligently in public discourse and debate about important issues that involve science and technology. And everyone deserves to share in the excitement and personal fulfillment that can come from understanding and learning about the natural world. ▮ Scientific literacy also is of increasing importance in the workplace. More and more jobs demand advanced skills, requiring that people be able to learn, reason, think creatively, make decisions, and solve problems. An understanding of science and the processes of science contributes in an essential way to these skills. Other countries are investing heavily to create scientifically and technically literate work forces. To keep pace in global markets, the United States needs to have an equally capable citizenry.

The *National Science Education Standards* present a vision of a scientifically literate populace. They outline what students need to know, understand, and be able to do to be scientifically literate at different grade levels. They describe an educational system in which all students demonstrate high levels of performance, in which teachers are empowered to make the decisions essential for effective learning, in which interlocking communities of teachers and students are focused on learning science, and in which supportive educational programs and systems nurture achievement. The *Standards* point toward a future that is challenging but attainable—which is why they are written in the present tense.

The intent of the *Standards* can be expressed in a single phrase: Science standards for all students. The phrase embodies both excellence and equity. The *Standards* apply to all students, regardless of age, gender, cultural or ethnic background, disabilities, aspirations, or interest and motivation in science. Different students will achieve understanding in different ways, and different students will achieve different degrees of depth and breadth of understanding depending on interest, ability, and context. But all students can develop the knowledge and skills described in the *Standards*, even as some students go well beyond these levels.

By emphasizing both excellence and equity, the *Standards* also highlight the need to give students the opportunity to learn science. Students cannot achieve high levels of performance without access to skilled professional teachers, adequate classroom time,

a rich array of learning materials, accommodating work spaces, and the resources of the communities surrounding their schools. Responsibility for providing this support falls on all those involved with the science education system.

Implementing the *Standards* will require major changes in much of this country's science education. The *Standards* rest on the premise that science is an active process. Learning science is something that students do, not something that is done to them. "Hands-on" activities, while essential, are not enough. Students must have "minds-on" experiences as well.

The *Standards* call for more than "science as process," in which students learn such skills as observing, inferring, and experimenting. Inquiry is central to science learning. When engaging in inquiry, students describe objects and events, ask questions, construct explanations, test those explanations against current scientific knowledge, and communicate their ideas to others. They identify their assumptions, use critical and logical thinking, and consider alternative explanations. In this way, students actively develop their understanding of science by combining scientific knowledge with reasoning and thinking skills.

The importance of inquiry does not imply that all teachers should pursue a single approach to teaching science. Just as inquiry has many different facets, so teachers need to use many different strategies to develop the understandings and abilities described in the *Standards*.

Nor should the *Standards* be seen as requiring a specific curriculum. A curriculum is the way content is organized and presented in the classroom. The content embodied in the *Standards* can be organized and presented with many different emphases and perspectives in many different curricula.

Instead, the *Standards* provide criteria that people at the local, state, and national levels can use to judge whether particular actions will serve the vision of a scientifically literate society. They bring coordination, consistency, and coherence to the improvement of science education. If people take risks in the name of improving science education, they know they will be supported by policies and procedures throughout the system. By moving the practices of extraordinary teachers and administrators to the forefront of science education, the *Standards* take science education beyond the constraints of the present and toward a shared vision of the future.

Hundreds of people cooperated in developing the *Standards*, including teachers, school administrators, parents, curriculum developers, college faculty and administrators, scientists, engineers, and government officials. These individuals drew heavily upon earlier reform efforts, research into teaching and learning, accounts of exemplary practice, and their own personal experience and insights. In turn, thousands of people reviewed various drafts of the standards. That open, iterative process produced a broad consensus about the elements of science education needed to permit all students to achieve excellence.

Continuing dialogues between those who set and implement standards at the national, state, and local levels will ensure that the *Standards* evolve to meet the needs of students, educators, and society at large. The *National Science Education Standards* should

be seen as a dynamic understanding that is always open to review and revision.

Organization of the *Standards*

After an introductory chapter and a chapter giving broad principles and definitions of terms, the *National Science Education Standards* are presented in six chapters:

- **Standards for science teaching (Chapter 3).**
- **Standards for professional development for teachers of science (Chapter 4).**
- **Standards for assessment in science education (Chapter 5).**
- **Standards for science content (Chapter 6).**
- **Standards for science education programs (Chapter 7).**
- **Standards for science education systems (Chapter 8).**

For the vision of science education described in the *Standards* to be attained, the standards contained in all six chapters need to be implemented. But the *Standards* document has been designed so that different people can read the standards in different ways. Teachers, for example, might want to read the teaching, content, and program standards before turning to the professional development, assessment, and systems standards. Policy makers might want to read the system and program standards first, while faculty of higher education might want to read the professional development and teaching standards first, before turning to the remaining standards.

Science Teaching Standards

The science teaching standards describe what teachers of science at all grade levels should know and be able to do. They are divided into six areas:

- **The planning of inquiry-based science programs.**
- **The actions taken to guide and facilitate student learning.**
- **The assessments made of teaching and student learning.**
- **The development of environments that enable students to learn science.**
- **The creation of communities of science learners.**
- **The planning and development of the school science program.**

Effective teaching is at the heart of science education, which is why the science teaching standards are presented first. Good teachers of science create environments in which they and their students work together as active learners. They have continually expanding theoretical and practical knowledge about science, learning, and science teaching. They use assessments of students and of their own teaching to plan and conduct their teaching. They build strong, sustained relationships with students that are grounded in their knowledge of students' similarities and differences. And they are active as members of science-learning communities.

In each of these areas, teachers need support from the rest of the educational system if they are to achieve the objectives embodied in the *Standards*. Schools, districts, local communities, and states need to provide teachers with the necessary resources— including time, appropriate numbers of students per teacher, materials, and schedules. For teachers to design and implement new ways of teaching and learning science, the practices, policies, and overall culture of most schools must change. Such reforms cannot be accomplished on a piecemeal or ad hoc basis.

Considerations of equity are critical in the science teaching standards. All students are capable of full participation and of making meaningful contributions in science classes. The diversity of students' needs, experiences, and backgrounds requires that teachers and schools support varied, high-quality opportunities for all students to learn science.

Professional Development Standards

The professional development standards present a vision for the development of professional knowledge and skill among teachers. They focus on four areas:

- **The learning of science content through inquiry.**
- **The integration of knowledge about science with knowledge about learning, pedagogy, and students.**
- **The development of the understanding and ability for lifelong learning.**

- **The coherence and integration of professional development programs.**

As envisioned by the standards, teachers partake in development experiences appropriate to their status as professionals. Beginning with preservice experiences and continuing as an integral part of teachers' professional practice, teachers have opportunities to work with master educators and reflect on teaching practice. They learn how students with diverse interests, abilities, and experiences make sense of scientific ideas and what a teacher does to support and guide all students. They study and engage in research on science teaching and learning, regularly sharing with colleagues what they have learned. They become students of the discipline of teaching.

Reforming science education requires substantive changes in how science is taught, which requires equally substantive change in professional development practices at all levels. Prospective and practicing teachers need opportunities to become both sources of their own growth and supporters of the growth of others. They should be provided with opportunities to develop theoretical and practical understanding and ability, not just technical proficiencies. Professional development activities need to be clearly and appropriately connected to teachers' work in the context of the school. In this way, teachers gain the knowledge, understanding, and ability to implement the *Standards*.

Assessment Standards

The assessment standards provide criteria against which to judge the quality of assessment practices. They cover five areas:

- **The consistency of assessments with the decisions they are designed to inform.**
- **The assessment of both achievement and opportunity to learn science.**
- **The match between the technical quality of the data collected and the consequences of the actions taken on the basis of those data.**
- **The fairness of assessment practices.**
- **The soundness of inferences made from assessments about student achievement and opportunity to learn.**

In the vision described by the *Standards*, assessments are the primary feedback mechanism in the science education system. They provide students with feedback on how well they are meeting expectations, teachers with feedback on how well their students are learning, school districts with feedback on the effectiveness of their teachers and programs, and policy makers with feedback on how well policies are working. This feedback in turn stimulates changes in policy, guides the professional development of teachers, and encourages students to improve their understanding of science.

Ideas about assessments have undergone important changes in recent years. In the new view, assessment and learning are two sides of the same coin. Assessments provide an operational definition of standards, in that they define in measurable terms what teachers should teach and students should learn. When students engage in assessments, they should learn from those assessments.

Furthermore, assessments have become more sophisticated and varied as they have focused on higher-order skills. Rather than simply checking whether students have memorized certain items of information, new assessments probe for students understanding, reasoning, and use of that knowledge—the skills that are developed through inquiry. A particular challenge to teachers is to communicate to parents and policy makers the advantages of new assessment methods.

Assessments can be done in many different ways. Besides conventional paper and pencil tests, assessments might include performances, portfolios, interviews, investigative reports, or written essays. They need to be developmentally appropriate, set in contexts familiar to students, and as free from bias as possible. At the district, state, and national levels, assessments need to involve teachers in their design and administration, have well-thought-out goals, and reach representative groups to avoid sampling bias.

Assessments also need to measure the opportunity of students to learn science. Such assessments might measure teachers' professional knowledge, the time available to teach science, and the resources available to students. Although difficult, such evaluations are a critical part of the *Standards*.

Science Content Standards

The science content standards outline what students should know, understand, and be able to do in the natural sciences over the course of K-12 education. They are divided into eight categories:

- **Unifying concepts and processes in science.**
- **Science as inquiry.**
- **Physical science.**
- **Life science.**
- **Earth and space science.**
- **Science and technology.**
- **Science in personal and social perspective.**
- **History and nature of science.**

The first category is presented for all grade levels, because the understandings and abilities associated with these concepts need to be developed throughout a student's educational experiences. The other seven categories are clustered for grade levels K-4, 5-8, and 9-12.

Each content standard states that as a result of activities provided for all students in those grade levels, the content of the standard is to be understood or certain abilities are to be developed. The standards refer to broad areas of content, such as objects in the sky, the interdependence of organisms, or the nature of scientific knowledge. Following each standard is a discussion of how students can learn that material, but these discussions are illustrative, not proscriptive. Similarly, the discussion of each standard concludes with a guide to the fundamental ideas that underlie that standard, but these ideas are designed to be illustrative of the standard, not part of the standard itself.

Because each content standard subsumes the knowledge and skills of other standards, they are designed to be used as a whole. Although material can be added to the content standards, using only a subset of the standards will leave gaps in the scientific literacy expected of students.

Science Education Program Standards

The science education program standards describe the conditions necessary for quality school science programs. They focus on six areas:

- The consistency of the science program with the other standards and across grade levels.
- The inclusion of all content standards in a variety of curricula that are developmentally appropriate, interesting, relevant to student's lives, organized around inquiry, and connected with other school subjects.
- The coordination of the science program with mathematics education.
- The provision of appropriate and sufficient resources to all students.
- The provision of equitable opportunities for all students to learn the standards.
- The development of communities that encourage, support, and sustain teachers.

Program standards deal with issues at the school and district level that relate to opportunities for students to learn and opportunities for teachers to teach science. The first three standards address individuals and groups responsible for the design, development, selection, and adaptation of science programs—including teachers, curriculum directors, administrators, publishers, and school committees. The last three standards describe the conditions necessary if science programs are to provide appropriate opportunities for all students to learn science.

Each school and district must translate the *National Science Education Standards* into a program that reflects local contexts and policies. The program standards discuss the planning and actions needed to provide comprehensive and coordinated experiences for all students across all grade levels. This can be done in many ways, because the *Standards* do not dictate the order, organization, or framework for science programs.

Science Education System Standards

The science education system standards consist of criteria for judging the performance of the overall science education system. They consider seven areas:

- **The congruency of policies that influence science education with the teaching, professional development, assessment, content, and program standards.**
- **The coordination of science education policies within and across agencies, institutions, and organizations.**
- **The continuity of science education policies over time.**
- **The provision of resources to support science education policies.**
- **The equity embodied in science education policies.**
- **The possible unanticipated effects of policies on science education.**
- **The responsibility of individuals to achieve the new vision of science education portrayed in the standards.**

Schools are part of hierarchical systems that include school districts, state school systems, and the national education system. Schools also are part of communities that contain organizations that influence science education, including colleges and universities, nature centers, parks and museums, businesses, laboratories, community organizations, and various media.

Although the school is the central institution for public education, all parts of the extended system have a responsibility for improving science literacy. For example, functions generally decided at the state (but sometimes at the local) level include the content of the school science curriculum, the characteristics of the science program, the nature of science teaching, and assessment practices. These policies need to be consistent with the vision of science education described in the *Standards* for the vision as a whole to be realized.

Today, different parts of the education system often work at cross purposes, resulting in waste and conflict. Only when most individuals and organizations share a common vision can we expect true excellence in science education to be achieved.

Toward the Future

Implementing the *National Science Education Standards* is a large and significant process that will extend over many years. But through the combined and continued support of all Americans, it can be achieved. Change will occur locally, and differences in individuals, schools, and communities will produce different pathways to reform, different rates of progress, and different final emphases. Nevertheless, with the common vision of the *Standards*, we can expect deliberate movement over time, leading to reform that is pervasive and permanent.

No one group can implement the *Standards*. The challenge extends to everyone within the education system, including teachers, administrators, science teacher educators, curriculum designers, assessment specialists, local school boards, state departments of education, and the federal government. It also extends to all those outside the system who have an influence on science education, including students, parents, scientists, engineers, businesspeople, taxpayers, legislators, and other public officials. All of these individuals have unique and complementary roles to play in improving the education that we provide to our children.

Efforts to achieve the vision of science education set forth in the *Standards* will be time-consuming, expensive, and sometimes uncomfortable. They also will be exhilarating and deeply rewarding. Above all, the great potential benefit to students requires that we act now. There is no more important task before us as a nation.

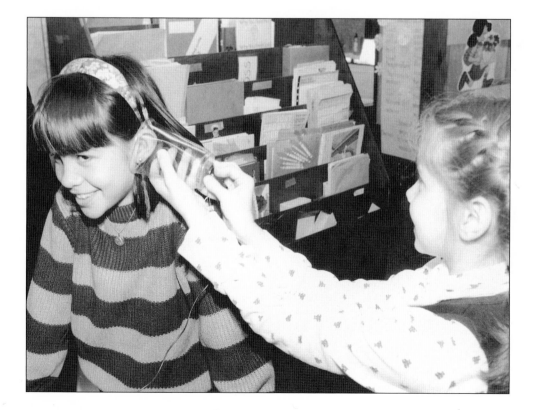

Learn
Interact

By building on the
best of current
practice, standards
aim to take us beyond
the constraints of
present structures of
schooling toward a
shared vision of
excellence.

Introduction

The *National Science Education Standards* are designed to guide our nation toward a scientifically literate society. Founded in exemplary practice and research, the *Standards* describe a vision of the scientifically literate person and present criteria for science education that will allow that vision to become reality. ▌ Why is science literacy important? First, an understanding of science offers personal fulfillment and excitement—benefits that should be shared by everyone. Second, Americans are confronted increasingly with questions in their lives that require scientific information and scientific ways of thinking for informed decision making. And the collective judgment of our people will determine how we manage shared resources—such as air, water, and national forests.

Science understanding and ability also will enhance the capability of all students to hold meaningful and productive jobs in the future. The business community needs entry-level workers with the ability to learn, reason, think creatively, make decisions, and solve problems. In addition, concerns regarding economic competitiveness stress the central importance of science and mathematics education that will allow us to keep pace with our global competitors.

Why National Science Education Standards?

The term "standard" has multiple meanings. Science education standards are criteria to judge quality: the quality of what students know and are able to do; the quality of the science programs that provide the opportunity for students to learn science; the quality of science teaching; the quality of the system that supports science teachers and programs; and the quality of assessment practices and policies. Science education standards provide criteria to judge progress toward a national vision of learning and teaching science in a system that promotes excellence, providing a banner around which reformers can rally.

A hallmark of American education is local control, where boards of education and teachers make decisions about what students will learn. National standards present criteria by which judgments can be made by state and local school personnel and communi-

ties, helping them to decide which curriculum, staff development activity, or assessment program is appropriate. National standards encourage policies that will bring coordination, consistency, and coherence to the improvement of science education: They allow everyone to move in the same direction, with the assurance that the risks they take in the name of improving science education will be supported by policies and practices throughout the system.

Some outstanding things happen in science classrooms today, even without national standards. But they happen because extraordinary teachers do what needs to be done despite conventional practice. Many generous teachers spend their own money on science supplies, knowing that students learn best by investigation. These teachers ignore the vocabulary-dense textbooks and encourage student inquiry. They also make their science courses relevant to students' lives, instead of simply being preparation for another school science course.

Implementation of the *National Science Education Standards* will highlight and promote the best practices of those extraordinary teachers and give them the recognition and support they deserve. School principals who find money in their budgets for field trips, parents whose bake-sale proceeds purchase science equipment, and publishers who are pioneering authentic assessments despite the market for multiple-choice tests will also be recognized and encouraged.

The *Standards* help to chart the course into the future. By building on the best of current practice, they aim to take us beyond the constraints of present structures of schooling toward a shared vision of excellence.

Goals for School Science

The goals for school science that underlie the *National Science Education Standards* are to educate students who are able to

- experience the richness and excitement of knowing about and understanding the natural world;
- use appropriate scientific processes and principles in making personal decisions;
- engage intelligently in public discourse and debate about matters of scientific and technological concern; and
- increase their economic productivity through the use of the knowledge, understanding, and skills of the scientifically literate person in their careers.

These goals define a scientifically literate society. The standards for content define what the scientifically literate person should know, understand, and be able to do after 13 years of school science. The separate standards for assessment, teaching, program, and system describe the conditions necessary to achieve the goal of scientific literacy for all students that is described in the content standards.

Schools that implement the *Standards* will have students learning science by actively engaging in inquiries that are interesting and important to them. Students thereby will establish a knowledge base for understanding science. In these schools, teachers will be empowered to make decisions about what students learn, how they learn it, and how resources are allocated. Teachers and students together will be members of a community focused on learning science while being nurtured by a supportive education system.

Students could not achieve the standards in most of today's schools. Implementation of the *Standards* will require a sustained, long-term commitment to change.

History of the *National Science Education Standards*

Setting national goals and developing national standards to meet them are recent strategies in our education reform policy. Support for national education standards by state governments originated in 1989, when the National Governors Association endorsed national education goals. President George Bush immediately added his support by forming the National Education Goals Panel. The support for standards was continued by the new administration after the election of President William Clinton.

The first standards appeared in 1989, when mathematics educators and mathematicians addressed the subject of national standards with two publications: *Curriculum and Evaluation Standards for School Mathematics*, by the National Council of Teachers of Mathematics (NCTM) (1989); and *Everybody Counts: A Report to the Nation on the Future of Mathematics Education*, by the National Research Council (1989). The NCTM experience was important in the development of other education standards, and it demonstrated that participation in the development of standards had to be open to all interested parties, especially those responsible for their realization.

The *National Science Education Standards* had several important precursors. In 1983, *A Nation at Risk* was published, calling for reconsideration and reform of the U.S. education system. In the 1980s, the American Chemical Society (ACS), the Biological Sciences Curriculum Study, the Education Development Center, the Lawrence Hall of Science, the National Science Resources Center (NSRC), and the Technical Education Resources Center all developed innovative science curricula. In 1989, the American Association for the Advancement of Science (AAAS), through its Project 2061, published *Science for All Americans,* defining scientific literacy for all high school graduates. Somewhat later, the National Science Teachers Association (NSTA), through its Scope, Sequence & Coordination Project, published *The Content Core.*

In the spring of 1991, the NSTA president, reflecting a unanimous vote of the NSTA board, wrote to Dr. Frank Press—president of the National Academy of Sciences and chairman of the National Research Council (NRC)—asking the NRC to coordinate development of national science education standards. The presidents of several leading science and science education associations, the U.S. secretary of education, the assistant director for education and human resources at the National Science Foundation, and the cochairs of the National Education Goals Panel all encouraged the NRC to play a leading role in the effort to develop national standards for sci-

ence education in content, teaching, and assessment. Shortly thereafter, major funding for this project was provided by the Department of Education and the National Science Foundation.

To oversee the important process of standards development, the NRC established the National Committee on Science Education Standards and Assessment (NCSESA). The committee was chaired successively by Dr. James Ebert and (from November 1993) Dr. Richard Klausner. In addition, the Chair's Advisory Committee was formed, consisting of representatives from NSTA, AAAS, ACS, NSRC, the American Association of Physics Teachers, the Council of State Science Supervisors, the Earth Science Education Coalition, and the National Association of Biology Teachers. This group helped to identify and recruit staff and volunteers for all of the committees and working groups that were required.

The oversight committee (NCSESA) first met in May 1992, and the three working groups (content, teaching, and assessment) each held intense working sessions over the summer. An initial phase of standards development lasted through the fall of 1993. During that 18 months, input to the standards was solicited from large numbers of science teachers, scientists, science educators, and many others interested in science education. More than 150 public presentations were made to promote discussion about issues in science education reform and the nature and content of science education standards.

Late in 1993, work began on the production of a complete "predraft" of the science education standards. This predraft was released in May 1994 to a selected set of focus groups for their critique and review. Each organization represented on the Chair's Advisory Committee joined by two additional organizations (NCTM and the New Standards Project) formed focus groups. In addition, the NRC convened five focus groups that were composed entirely of individuals who had not yet been involved in the project to critique the predraft. In this NRC-organized review, separate groups of experts reviewed the content, teaching, assessment, program, and system standards present in the predraft.

After the many suggestions for improving the predraft were collated and analyzed, an extensively revised standards document was prepared as a public document. This draft was released for nationwide review in December 1994. More than 40,000 copies of the draft *National Science Education Standards* were distributed to some 18,000 individuals and 250 groups. The comments of the many individuals and groups who reviewed this draft were again collated and analyzed; these were used to prepare the final *National Science Education Standards* that are presented here.

The many individuals who developed the content standards sections of the *National Science Education Standards* made independent use and interpretation of the statements of what all students should know and be able to do that are published in *Science for All Americans* and *Benchmarks for Science Literacy*. The National Research Council of the National Academy of Sciences gratefully acknowledges its indebtedness to the seminal work by the American Association for the Advancement of Science's Project 2061 and believes that

use of *Benchmarks for Science Literacy* by state framework committees, school and school-district curriculum committees, and developers of instructional and assessment materials complies fully with the spirit of the content standards.

Organization

The *Standards* are organized into seven chapters. The next chapter (Chapter 2) lays out a set of overarching principles that underlie the vision of scientific literacy for all students. These principles, as well as definitions for key terms, provide the conceptual basis for the *Standards*.

Teaching and teachers are at the center of the reform in science education. The standards for science teaching are, therefore, the standards presented first. Found in Chapter 3, these standards focus on what teachers know and do. The standards for the professional development of teachers are presented next: Chapter 4 focuses on how teachers develop professional knowledge and skill. Together, the standards in Chapters 3 and 4 present a broad and deep view of science teaching that is based on the conviction that scientific inquiry is at the heart of science and science learning.

The science education assessment standards are presented in Chapter 5 as criteria for judging the quality of assessment practices. The assessment standards are also designed to be used as guides in developing assessment practices and policy. These standards apply equally to classroom-based and externally designed assessments and to formative and summative assessments.

The content standards, organized by K-4, 5-8, and 9-12 grade levels, are found in Chapter 6. These standards provide expectations for the development of student understanding and ability over the course of K-12 education. Content is defined to include inquiry; the traditional subject areas of physical, life, and earth and space sciences; connections between science and technology; science in personal and social perspectives; and the history and nature of science. The content standards are supplemented with information on developing student understanding, and they include fundamental concepts that underlie each standard.

Chapter 7 contains the program standards, which provide criteria for judging the quality of school and district science programs. The program standards focus on issues that relate to opportunities for students to learn and teachers to teach science as described in the *Standards*.

The system standards in Chapter 8 consist of criteria for judging the performance of components of the science education system beyond the school and district: the people and entities, including education professionals and the broader community that supports the schools.

Throughout the *Standards*, examples have been supplied that are based in actual practice. These examples demonstrate that the vision is attainable. Each example includes a brief description of some of its features and lists the standards that might be highlighted by the example. Many of the examples are appropriate only if students have been involved in the type of science education described in the *Standards*. For instance, the assessment exercises are appropriate if students have had the opportunity to gain the understanding and skills being assessed.

The *National Science Education Standards* are standards for all Americans: Equity is an underlying principle for the *Standards* and should pervade all aspects of science education.

Guidance for Readers

The *National Science Education Standards* are intended to serve as a responsible guide to the creation of a scientifically literate society. Because the *Standards* present a vision for scientific literacy that will require changes in the entire education system, it is expected that different individuals will read the *Standards* for different purposes. It is important that all readers read Chapter 2, *Principles and Definitions*, which sets the foundation for the vision of science education reform. The order of reading then might differ, depending on the reader's purpose. The brief guide below (Table 1.1) provides direction for locating different types of information.

TABLE 1.1. GUIDE TO USING THE *STANDARDS*

PURPOSE

Defining scientific literacy

Principles and Definitions (Chapter 2)
Content Standards (Chapter 6)

Providing guidance for teachers and other science educators

Teaching Standards (Chapter 3)
Assessment Standards (Chapter 5)
Professional Development Standards (Chapter 4)

Clarifying the responsibility of policy makers and the community

Program Standards (Chapter 7)
System Standards (Chapter 8)

References for Further Reading

AAAS (American Association for the Advancement of Science). 1993. Benchmarks for Science Literacy. New York: Oxford University Press.

AAAS (American Association for the Advancement of Science). 1989. Science for All Americans. New York: Oxford University Press.

National Commission on Excellence in Education. 1983. A Nation at Risk: The Imperative for Educational Reform. Washington, DC: U.S. Government Printing Office.

NCTM (National Council of Teachers of Mathematics). 1989. Curriculum and Evaluation Standards for School Mathematics. Reston, VA: NCTM.

NRC (National Research Council). 1989. Everybody Counts: A Report to the Nation of the Future of Mathematics Education. Washington, DC: National Academy Press.

NSTA (National Science Teachers Association). 1992. Scope, Sequence and Coordination of Secondary School Science. Vol.1. The Content Core: A Guide for Curriculum Developers. Washington, DC: NSTA.

SCANS (Secretary's Commission on Achieving Necessary Skills). 1991. What Work Requires of Schools. Washington, DC: U.S. Government Printing Office.

observe

change

Learn

interact

Lifelong scientific
literacy begins
with attitudes
and values
established in the
earliest years.

Principles and Definitions

The development of the *National Science Education Standards* was guided by certain principles. Those principles are

- **Science is for all students.**

- **Learning science is an active process.**

- **School science reflects the intellectual and cultural traditions that characterize the practice of contemporary science.**

- **Improving science education is part of systemic education reform.**

Tension inevitably accompanied the incorporation of these principles into standards. Tension also will arise as the principles are applied in school science programs and classrooms. The following discussion elaborates upon the principles and clarifies some of the associated difficulties.

**See Teaching
Standard B,
Assessment
Standard D,
Program Standard
E, and System
Standard E**

SCIENCE IS FOR ALL STUDENTS. This principle is one of equity and excellence. Science in our schools must be for all students: All students, regardless of age, sex, cultural or ethnic background, disabilities, aspirations, or interest and motivation in science, should have the opportunity to attain high levels of scientific literacy.

The *Standards* assume the inclusion of all students in challenging science learning opportunities and define levels of understanding and abilities that all should develop. They emphatically reject any situation in science education where some people—for example, members of certain populations—are discouraged from pursuing science and excluded from opportunities to learn science.

Excellence in science education embodies the ideal that all students can achieve understanding of science if they are given the opportunity. The content standards describe outcomes—what students should understand and be able to do, not the manner in which students will achieve those outcomes. Students will achieve understanding in different ways and at different depths as they answer questions about the natural world. And students will achieve the outcomes at different rates, some sooner than others. But all should have opportunities in the form of multiple experiences over several years to develop the understanding associated with the *Standards*.

**See Program
Standard D and
System Standard D**

The commitment to science for all students has implications for both program design and the education system. In particular, resources must be allocated to ensure that the *Standards* do not exacerbate the differences in opportunities to learn that currently exist between advantaged and disadvantaged students.

LEARNING SCIENCE IS AN ACTIVE PROCESS. Learning science is something students do, not something that is done to them. In learning science, students describe objects and events, ask questions, acquire knowledge, construct explanations of natural phenomena, test those explanations in many different ways, and communicate their ideas to others.

**See Teaching
Standard B**

In the *National Science Education Standards*, the term "active process" implies physical and mental activity. Hands-on activities are not enough—students also must have "minds-on" experiences. Science

Learning science is something students do, not something that is done to them.

teaching must involve students in inquiry-oriented investigations in which they interact with their teachers and peers. Students establish connections between their current knowledge of science and the scientific knowledge found in many sources; they apply science content to new questions; they engage in problem solving, planning, decision making, and group discussions; and they experience assessments that are consistent with an active approach to learning.

Emphasizing active science learning means shifting emphasis away from teachers presenting information and covering science topics. The perceived need to include all the topics, vocabulary, and information in textbooks is in direct conflict with the central goal of having students learn scientific knowledge with understanding.

SCHOOL SCIENCE REFLECTS THE INTELLECTUAL AND CULTURAL TRADITIONS THAT CHARACTERIZE THE PRACTICE OF CONTEMPORARY SCIENCE. To develop a rich knowledge of science and the natural world, students must become familiar with modes of scientific inquiry, rules of evidence, ways of formulating questions, and

> *Students should develop an understanding of what science is, what science is not, what science can and cannot do, and how science contributes to culture.*

ways of proposing explanations. The relation of science to mathematics and to technology and an understanding of the nature of science should also be part of their education.

An explicit goal of the *National Science Education Standards* is to establish high levels of scientific literacy in the United States. An essential aspect of scientific literacy is greater knowledge and understanding of science subject matter, that is, the knowledge specifically associated with the physical, life, and earth sciences. Scientific literacy also includes understanding the nature of science, the scientific enterprise, and the role of science in society and personal life. The *Standards* recognize that many individuals have contributed to the

See definition of science literacy

traditions of science and that, in historical perspective, science has been practiced in many different cultures.

Science is a way of knowing that is characterized by empirical criteria, logical argument, and skeptical review. Students should develop an understanding of what science is, what science is not, what science can and cannot do, and how science contributes to culture.

IMPROVING SCIENCE EDUCATION IS PART OF SYSTEMIC EDUCATION REFORM. National goals and standards contribute to state and local systemic initiatives, and the national and local reform efforts complement each other. Within the larger education system, we can view science education as a subsystem with both shared and unique components. The components include students and teachers; schools with principals, superintendents, and school boards; teacher education programs in colleges and universities; textbooks and textbook publishers; communities of parents and of students; scientists and engineers; science museums; business and industry; and legislators. The *National Science Education Standards* provide the unity of purpose and vision required to focus all of those components effectively on the important task of improving science education for all students, supplying a consistency that is needed for the long-term changes required.

Perspectives and Terms in the *National Science Education Standards*

Although terms such as "scientific literacy" and "science content and curriculum" frequently appear in education discussions and in the popular press without definition, those terms have a specific meaning as used in the *National Science Education Standards.*

SCIENTIFIC LITERACY. Scientific literacy is the knowledge and understanding of scientific concepts and processes required for personal decision making, participation in civic and cultural affairs, and economic productivity. It also includes specific types of abilities. In the *National Science Education Standards*, the content standards define scientific literacy.

Scientific literacy means that a person can ask, find, or determine answers to questions derived from curiosity about everyday experiences. It means that a person has the ability to describe, explain, and predict natural phenomena. Scientific literacy entails being able to read with understanding articles about science in the popular press and to engage in social conversation about the validity of the conclusions. Scientific literacy implies that a person can identify scientific issues underlying national and local decisions and express positions that are scientifically and technologically informed. A liter-

ate citizen should be able to evaluate the quality of scientific information on the basis of its source and the methods used to generate it. Scientific literacy also implies the capacity to pose and evaluate arguments based on evidence and to apply conclusions from such arguments appropriately.

Individuals will display their scientific literacy in different ways, such as appropriately using technical terms, or applying scientific concepts and processes. And individuals often will have differences in literacy in different domains, such as more understanding of life-science concepts and words, and less understanding of physical-science concepts and words.

Scientific literacy has different degrees and forms; it expands and deepens over a lifetime, not just during the years in school. But the attitudes and values established toward science in the early years will shape a person's development of scientific literacy as an adult.

CONTENT AND CURRICULUM. The content of school science is broadly defined to include specific capacities, understandings, and abilities in science. The content standards are not a science curriculum. Curriculum is the way content is delivered: It includes the structure, organization, balance, and presentation of the content in the classroom.

The content standards are not science lessons, classes, courses of study, or school science programs. The components of the science content described can be organized with a variety of emphases and perspectives into many different curricula. The organizational schemes of the content standards are not intended to be used as curricula;

See Program Standard B

instead, the scope, sequence, and coordination of concepts, processes, and topics are left to those who design and implement curricula in science programs.

Curricula often will integrate topics from different subject-matter areas—such as life and physical sciences—from different content standards—such as life sciences and sci-

Scientific literacy implies that a person can identify scientific issues underlying national and local decisions and express positions that are scientifically and technologically informed.

ence in personal and social perspectives—and from different school subjects—such as science and mathematics, science and language arts, or science and history.

KNOWLEDGE AND UNDERSTANDING. Implementing the *National Science Education Standards* implies the acquisition of scientific knowledge and the development of understanding. Scientific knowledge refers to facts, concepts, principles, laws, theories, and models and can be acquired in many ways. Understanding science requires that an individual integrate a complex structure of many types of knowledge, including the ideas of science, relationships between ideas, reasons for these relationships, ways to use the ideas to explain and predict other natural phenomena, and ways to apply them to many events. Understanding encompasses the ability to use knowledge, and it entails the ability to distinguish between what is and what is not a scientific idea. Developing understanding

presupposes that students are actively engaged with the ideas of science and have many experiences with the natural world.

INQUIRY. Scientific inquiry refers to the diverse ways in which scientists study the natural world and propose explanations based on the evidence derived from their work. Inquiry also refers to the activities of students in which they develop knowledge and understanding of scientific ideas, as well as an understanding of how scientists study the natural world.

See Content Standards A & G (all grade levels)

See Teaching Standard B

Inquiry is a multifaceted activity that involves making observations; posing questions; examining books and other sources of information to see what is already known; planning investigations; reviewing what is already known in light of experimental evidence; using tools to gather, analyze, and interpret data; proposing answers, explanations, and predictions; and communicating the results. Inquiry requires identification of assumptions, use of critical and logical thinking, and consideration of alternative explanations. Students will engage in selected aspects of inquiry as they learn the scientific way of knowing the natural world, but they also should develop the capacity to conduct complete inquiries.

Although the *Standards* emphasize inquiry, this should not be interpreted as recommending a single approach to science teaching. Teachers should use different strategies to develop the knowledge, understandings, and abilities described in the content standards. Conducting hands-on science activities does not guarantee inquiry, nor is reading about science incompatible with inquiry. Attaining the understandings and abilities described in Chapter 6 cannot be achieved by any single teaching strategy or learning experience.

SCIENCE AND TECHNOLOGY. As used in the *Standards*, the central distinguishing characteristic between science and technology is a difference in goal: The goal of science is to understand the natural world, and the goal of technology is to make modifications in the world to meet human needs. Technology as design is included in the *Standards* as parallel to science as inquiry.

Technology and science are closely related. A single problem often has both scientific and technological aspects. The need to answer questions in the natural world drives the development of technological products; moreover, technological needs can drive scientific research. And technological products, from pencils to computers, provide tools that promote the understanding of natural phenomena.

See Content Standard E (all grade levels)

The use of "technology" in the *Standards* is not to be confused with "instructional technology," which provides students and teachers with exciting tools—such as computers—to conduct inquiry and to understand science.

Additional terms important to the *National Science Education Standards*, such as "teaching," "assessment," and "opportunity to learn," are defined in the chapters and sections where they are used. Throughout, we have tried to avoid using terms that have different meanings to the many different groups that will be involved in implementing the *Standards*.

References for Further Reading

AAUW (American Association of University Women). 1992. How Schools Shortchange Girls. Washington, DC: AAUW.

Beane, D.B. 1988. Mathematics and Science: Critical Filters for the Future of Minority Students. Washington, DC: The Mid-Atlantic Center for Race Equity.

Brown, A.L. 1992. Design experiments: Theoretical and methodological challenges in creating complex interventions in classroom settings. The Journal of the Learning Sciences, 2: 141-178.

Brown, J.S., A. Collins, and P. Duguid. 1989. Situated cognition and the culture of learning. Educational Researcher, 18: 32-42.

Bruer, J.T. 1993. Schools for Thought: A Science of Learning in the Classroom. Cambridge, MA: The MIT Press/Bradford Books.

Bybee, R.W. 1994. Reforming Science Education: Social Perspectives and Personal Reflections. New York: Teachers College Press, Columbia University.

Bybee, R.W., and G. DeBoer. 1994. Research as goals for the science curriculum. In Handbook on Research on Science Teaching and Learning, D. Gabel, ed. New York: MacMillan Publishing Company.

Champagne, A.B., and L.E. Hornig. 1987. Practical Application of Theories About Learning. In This Year in School Science 1987: The Report of the National Forum for School Science, A.B. Champagne and L.E. Hornig, eds. Washington, DC: American Association for the Advancement of Science.

Clewell, B.C., B.T. Anderson, and M.E. Thorpe. 1992. Breaking the Barriers: Helping Female and Minority Students Succeed in Mathematics and Science. San Francisco: Jossey-Bass.

DeBoer, G. 1991. A History of Ideas in Science Education: Implications for Practice. New York: Teachers College Press.

Forman, E.A., and C.B. Cazden. 1985. Exploring Vygotskian perspectives in education: The cognitive value of peer interaction. In Culture, Communication, and Cognition: Vygotskian Perspectives, J.V. Wertsch, ed: 323-347. New York: Cambridge University Press.

Frederiksen, N. 1984. Implications of cognitive theory for instruction in problem solving. Review of Educational Research, 54: 363-407.

Greeno, J.G. 1989. Situations, mental models, and generative knowledge. In Complex Information Processing: The Impact of Herbert A. Simon. D. Klahr and K. Kotovsky eds. Hillsdale, NJ: Lawrence Erlbaum and Associates.

Gross, P. R., and N. Levitt. 1994. Higher Superstition: The Academic Left and Its Quarrels With Science. Baltimore, MD: Johns Hopkins University Press.

Holton, G. 1993. Science and Anti-science. Cambridge, MA: Harvard University Press.

Johnson, D.W., and F. Johnson. 1994. Joining Together: Group Theory and Group Skills, 5th ed. Boston: Allyn and Bacon.

Kahle, J.B. 1988. Gender and science education II. In Development and Dilemmas in Science Education, P. Fensham, ed. New York: Falmer Press.

Lee, O., and C.W. Anderson. 1993. Task engagement and conceptual change in middle school science classrooms. American Educational Research Journal, 30: 585-610.

NCTM (National Council of Teachers of Mathematics). 1989. Curriculum and Evaluation Standards for School Mathematics. Reston, VA: NCTM.

NRC (National Research Council). 1989. High-School Biology Today and Tomorrow. Washington, DC: National Academy Press.

NRC (National Research Council). 1987. Education and Learning to Think, L. Resnick, ed. Washington, DC: National Academy Press.

NSF (National Science Foundation). 1992. The Influence of Testing on Teaching Math and Science in Grades 4-12: Report of a Study. Chestnut Hill, MA: Center for the Study of Testing, Evaluation, and Educational Policy.

Oakes, J. 1990. Lost Talent: The Underparticipation of Women, Minorities, and Disabled Persons in Science. Santa Monica, CA: RAND Corporation.

Ohlsson, S. 1992. The Cognitive Skill of Theory Articulation: A Neglected Aspect of Science Education. Science & Education, 1 (2): 121-92.

Piaget, J. 1970. Genetic Epistemology. Translated by Eleanor Duckworth. New York: Columbia University Press.

Piaget, J. 1954. The Construction of Reality in the Child. Translated by M. Cook. New York: Ballantine Books.

Resnick, L.B., and L.E. Klopfer, eds. 1989. Toward the Thinking Curriculum: Current Cognitive Research. Alexandria, VA: Association for Supervision and Curriculum Development.

Shayer, M., and P. Adey. 1981. Towards a Science of Science Teaching: Cognitive Development and Curriculum Demand. London: Heinemann Educational Books.

Tyson-Bernstein, H. 1988. America's Textbook Fiasco: A Conspiracy of Good Intentions. Washington, DC: Council for Basic Education.

Vera, A.H., and H.A. Simon. 1993. Situated action: a symbolic interpretation. Cognitive Science, 17: 7-48.

White, B.Y. 1993. Thinkertools: Causal models, conceptual change, and science education. Cognition and Instruction, 10: 1-100.

observe

Change

Learn

Interact

Envisioned is a new order where teachers and students can work together as active learners.

Science Teaching Standards

Science teaching is a complex activity that lies at the heart of the vision of science education presented in the *Standards*. The teaching standards provide criteria for making judgments about progress toward the vision; they describe what teachers of science at all grade levels should understand and be able to do. ▌ To highlight the importance of teachers in science education, these standards are presented first. However, to attain the vision of science education described in the *Standards*, change is needed in the entire system. Teachers are central to education, but they must not be placed in the position of being solely responsible for reform. Teachers will need to work within a collegial, organizational, and policy context that is supportive of good science teaching. In addition, students must accept and share responsibility for their own learning.

In the vision of science education portrayed by the *Standards*, effective teachers of science create an environment in which they and students work together as active learners. While students are engaged in learning about the natural world and the scientific principles needed to understand it, teachers are working with their colleagues to expand their knowledge about science teaching. To teach science as portrayed by the *Standards*, teachers must have theoretical and practical knowledge and abilities about science, learning, and science teaching.

The standards for science teaching are grounded in five assumptions.

- **The vision of science education described by the *Standards* requires changes throughout the entire system.**
- **What students learn is greatly influenced by how they are taught.**
- **The actions of teachers are deeply influenced by their perceptions of science as an enterprise and as a subject to be taught and learned.**
- **Student understanding is actively constructed through individual and social processes.**
- **Actions of teachers are deeply influenced by their understanding of and relationships with students.**

THE VISION OF SCIENCE EDUCATION DESCRIBED BY THE STANDARDS REQUIRES CHANGES THROUGHOUT THE ENTIRE SYSTEM. The educational system must act to sustain effective teaching. The routines, rewards, structures, and expectations of the system must endorse the vision of science teaching portrayed by the *Standards*. Teachers must be provided with resources, time, and opportunities to make

change as described in the program and system standards. They must work within a framework that encourages their efforts.

The changes required in the educational system to support quality science teaching are major ones. Each component of the system will change at a different pace, and most changes will be incremental. Nonetheless, changes in teaching must begin before all of the systemic problems are solved.

WHAT STUDENTS LEARN IS GREATLY INFLUENCED BY HOW THEY ARE TAUGHT. The decisions about content and activities that teachers make, their interactions with students, the selection of assessments, the habits of mind that teacher

Teachers must have theoretical and practical knowledge and abilities about science, learning, and science teaching.

demonstrate and nurture among their students, and the attitudes conveyed wittingly and unwittingly all affect the knowledge, understanding, abilities, and attitudes that students develop.

THE ACTIONS OF TEACHERS ARE DEEPLY INFLUENCED BY THEIR PERCEPTIONS OF SCIENCE AS AN ENTERPRISE AND AS A SUBJECT TO BE TAUGHT AND LEARNED. All teachers of science have implicit and explicit beliefs about science, learning, and teaching. Teachers can be effective guides for students learning science only if they have the opportunity to examine their own beliefs, as well as to develop an understanding of the tenets on which the *Standards* are based.

See Professional Development Standard A

STUDENT UNDERSTANDING IS ACTIVE-LY CONSTRUCTED THROUGH INDIVID-UAL AND SOCIAL PROCESSES. In the same way that scientists develop their knowledge and understanding as they seek answers to questions about the natural world, students develop an understanding of the natural world when they are actively engaged in scientific inquiry—alone and with others.

See Teaching
Standard D

ACTIONS OF TEACHERS ARE DEEPLY INFLUENCED BY THEIR UNDERSTAND-ING OF AND RELATIONSHIPS WITH STUDENTS. The standards for science teaching require building strong, sustained relationships with students. These relation-ships are grounded in knowledge and awareness of the similarities and differ-ences in students' backgrounds, experi-ences, and current views of science. The diversity of today's student population and the commitment to science education for all requires a firm belief that all students can learn science.

The Standards

Dividing science teaching into separate components oversimplifies a complex process; nevertheless, some division is required to manage the presentation of cri-teria for good science teaching, accepting that this leaves some overlap. In addition, the teaching standards cannot possibly address all the understanding and abilities that masterful teachers display. Therefore, the teaching standards focus on the qualities that are most closely associated with science

teaching and with the vision of science edu-cation described in the *Standards*.

The teaching standards begin with a focus on the long-term planning that teachers do. The discussion then moves to facilitating learning, assessment, and the classroom envi-ronment. Finally, the teaching standards address the teacher's role in the school com-munity. The standards are applicable at all grade levels, but the teaching at different grade levels will be different to reflect the capabilities and interests of students at different ages.

Teachers across the country will find some of their current practices reflected

A challenge to teachers of science is to balance and integrate immediate needs with the intentions of the yearlong framework of goals.

below. They also will find criteria that sug-gest new and different practices. Because change takes time and takes place at the local level, differences in individuals, schools, and communities will be reflected in different pathways to reform, different rates of progress, and different emphases. For example, a beginning teacher might focus on developing skills in managing the learning environment rather than on long-term planning, whereas a more experi-enced group of teachers might work together on new modes for assessing stu-dent achievement. Deliberate movement over time toward the vision of science teaching described here is important if reform is to be pervasive and permanent.

TEACHING STANDARD A:

Teachers of science plan an inquiry-based science program for their students. In doing this, teachers

- **Develop a framework of yearlong and short-term goals for students.**
- **Select science content and adapt and design curricula to meet the interests, knowledge, understanding, abilities, and experiences of students.**
- **Select teaching and assessment strategies that support the development of student understanding and nurture a community of science learners.**
- **Work together as colleagues within and across disciplines and grade levels.**

DEVELOP A FRAMEWORK OF YEARLONG AND SHORT-TERM GOALS FOR STUDENTS. All teachers know that planning is a critical component of effective teaching. One important aspect of planning is setting goals. In the vision of science education described in the *Standards*, teachers of science take responsibility for setting yearlong and short-term goals; in doing so, they adapt school and district program goals, as well as state and national goals, to the experiences and interests of their students individually and as a group.

Once teachers have devised a framework of goals, plans remain flexible. Decisions are visited and revisited in the light of experience. Teaching for understanding requires responsiveness to students, so activities and strategies are continuously adapted and refined to address topics arising from student inquiries and experiences, as well as school, community, and national events.

Teachers also change their plans based on the assessment and analysis of student achievement and the prior knowledge and beliefs students have demonstrated. Thus, an inquiry might be extended because it sparks the interest of students, an activity might be added because a particular concept has not been understood, or more group work might be incorporated into the plan to encourage communication. A challenge to teachers of science is to balance and integrate immediate needs with the intentions of the yearlong framework of goals.

During planning, goals are translated into a curriculum of specific topics, units, and sequenced activities that help students make sense of their world and understand the fundamental ideas of science. The content standards, as well as state, district, and school frameworks, provide guides for teachers as they select specific science topics. Some frameworks allow teachers choices in determining topics, sequences, activities, and materials. Others mandate goals, objectives, content, and materials. In either case, teachers examine the extent to which a curriculum includes inquiry and direct experimentation as methods for developing understanding. In planning and choosing curricula, teachers strive to balance breadth of topics with depth of understanding.

See Program Standard B

SELECT SCIENCE CONTENT AND ADAPT AND DESIGN CURRICULA TO MEET THE INTERESTS, KNOWLEDGE, UNDERSTANDING, ABILITIES, AND EXPERIENCES OF STUDENTS. In determining the specific science content and activities that make up a curriculum, teachers consider the students who will be learning the science. Whether working with mandated content and activities, selecting from extant activities, or creating original activities, teachers plan to meet the particular interests, knowledge, and skills of their students and build on their questions and ideas. Such decisions rely heavily on a teacher's knowledge of students' cognitive potential, developmental level, physical attributes, affective development, and motivation—and how they learn. Teachers are aware of and understand common naive concepts in science for given grade levels, as well as the cultural and experiential background of students and the effects these have on learning. Teachers also consider their own strengths and interests and take into account available resources in the local environment. For example, in Cleveland, the study of Lake Erie, its pollution, and

See Program Standard E and System Standard E

Inquiry into authentic questions generated from student experiences is the central strategy for teaching science.

cleanup is an important part of a science curriculum, as is the study of earthquakes in the Los Angeles area. Teachers can work with local personnel, such as those at science-rich centers (museums, industries, universities, etc.), to plan for the use of exhibits and educational programs that enhance the study of a particular topic.

SELECT TEACHING AND ASSESSMENT STRATEGIES THAT SUPPORT THE DEVELOPMENT OF STUDENT UNDERSTANDING AND NURTURE A COMMUNITY OF SCIENCE LEARNERS. Over the years, educators have developed many

teaching and learning models relevant to classroom science teaching. Knowing the strengths and weaknesses of these models, teachers examine the relationship between the science content and how that content is to be taught. Teachers of science integrate a sound model of teaching and learning, a practical structure for the sequence of activities, and the content to be learned.

Inquiry into authentic questions generated from student experiences is the central strategy for teaching science. Teachers focus inquiry predominantly on real phenomena, in classrooms, outdoors, or in laboratory settings, where students are given investigations or guided toward fashioning investigations that are demanding but within their capabilities.

As more complex topics are addressed, students cannot always return to basic phenomena for every conceptual understanding. Nevertheless, teachers can take an inquiry approach as they guide students in acquiring and interpreting information from sources such as libraries, government documents, and computer databases—or as they gather information from experts from industry, the community, and government. Other teaching strategies rely on teachers, texts, and secondary sources—such as video, film, and computer simulations. When secondary sources of scientific knowledge are used, students need to be made aware of the processes by which the knowledge presented in these sources was acquired and to understand that the sources are authoritative and accepted within the scientific community.

Another dimension of planning relates to the organization of students. Science often is a collaborative endeavor, and all science

See Teaching Standard E

depends on the ultimate sharing and debating of ideas. When carefully guided by teachers to ensure full participation by all, interactions among individuals and groups in the classroom can be vital in deepening the understanding of scientific concepts and the nature of scientific endeavors. The size of a group depends on age, resources, and the nature of the inquiry.

Teachers of science must decide when and for what purposes to use whole-class instruction, small-group collaboration, and individual work. For example, investigating simple electric circuits initially might best be explored individually. As students move toward building complex circuits, small group interactions might be more effective to share ideas and materials, and a full-class discussion then might be used to verify experiences and draw conclusions.

The plans of teachers provide opportunities for all students to learn science. Therefore, planning is heavily dependent on the teacher's awareness and understanding of the diverse abilities, interests, and cultural backgrounds of students in the classroom. Planning also takes into account the social structure of the classroom and the challenges posed by diverse student groups. Effective planning includes sensitivity to student views that might conflict with current scientific knowledge and strategies that help to support alternative ways of making sense of the world while developing the scientific explanations.

Teachers plan activities that they and the students will use to assess the understanding and abilities that students hold when they begin a learning activity. In addition, appropriate ways are designed to monitor the development of knowledge, understanding, and abilities as students pursue their work throughout the academic year.

WORK TOGETHER AS COLLEAGUES WITHIN AND ACROSS DISCIPLINES AND GRADE LEVELS. Individual and collective planning is a cornerstone of science teaching; it is a vehicle for professional support and growth. In the vision of science education described in the *Standards*, many planning decisions are made by groups of teachers at grade and building levels to construct coherent and articulated programs within and across grades. Schools must provide teachers with time and access to their colleagues and others who can serve as resources if collaborative planning is to occur.

See Program
Standard F

TEACHING STANDARD B:
Teachers of science guide and facilitate learning. In doing this, teachers

- Focus and support inquiries while interacting with students.
- Orchestrate discourse among students about scientific ideas.
- Challenge students to accept and share responsibility for their own learning.
- Recognize and respond to student diversity and encourage all students to participate fully in science learning.
- Encourage and model the skills of scientific inquiry, as well as the curiosity, openness to new ideas and data, and skepticism that characterize science.

Coordinating people, ideas, materials, and the science classroom environment are difficult, continual tasks. This standard focuses on the work that teachers do as they implement the plans of Standard A in the classroom.

Teachers of science constantly make decisions, such as when to change the direction of a discussion, how to engage a particular

At all stages of inquiry, teachers guide, focus, challenge, and encourage student learning.

student, when to let a student pursue a particular interest, and how to use an opportunity to model scientific skills and attitudes. Teachers must struggle with the tension between guiding students toward a set of predetermined goals and allowing students to set and meet their own goals. Teachers face a similar tension between taking the time to allow students to pursue an interest in greater depth and the need to move on to new areas to be studied. Furthermore, teachers constantly strike a balance among the demands of the understanding and ability to be acquired and the demands of student-centered developmental learning. The result of making these decisions is the enacted curriculum—the planned curriculum as it is modified and shaped by the interactions of students, teachers, materials, and daily life in the classroom.

FOCUS AND SUPPORT INQUIRIES.

See Content Standard A (all grade levels)
Student inquiry in the science classroom encompasses a range of activities. Some activities provide a basis for observation, data collection, reflection, and analysis of firsthand events and phenomena. Other activities encourage the critical analysis of

secondary sources—including media, books, and journals in a library.

In successful science classrooms, teachers and students collaborate in the pursuit of ideas, and students quite often initiate new activities related to an inquiry. Students formulate questions and devise ways to answer them, they collect data and decide how to represent it, they organize data to generate knowledge, and they test the reliability of the knowledge they have generated. As they proceed, students explain and justify their work to themselves and to one another, learn to cope with problems such as the limitations of equipment, and react to challenges posed by the teacher and by classmates. Students assess the efficacy of their efforts—they evaluate the data they have collected, re-examining or collecting more if necessary, and making statements about the generalizability of their findings. They plan and make presentations to the rest of the class about their work and accept and react to the constructive criticism of others.

See Teaching Standard E

At all stages of inquiry, teachers guide, focus, challenge, and encourage student learning. Successful teachers are skilled observers of students, as well as knowledgeable about science and how it is learned. Teachers match their actions to the particular needs of the students, deciding when and how to guide—when to demand more rigorous grappling by the students, when to provide information, when to provide particular tools, and when to connect students with other sources.

In the science classroom envisioned by the *Standards*, effective teachers continually create opportunities that challenge students and promote inquiry by asking questions.

See Program Standard E and System Standard E

Earthworms

Ms. F. is planning and teaching a unit that provides students with the opportunity to understand the science in the K-4 Life Science Content Standard. She plans to do this through inquiry. Of the many organisms she might choose to use, she selects an organism that is familiar to the students, one that they have observed in the schoolyard. As a life-long learner, Ms. F. uses the resources in the community, a local museum, to increase her knowledge and help with her planning. She also uses the resources of the school—materials available for science and media in the school library. She models the habits and values of science by the care provided to the animals. Students write and draw their observations. Developing communication skills in science and in language arts reinforce one another.

[This example highlights some elements of Teaching Standards A, B, D, and E; Professional Development Standard C; K-4 Content Standards A and C; Program Standards B and D; and System Standard D.]

While studying a vacant lot near school, several of Ms. F.'s third-grade students became fascinated with earthworms. Although she had never used earthworms in the science classroom before, and she knew she could use any of a number of small animals to meet her goals, Ms. F. felt she could draw from her experience and knowledge working with other small animals in the classroom. She called the local museum of natural history to talk with personnel to be sure she knew enough about earthworms to care for them and to guide the children's explorations. She learned that it was relatively easy to house earthworms over long periods. She was told that if she ordered the earthworms from a biological supply house, they would come with egg cases and baby earthworms and the children would be able to observe the adult earthworms, the egg cases, the young earthworms, and some of the animal's habits.

Before preparing a habitat for the earthworms, students spent time outdoors closely examining the environment where the worms had been found. This fieldtrip was followed by a discussion about important aspects of keeping earthworms in the classroom: How would students create a place for the earthworms that closely resembled the natural setting? An earthworm from outside was settled into a large terrarium away from direct sun; black paper was secured over the sides of the terrarium into which the children had put soil, leaves, and grass. A week later the earthworms arrived from the supply company and were added to the habitat.

Ms. F. had been thinking about what she wanted the children to achieve and the guidance she needed to give. She wanted the students to become familiar with the basic needs of the earthworms and how to care for them. It was important that the children develop a sense of responsibility toward living things as well as enhance their skills of observation and recording. She also felt that this third grade class would be able to design simple experiments that would help the students learn about some of the behaviors of the earthworms.

In the first 2 weeks, the students began closely observing the earthworms and recording their habits. The students recorded what the earthworms looked like, how they moved, and what the students thought the earthworms were doing. The students described color and shape; they weighed and measured the earthworms and kept a large chart of the class data, which provoked a discussion about variation. They observed and described how the earthworms moved on a surface and in the soil. Questions and ideas about the earthworms came up continually. Ms. F. recorded these thoughts on a chart, but she kept the students focused on their descriptive work. Then Ms. F. turned to what else the children might want to find out about earthworms and how they might go about doing so. Among the many questions on the chart were: How do the earthworms have babies? Do they like to live in some kinds of soil better than others? What are those funny things on the top of the soil? Do they really like the dark? How do they go through the dirt? How big can an earthworm get?

Ms. F. let all the questions flow in a discussion, and then she asked the students to divide into groups and to see if they could come up with a question or topic that they would like to explore. When the class reconvened, each group shared what they were going to explore and how they might investigate the topic. The students engaged in lively discussion as they shared their proposed explorations. Ms. F. then told the students that they should think about how they might conduct their investigations and that they would share these ideas in the next class.

A week later, the investigations were well under way. One group had chosen to investigate the life cycle of earthworms and had found egg cases in the soil. While waiting for baby earthworms to hatch, they had checked books about earthworms out of the library. They had also removed several very young (very small) earthworms from the terrarium and were trying to decide how they might keep track of the growth.

Two groups were investigating what kind of environment the earthworms liked best. Both were struggling with several variables at once—moisture, light, and temperature. Ms. F. planned to let groups struggle before suggesting that students focus on one variable at a time. She hoped they might come to this idea on their own.

A fourth group was trying to decide what the earthworms liked to eat. The students had been to the library twice and now were ready to test some foods.

The last two groups were working on setting up an old ant farm with transparent sides to house earthworms, because they were interested in observing what the earthworms actually did in the soil and what happened in different kinds of soil.

In their study of earthworms, Mrs. F.'s students learned about the basic needs of animals, about some of the structures and functions of one animal, some features of animal behavior, and about life cycles. They also asked and answered questions and communicated their understandings to one another. They observed the outdoors and used the library and a classroom well equipped to teach science.

Although open exploration is useful for students when they encounter new materials and phenomena, teachers need to intervene to focus and challenge the students, or the exploration might not lead to understanding. Premature intervention deprives students of the opportunity to confront problems and find solutions, but intervention that occurs too late risks student frustration. Teachers also must decide when to challenge students to make sense of their experiences: At these points, students should be asked to explain, clarify, and critically examine and assess their work.

ORCHESTRATE DISCOURSE AMONG STUDENTS ABOUT SCIENTIFIC IDEAS. An important stage of inquiry and of student science learning is the oral and written discourse that focuses the attention of students on how they know what they know and how their knowledge connects to larger ideas, other domains, and the world beyond the classroom. Teachers directly support and guide this discourse in two ways: They require students to record their work—teaching the necessary skills as appropriate—and they promote many different forms of communication (for example, spoken, written, pictorial, graphic, mathematical, and electronic).

Using a collaborative group structure, teachers encourage interdependency among group members, assisting students to work together in small groups so that all participate in sharing data and in developing group reports. Teachers also give groups opportunities to make presentations of their work and to engage with their classmates in explaining, clarifying, and justifying what they have learned. The teacher's role in these small and larger group interactions is to listen, encourage broad participation, and judge how to guide discussion—determining ideas to follow, ideas to question, information to provide, and connections to make. In the hands of a skilled teacher, such group work leads students to recognize the expertise that different members of the group bring to each endeavor and the greater value of evidence and argument over personality and style.

CHALLENGE STUDENTS TO ACCEPT AND SHARE RESPONSIBILITY FOR THEIR OWN LEARNING. Teachers make it clear that each student must take responsibility for his or her work. The teacher also creates opportunities for students to take responsibility for their own learning, individually and as members of groups. Teachers do so by supporting student ideas and questions and by encouraging students to pursue them. Teachers give individual students active roles in the design and implementation of investigations, in the preparation and presentation of student work to their peers, and in student assessment of their own work.

RECOGNIZE AND RESPOND TO STUDENT DIVERSITY AND ENCOURAGE ALL STUDENTS TO PARTICIPATE FULLY IN SCIENCE LEARNING. In all aspects of science learning as envisioned by the *Standards*, skilled teachers recognize the diversity in their classes and organize the classroom so that all students have the opportunity to participate fully. Teachers monitor the participation of all students, carefully determining, for instance, if all members of a collaborative group are working with materials or if one student is making all the decisions. This monitoring can be particularly important in classes of diverse students, where social issues of status and authority can be a factor.

Teachers of science orchestrate their classes so that all students have equal opportunities to participate in learning activities. Students with physical disabilities might

Teachers who are enthusiastic, interested, and who speak of the power and beauty of scientific understanding instill in their students some of those same attitudes.

require modified equipment; students with limited English ability might be encouraged to use their own language as well as English and to use forms of presenting data such as pictures and graphs that require less language proficiency; students with learning disabilities might need more time to complete science activities.

ENCOURAGE AND MODEL THE SKILLS OF SCIENTIFIC INQUIRY, AS WELL AS THE CURIOSITY, OPENNESS TO NEW IDEAS, AND SKEPTICISM THAT CHARACTERIZE SCIENCE. Implementing the recommendations above requires a range of actions based on careful assessments of students, knowledge of science, and a repertoire of science-teaching strategies. One aspect of the teacher's role is less tangible: teachers are models for the students they teach. A teacher who engages in inquiry with students models the skills needed for

inquiry. Teachers who exhibit enthusiasm and interest and who speak to the power and beauty of scientific understanding instill in their students some of those same attitudes toward science. Teachers whose actions demonstrate respect for differing ideas, attitudes, and values support a disposition fundamental to science and to science classrooms that also is important in many everyday situations.

The ability of teachers to do all that is required by Standard B requires a sophisticated set of judgments about science, students, learning, and teaching. To develop these judgments, successful teachers must have the opportunity to work with colleagues to discuss, share, and increase their knowledge. They are also more likely to succeed if the fundamental beliefs about students and about learning are shared across their school community in all learning domains. Successful implementation of this vision of science teaching and learning also requires that the school and district provide the necessary resources, including time, science materials, professional development opportunities, appropriate numbers of students per teacher, and appropriate schedules. For example, class periods must be long enough to enable the type of inquiry teaching described here to be achieved.

TEACHING STANDARD C:
Teachers of science engage in ongoing assessment of their teaching and of student learning. In doing this, teachers
- Use multiple methods and systematically gather data about student understanding and ability.

- Analyze assessment data to guide teaching.
- Guide students in self-assessment.
- Use student data, observations of teaching, and interactions with colleagues to reflect on and improve teaching practice.
- Use student data, observations of teaching, and interactions with colleagues to report student achievement and opportunities to learn to students, teachers, parents, policy makers, and the general public.

The word "assessment" is commonly equated with testing, grading, and providing feedback to students and parents. However, these are only some of the uses of assessment data. Assessment of students and of teaching—formal and informal—provides teachers with the data they need to make the many decisions that are required to plan and conduct their teaching. Assessment data also provide information for communicating about student progress with individual students and with adults, including parents, other teachers, and administrators.

USE MULTIPLE METHODS AND SYSTEMATICALLY GATHER DATA ON STUDENT UNDERSTANDING AND ABILITY.

During the ordinary operation of a class, information about students' understanding of science is needed almost continuously. Assessment tasks are not afterthoughts to instructional planning but are built into the design of the teaching. Because assessment information is a powerful tool for monitoring the development of student understanding, modifying activities, and promoting student self-reflection, the effective teacher of science carefully selects and uses assessment

tasks that are also good learning experiences. These assessment tasks focus on important content and performance goals and provide students with an opportunity to demonstrate their understanding and ability to conduct science. Also, teachers use many strategies to gather and interpret the large amount of information about student understanding of science that is present in thoughtful instructional activities.

Classroom assessments can take many forms. Teachers observe and listen to students as they work individually and in groups. They interview students and require formal performance tasks, investigative reports, written reports, pictorial work, models, inventions, and other creative expressions of understanding. They examine portfolios of student work, as well as more traditional paper-and-pencil tests. Each mode of assessment serves particular purposes and particular students. Each has particular strengths and weaknesses and is used to gather different kinds of information about student understanding and ability. The teacher of science chooses the form of the assessment in relationship to the particular learning goals of the class and the experiences of the students.

ANALYZE ASSESSMENT DATA TO GUIDE TEACHING.

Analysis of student assessment data provides teachers with knowledge to meet the needs of each student. It gives them indicators of each student's current understanding, the nature of each student's thinking, and the origin of what each knows. This knowledge leads to decisions about individual teacher-student interactions, to modifications of learning activities to meet diverse student needs and learning approaches, and

See *Assessment in Science Education* in Chapter 5

3 SCIENCE TEACHING STANDARDS

Science Olympiad

This example illustrates the close relationship between teaching and assessment. The assessment tasks are developmentally appropriate for young children, including recognition of students' physicals skills and cognitive abilities. The titles in this example (e.g., "Science Content") emphasize some important components of the assessment process. As students move from station to station displaying their understanding and ability in science, members of the community evaluate the students' science achievement and can observe that the students have had the opportunity to learn science. An Olympiad entails extensive planning, and even when the resources are common and readily available, it takes time to design and set up an Olympiad.

[This example highlights some elements of Teaching Standards A, C, and D; Assessment Standards A, B, C, and E; K-4 Content Standards A and B; Program Standards D and F; and System Standards D and G.]

SCIENCE CONTENT: The K-4 Content Standard for Science as Inquiry sets the criterion that students should be able to use simple equipment and tools to gather data. In this assessment exercise, four tasks use common materials to allow students to demonstrate their abilities.

ASSESSMENT ACTIVITY: Students make and record observations.

ASSESSMENT TYPE: Performance, public, authentic, individual.

ASSESSMENT PURPOSE: This assessment activity provides the teacher with information about student achievement. That information can be used to assign grades to students and to make promotion decisions. By involving the community, parents, and older siblings in the assessment process, the activity increases the community's understanding of and support for the elementary school science program.

DATA: Student records in science laboratory notebooks
Teachers' observations of students
Community members' observations of students

CONTEXT: Assessment activities of this general form are appropriate as an end-of-the-year activity for grades 1-4. The public performance involves students engaging in inquiry process skills at several stations located in and around the science classroom. Parents, local business persons, community leaders, and faculty from higher education act as judges of student performance. Benefits to the students and to the school and the science program, such as increased parental and community involvement, are well worth the costs of the considerable planning and organization on the part of the teacher. Planning includes 1) selecting appropriate tasks, 2) collecting necessary equipment, 3) making task cards, 4) checking the equipment, 5) obtaining and training judges, and 6) preparing students for public performance.

Assessment Exercise:

STATION A.   Measuring Wind Speed

a. Equipment

  1. Small, battery-operated fan
  2. Wind gauge
  3. Table marked with a letter-by-number grid
  4. Task cards with directions

b. Task

  1. Place the wind gauge at position D-4 on the grid.
  2. Place the fan at position G-6 facing the wind gauge.
  3. Turn the fan on to medium speed.
  4. Record the wind speed and direction in your laboratory notebook.

STATION B.   Rolling Cylinders

a. Equipment

  1. Four small clear plastic cylinders— one filled with sand, one empty, one 1/4 filled with sand, and one 1/2 filled with sand
  2. Adjustable incline
  3. Strips of colored paper of various lengths
  4. Task cards with directions

b. Task 1

  1. Roll each cylinder down the incline.
  2. Describe the motion of the cylinders and their relation to each other.

c. Task 2

  1. Place the blue strip of paper at the bottom of the incline.
  2. Select one of the cylinders, and adjust the angle of the incline so that the cylinder consistently rolls just to the end of the blue strip.

STATION C.   Comparing Weights

a. Equipment

  1. Balance
  2. Collections of objects in bags (Teachers select objects that have irregular shapes and are made of materials of different densities so that volume and mass are not correlated.)
  3. Task card with directions

b. Task

  1. Arrange the objects in one bag in order of their weights.
  2. Describe how you arranged the objects.

STATION D.   Measuring Volumes

a. Equipment

  1. Graduated cylinder, calibrated in half cubic centimeters.
  2. Numbered stones of various colors, shapes, and sizes but small enough to fit into the cylinder.
  3. Several containers marked A, B, C, and D.
  4. Task cards with directions

b. Task 1

  1. Measure the volume of container A.
  2. Record your measurement in your laboratory notebook.

c. Task 2

  1. Measure the volume of the stone marked 1.
  2. Record your measurement in your laboratory notebook.

EVALUATING STUDENT PERFORMANCE

Aspects of a student's performance and criteria for evaluation include:

PERFORMANCE INDICATOR	EVIDENCE
Following directions	Student follows the directions.
Measuring and recording data	Measurements are reasonably accurate and include correct units
Planning	Student organizes the work: (1) observations of the rolling cylinders are sequenced logically, (2) student selects the cylinder with the most predictable motion for Part 2 of the rolling-cylinders task, (3) student records the weights of the objects before attempting to order them in the ordering-by-weight task.
Elegance of approach	Student invents a sophisticated way of collecting, recording, or reporting observations.
Evidence of reflection	Student comments on observations in ways that indicate that he/she is attempting to find patterns and causal relationships.
Quality of observations	Observations are appropriate to the task, complete, accurate, and have some basis in experience or scientific understanding.
Behavior in the face of adversity	The student seeks help and does not panic if sand or water is spilled or glassware is broken, but proceeds to clean up, get replacements, and continue the task.

to the design of learning activities that build from student experience, culture, and prior understanding.

See *Inproving Classroom Pratice* in Chapter 5

GUIDE STUDENTS IN SELF-ASSESS-MENT. Skilled teachers guide students to understand the purposes for their own learning and to formulate self-assessment strategies. Teachers provide students with opportunities to develop their abilities to assess and reflect on their own scientific accomplishments. This process provides teachers with additional perspectives on student learning, and it deepens each student's

> *Skilled teachers guide students to understand the purposes for their own learning and to formulate self-assessment strategies.*

understanding of the content and its applications. The interactions of teachers and students concerning evaluation criteria helps students understand the expectations for their work, as well as giving them experience in applying standards of scientific practice to their own and others' scientific efforts. The internalization of such standards is critical to student achievement in science.

Involving students in the assessment process does not diminish the responsibilities of the teacher—it increases them. It requires teachers to help students develop skills in self-reflection by building a learning environment where students review each other's work, offer suggestions, and challenge mistakes in investigative processes, faulty reasoning, or poorly supported conclusions.

USE STUDENT DATA, OBSERVATIONS OF TEACHING, AND INTERACTIONS WITH COLLEAGUES TO REFLECT ON AND IMPROVE TEACHING PRACTICE. In the science education envisioned by the *Standards*, teachers of science approach their teaching in a spirit of inquiry—assessing, reflecting on, and learning from their own practice. They seek to understand which plans, decisions, and actions are effective in helping students and which are not. They ask and answer such questions as: "Why is this content important for this group of students at this stage of their development? Why did I select these particular learning activities? Did I choose good examples? How do the activities tie in with student needs and interests? How do they build on what students already know? Do they evoke the level of reasoning that I wanted? What evidence of effect on students do I expect?"

As teachers engage in study and research about their teaching, they gather data from classroom and external assessments of student achievement, from peer observations and supervisory evaluations, and from self-questioning. They use self-reflection and discussion with peers to understand more fully what is happening in the classroom and to explore strategies for improvement. To engage in reflection on teaching, teachers must have a structure that guides and encourages it—a structure that provides opportunities to have formal and informal dialogues about student learning and their science teaching practices in forums with peers and others; opportunities to read and discuss the research literature about science

See Program Standard F

content and pedagogy with other education professionals; opportunities to design and revise learning experiences that will help students to attain the desired learning; opportunities to practice, observe, critique, and analyze effective teaching models and the challenges of implementing exemplary strategies; and opportunities to build the skills of self-reflection as an ongoing process throughout each teacher's professional life.

USE STUDENT DATA, OBSERVATIONS OF TEACHING, AND INTERACTIONS WITH COLLEAGUES TO REPORT STUDENT ACHIEVEMENT AND OPPORTUNITIES TO LEARN TO STUDENTS, TEACHERS, PARENTS, POLICY MAKERS, AND THE GENERAL PUBLIC. Teachers have the obligation to report student achievement data to many individuals and agencies, including the students and their parents, certification agencies, employers, policy makers, and taxpayers. Although reports might include grades, teachers might also prepare profiles of student achievement. The opportunity that students have had to learn science is also an essential component of reports on student achievement in science understanding and ability.

TEACHING STANDARD D: Teachers of science design and manage learning environments that provide students with the time, space, and resources needed for learning science. In doing this, teachers

- Structure the time available so that students are able to engage in extended investigations.

See Program Standard D and System Standard D

- Create a setting for student work that is flexible and supportive of science inquiry.
- Ensure a safe working environment.
- Make the available science tools, materials, media, and technological resources accessible to students.
- Identify and use resources outside the school.
- Engage students in designing the learning environment.

Time, space, and materials are critical components of an effective science learning environment that promotes sustained inquiry and understanding. Creating an adequate environment for science teaching is a shared responsibility. Teachers lead the way in the design and use of resources, but school administrators, students, parents,

Teachers of science need regular, adequate space for science.

and community members must meet their responsibility to ensure that the resources are available to be used. Developing a schedule that allows time for science investigations needs the cooperation of all in the school; acquiring materials requires the appropriation of funds; maintaining scientific equipment is the shared responsibility of students and adults alike; and designing appropriate use of the scientific institutions and resources in the local community requires the participation of the school and those institutions and individuals.

This standard addresses the classroom use of time, space, and resources—the ways in which teachers make decisions about how to design and manage them to create the best possible opportunities for students to learn science.

STRUCTURE THE TIME AVAILABLE SO THAT STUDENTS ARE ABLE TO ENGAGE IN EXTENDED INVESTIGATIONS. Building scientific understanding takes time on a daily basis and over the long term. Schools must restructure schedules so that teachers can use blocks of time, interdisciplinary strategies, and field experiences to give students many opportunities to engage in serious scientific investigation as an integral part of their science learning. When considering how to structure available time, skilled teachers realize that students need time to try out ideas, to make mistakes, to ponder, and to discuss with one another. Given a voice in scheduling, teachers plan for adequate blocks of time for students to set up scientific equipment and carry out experiments, to go on field trips, or to reflect and share with each other. Teachers make time for students to work in varied groupings— alone, in pairs, in small groups, as a whole class—and on varied tasks, such as reading, conducting experiments, reflecting, writing, and discussing.

See Program Standard F

CREATE A SETTING FOR STUDENT WORK THAT IS FLEXIBLE AND SUPPORTIVE OF SCIENCE INQUIRY. The arrangement of available space and furnishings in the classroom or laboratory influences the nature of the learning that takes place. Teachers of science need regular, adequate space for science. They plan the use of this space to allow students to work safely in groups of various sizes at various tasks, to maintain their work in progress, and to dis-

play their results. Teachers also provide students with the opportunity to contribute their ideas about use of space and furnishings.

ENSURE A SAFE WORKING ENVIRONMENT. Safety is a fundamental concern in all experimental science. Teachers of science must know and apply the necessary safety regulations in the storage, use, and care of the materials used by students. They adhere to safety rules and guidelines that are established by national organizations such as the American Chemical Society and the Occu-

See Program Standard D

Effective science teaching depends on the availability and organization of materials, equipment, media, and technology.

pational Safety and Health Administration, as well as by local and state regulatory agencies. They work with the school and district to ensure implementation and use of safety guidelines for which they are responsible, such as the presence of safety equipment and an appropriate class size. Teachers also teach students how to engage safely in investigations inside and outside the classroom.

MAKE THE AVAILABLE SCIENCE TOOLS, MATERIALS, MEDIA, AND TECHNOLOGICAL RESOURCES ACCESSIBLE TO STUDENTS. Effective science teaching depends on the availability and organization of materials, equipment, media, and technology. An effective science learning environment requires a broad range of basic scientific materials, as well as specific tools for particular topics and learning experiences.

See Program Standard D and System Standard D

Teachers must be given the resources and authority to select the most appropriate materials and to make decisions about when, where, and how to make them accessible. Such decisions balance safety, proper use, and availability with the need for students to participate actively in designing experiments, selecting tools, and constructing apparatus, all of which are critical to the development of an understanding of inquiry.

It is also important for students to learn how to access scientific information from books, periodicals, videos, databases, electronic communication, and people with expert knowledge. Students are also taught to evaluate and interpret the information they have acquired through those resources. Teachers provide the opportunity for students to use contemporary technology as they develop their scientific understanding.

IDENTIFY AND USE RESOURCES OUTSIDE THE SCHOOL. The classroom is a limited environment. The school science program must extend beyond the walls of the school to the resources of the community. Our nation's communities have many specialists, including those in transportation, health-care delivery, communications, computer technologies, music, art, cooking, mechanics, and many other fields that have scientific aspects. Specialists often are available as resources for classes and for individual students. Many communities have access to science centers and museums, as well as to the science communities in higher education, national laboratories, and industry; these can contribute greatly to the understanding of science and encourage students to further their interests outside of school. In addition, the physical environment in

and around the school can be used as a living laboratory for the study of natural phenomena. Whether the school is located in a

The school science program must extend beyond the walls of the school to include the resources of the community.

densely populated urban area, a sprawling suburb, a small town, or a rural area, the environment can and should be used as a resource for science study. Working with others in their school and with the community, teachers build these resources into their work with students.

ENGAGE STUDENTS IN DESIGNING THE LEARNING ENVIRONMENT. As part of challenging students to take responsibility for their learning, teachers involve them in the design and management of the learning environment. Even the youngest students can and should participate in discussions and decisions about using time and space for work. With this sharing comes responsibility for care of space and resources. As students pursue their inquiries, they need access to resources and a voice in determining what is needed. The more independently students can access what they need, the more they can take responsibility for their own work. Students are also invaluable in identifying resources beyond the school.

TEACHING STANDARD E:
Teachers of science develop communities of science learners that reflect the intellectual rigor of scientific inquiry and the attitudes and social values conducive

to science learning. In doing this, teachers

- Display and demand respect for the diverse ideas, skills, and experiences of all students.
- Enable students to have a significant voice in decisions about the content and context of their work and require students to take responsibility for the learning of all members of the community.
- Nurture collaboration among students.
- Structure and facilitate ongoing formal and informal discussion based on a shared understanding of rules of scientific discourse.
- Model and emphasize the skills, attitudes, and values of scientific inquiry.

The focus of this standard is the social and intellectual environment that must be in place in the classroom if all students are to succeed in learning science and have the opportunity to develop the skills and dispositions for life-long learning. Elements of other standards are brought together by this standard to highlight the importance of the community of learners and what effective teachers do to foster its development. A community approach enhances learning: It helps to advance understanding, expand students' capabilities for investigation, enrich the questions that guide inquiry, and aid students in giving meaning to experiences.

See Teaching Standard B and Program Standard F

An assumption of the *Standards* is that all students should learn science through full participation and that all are capable of making meaningful contributions in science classes. The nature of the community in which students learn science is critical to making this assumption a reality.

DISPLAY AND DEMAND RESPECT FOR THE DIVERSE IDEAS, SKILLS, AND EXPERIENCES OF ALL STUDENTS. Respect for the ideas, activities, and thinking of all students is demonstrated by what teachers say and do, as well as by the flexibility with which they respond to student interests, ideas, strengths, and needs. Whether adjusting an activity to reflect the cultural background of particular students, providing resources for a small group to pursue an interest, or suggesting that an idea is valuable but cannot be pursued at the moment, teachers model what it means to respect and value the views of others. Teachers teach respect explicitly by focusing on their own and students' positive interactions, as well as confronting disrespect, stereotyping, and prejudice whenever it occurs in the school environment.

Science is a discipline in which creative and sometimes risky thought is important. New ideas and theories often are the result of creative leaps. For students to understand this aspect of science and be willing to express creative ideas, all of the members of the learning community must support and respect a diversity of experience, ideas, thought, and expression. Teachers work with students to develop an environment in which students feel safe in expressing ideas.

See Content Standards A & G (all grade levels)

ENABLE STUDENTS TO HAVE A SIGNIFICANT VOICE IN DECISIONS ABOUT THE CONTENT AND CONTEXT OF THEIR WORK AND GIVE STUDENTS SIGNIFICANT RESPONSIBILITY FOR THE LEARNING OF ALL MEMBERS OF THE COMMUNITY. A community of science learners is one in which students develop a sense of purpose and the ability to assume

Musical Instruments

This example includes a description of teaching and an assessment task, although the assessment task is indistinguishable from the teaching activity. The example begins with the teachers at King School working as a team involved in school reform. The team naturally builds on previous efforts; for example, the technology unit is modified from an existing unit. Other indicators that King School is working toward becoming a community of learners is the availability of older students to help the younger students with tasks beyond their physical abilities and the decision for one class to give a concert for another class. In her planning, Ms. R. integrates the study of the science of sound with the technology of producing sound. Recognizing the different interests and abilities of the students, Ms. R. allows students to work alone or in groups and plans a mixture of whole-class discussions and work time. She encourages the students in planning and communicating their designs. She imposes constraints on materials and time.

[This example highlights some elements of all of the Teaching Standards; Assessment Standard A; K-4 Content Standards B, E, and F; and Program Standards A, D, and E.]

The King School was reforming its science curriculum. After considerable research into existing curriculum materials and much discussion, the team decided to build a technology piece into some of the current science studies. The third-grade teacher on the team, Ms. R., said that she would like to work with two or three of her colleagues on the third-grade science curriculum. They selected three topics that they knew they would be teaching the following year: life cycles, sound, and water.

Ms. R. chose to introduce technology as part of the study of sound. That winter, when the end of the sound study neared, Ms. R. was ready with a new culminating activity—making musical instruments. She posed a question to the entire class: Having studied sound for almost 6 weeks, could they design and make musical instruments that would produce sounds for entertainment? Ms. R. had collected a variety of materials, which she now displayed on a table, including boxes, tubes, string, wire, hooks, scrap wood, dowels, plastic, rubber, fabric, and more. The students had been working in groups of four during the sound study, and Ms. R. asked them to gather into those groups to think about the kinds of instruments they would like to make. Ms. R. asked the students to think particularly about what they knew about sound, what kind of sound they would like their instruments to make, and what kind of instrument it would be. How would the sound be produced? What would make the sound? She suggested they might want to look at the materials she had brought in, but they could think about other materials too.

Ms. R. sent the students to work in their groups. Collaborative work had been the basis of most of the science inquiry the students had done; for this phase, Ms. R. felt that the students should work together to discuss and share ideas, but she suggested that each student might want to have an instrument at the end to play and to take home.

As the students began to talk in their groups, Ms. R. added elements to the activity. They would have only the following 2 weeks to make their instruments. Furthermore, any materials they needed beyond what was in the boxes had to be materials that were readily available and inexpensive.

Ms. R. knew that planning was a challenge for these third graders. She moved among groups, listening and adding comments. When she felt that discussions had gone as far as they could go, she asked each group to draw a picture of the instruments the children thought they would like to make, write a short piece on how they thought they would make them, and make a list of the materials that they would need. Ms. R. made a list of what was needed, noted which children and which groups might profit from discussing their ideas with one another, and suggested that the children think about their task, collect materials if they could, and come to school in the next week prepared to build their instruments.

Ms. R. invited several sixth graders to join the class during science time the following week, knowing that the third grade students might need their help in working with the materials. Some designs were simple and easy to implement; e.g., one group was making a rubber-band player by stretching different widths and lengths of rubber bands around a plastic gallon milk container with the top cut off. Another group was making drums of various sizes using some thick cardboard tubes and pieces of thin rubber roofing material. For many, the designs could not be translated into reality, and much change and trial and error ensued. One group planned to build a guitar and designed a special shape for the sound box, but after the glued sides of their original box collapsed twice, the group decided to use the

wooden box that someone had added to the supply table. In a few cases, the original design was abandoned, and a new design emerged as the instrument took shape.

At the end of the second week, Ms. R. set aside 2 days for the students to reflect on what they had done individually and as a class. On Friday, they were once again to draw and write about their instruments. Where groups had worked together on an instrument, one report was to be prepared. On the next Monday, each group was to make a brief presentation of the instrument, what it could do, how the design came to be, and what challenges had been faced. As a final effort, the class could prepare a concert for the other third grades.

In making the musical instruments, students relied on the knowledge and understanding developed while studying sound, as well as the principles of design, to make an instrument that produced sound.

The assessment task for the musical instruments follows. The titles emphasize some important components of the assessment process.

SCIENCE CONTENT: The K-4 science content standard on science and technology is supported by the idea that students should be able to communicate the purpose of a design. The K-4 physical science standard is supported by the fundamental understanding of the characteristics of sound, a form of energy.

ASSESSMENT ACTIVITY: Students demonstrate the products of their design work to their peers and reflect on what the project taught them about the nature of sound and the process of design.

ASSESSMENT TYPE: This can be public, group, or individual, embedded in teaching.

ASSESSMENT PURPOSE: This activity assesses student progress toward understanding the purpose and processes of design. The information will be used to plan the next design activity. The activity also permits the teacher to gather data about understanding of sound.

DATA: Observations of the student performances.

CONTEXT: Third-grade students have just completed a design project. Their task is to present the product of their work to their peers and talk about what they learned about sound and design as a result of doing the project. This is a challenging task for third-grade students, and the teacher will have to provide considerable guidance to the groups of students as they plan their presentations. The following directions provide a framework that students can use to plan their presentations.

1. Play your instrument for the class.
2. Show the class the part of the instrument that makes the sound.
3. Describe to the class the purpose (function) that other parts of the instrument have.
4. Show the class how you can make the sound louder.
5. Show the class how you can change the pitch (how high or how low the sound is) of the sound.
6. Tell the class about how you made the instrument, including
   a. What kind of instrument did you want to make?

b. How like the instrument you wanted to make is the one you actually made?
c. Why did you change your design?
d. What tools and materials did you use to make your instrument?

7. Explain why people make musical instruments.

EVALUATING STUDENT PERFORMANCE: Student understanding of sound will be revealed by understanding that the sound is produced in the instrument by the part of the instrument that *vibrates* (moves rapidly back and forth), that the *pitch* (how high or how low) can be changed by changing how rapidly the vibrating part moves, and the loudness can be changed by the force (how hard you pluck, tap, or blow the vibrating part) with which the vibrating part is set into motion. An average student performance would include the ability to identify the source of the vibration and ways to change either pitch or loudness in two directions (raise and lower the pitch of the instrument or make the instrument louder and softer) or change the pitch and loudness in one direction (make the pitch higher and the sound louder). An exemplary performance by a student would include not only the ability to identify the source of the vibration but also to change pitch and loudness in both directions.

Student understanding of the nature of technology will be revealed by the students' ability to reflect on why people make musical instruments—e.g., to improve the quality of life—as well as by their explanations of how they managed to make the instrument despite the constraints faced—that is, the ability to articulate why the conceptualization and design turned out to be different from the instrument actually made.

See *Improving Classroom Practice* in the Assessment Standards

responsibility for their learning. Teachers give students the opportunity to participate in setting goals, planning activities, assessing work, and designing the environment. In so doing, they give students responsibility for a significant part of their own learning, the learning of the group, and the functioning of the community.

See Content Standards A & G (all grade levels)

NURTURE COLLABORATION AMONG STUDENTS. Working collaboratively with others not only enhances the understanding of science, it also fosters the practice of many of the skills, attitudes, and values that characterize science. Effective teachers design many of the activities for learning science to require group work, not simply as an exercise, but as essential to the inquiry. The teacher's role is to structure the groups and to teach students the skills that are needed to work together.

STRUCTURE AND FACILITATE ONGOING FORMAL AND INFORMAL DISCUSSION BASED ON A SHARED UNDERSTANDING OF RULES OF SCIENTIFIC DISCOURSE. A fundamental aspect of a community of learners is communication. Effective communication requires a foundation of respect and trust among individuals. The ability to engage in the presentation of evidence, reasoned argument, and explanation comes from practice. Teachers encourage informal discussion and structure science activities so that students are required to explain and justify their understanding, argue from data and defend their conclusions, and critically assess and challenge the scientific explanations of one another.

MODEL AND EMPHASIZE THE SKILLS, ATTITUDES, AND VALUES OF SCIENTIFIC INQUIRY. Certain attitudes, such as wonder, curiosity, and respect toward nature are vital parts of the science learning community. Those attitudes are reinforced when the adults in the community engage in their own learning and when they share positive attitudes toward science. Environments that promote the development of appropriate attitudes are supported by the school administration and a local community that

See Content Standard A (all grade levels)

Effective teachers design many activities for group learning, not simply as an exercise but as collaboration essential to inquiry.

has taken responsibility for understanding the science program and supports students and teachers in its implementation.

Communities of learners do not emerge spontaneously; they require careful support from skillful teachers. The development of a community of learners is initiated on the first day that a new group comes together, when the teacher begins to develop with students a vision of the class environment they wish to form. This vision is communicated, discussed, and adapted so that all students come to share it and realize its value. Rules of conduct and expectations evolve as the community functions and takes shape over the weeks and months of the school year.

Some students will accommodate quickly; others will be more resistant because of the responsibilities required or because of discrepancies between their perceptions of what they should be doing in school and what is actually happening. The optimal environment for learning science is constructed by students and teachers together. Doing so requires time, persistence, and skill on everyone's part.

TEACHING STANDARD F:
Teachers of science actively participate in the ongoing planning and development of the school science program. In doing this, teachers

- Plan and develop the school science program.
- Participate in decisions concerning the allocation of time and other resources to the science program.
- Participate fully in planning and implementing professional growth and development strategies for themselves and their colleagues.

See Teaching Standard E

PLAN AND DEVELOP THE SCHOOL SCIENCE PROGRAM.   The teaching in individual science classrooms is part of a larger system that includes the school, district, state, and nation. Although some teachers might choose involvement at the district, state, and national levels, all teachers have a professional responsibility to be active in some way as members of a science learning community at the school level, working with colleagues and others to improve and maintain a quality science program for all students. Many teachers already assume these responsibilities within their schools. However, they usually do so under difficult circumstances. Time for such activities is minimal, and involvement often requires work after hours. Resources are likely to be scarce as well. Furthermore, the authority to plan and carry out necessary activities is not typically in the hands of teachers. Any improvement of science education will require that the structure and culture of schools change to support the collaboration of the entire school staff with resources in the community in planning, designing, and carrying out new practices for teaching and learning science.

Although individual teachers continually make adaptations in their classrooms, the school itself must have a coherent program of science study for students. In the vision described by the *National Science Education Standards*, the teachers in the school and school district have a major role in designing that program, working together across science disciplines and grade levels, as well as within levels. Teachers of science must also work with their colleagues to coordinate and integrate the learning of science understanding and abilities with learning in

Although individual teachers continually make adaptations in their classrooms, the school itself must have a coherent program of science study for students.

other disciplines. Teachers working together determine expectations for student learning, as well as strategies for assessing, recording, and reporting student progress. They also work together to create a learning community within the school.

PARTICIPATE IN DECISIONS CONCERNING THE ALLOCATION OF TIME AND OTHER RESOURCES TO THE SCIENCE PROGRAM. See Program Standard D Time and other resources are critical elements for effective science teaching.

Teachers of science need to have a significant role in the process by which decisions are made concerning the allocation of time and resources to various subject areas. However, to assume this responsibility, schools and districts must provide teachers with the opportunity to be leaders.

See Professional Development Standard D

PARTICIPATE FULLY IN PLANNING AND IMPLEMENTING PROFESSIONAL GROWTH AND DEVELOPMENT STRATEGIES FOR THEMSELVES AND THEIR COLLEAGUES. Working as colleagues, teachers are responsible for designing and implementing the ongoing professional development opportunities they need to enhance their skills in teaching science, as well as their abilities to improve the science programs in their schools. Often they employ the services of specialists in science, children, learning, curriculum, assessment, or other areas of interest. In doing so, they must have the support of their school districts.

CHANGING EMPHASES

The *National Science Education Standards* envision change throughout the system. The teaching standards encompass the following changes in emphases:

LESS EMPHASIS ON	MORE EMPHASIS ON
Treating all students alike and responding to the group as a whole	Understanding and responding to individual student's interests, strengths, experiences, and needs
Rigidly following curriculum	Selecting and adapting curriculum
Focusing on student acquisition of information	Focusing on student understanding and use of scientific knowledge, ideas, and inquiry processes
Presenting scientific knowledge through lecture, text, and demonstration	Guiding students in active and extended scientific inquiry
Asking for recitation of acquired knowledge	Providing opportunities for scientific discussion and debate among students
Testing students for factual information at the end of the unit or chapter	Continuously assessing student understanding
Maintaining responsibility and authority	Sharing responsibility for learning with students
Supporting competition	Supporting a classroom community with cooperation, shared responsibility, and respect
Working alone	Working with other teachers to enhance the science program

References for Further Reading

Bereiter, C., and M. Scardamalia. 1989. Intentional learning as a goal of instruction. In Knowing, Learning, and Instruction: Essays in Honor of Robert Glaser, L.B. Resnick, ed.: 361-392. Hillsdale, NJ: Lawrence Erlbaum and Associates.

Brown, A. 1994. The advancement of learning. Presidential Address, American Educational Research Association. Educational Researcher, 23: 4-12.

Brown, A.L., and J.C. Campione. 1994. Guided discovery in a community of learners. In Classroom Lessons: Integrating Cognitive Theory and Classroom Practice, K. McGilly, ed.: 229-270. Cambridge, MA: MIT Press.

Bruer, J.T. 1993. Schools for Thought: A Science of Learning in the Classroom. Cambridge, MA: MIT Press.

Carey, S. 1985. Conceptual Change in Childhood. Cambridge, MA: MIT Press.

Carey, S., and R. Gelman, eds. 1991. The Epigenesis of Mind: Essays on Biology and Cognition. Hillsdale, NJ: Lawrence Erlbaum and Associates.

Champagne, A.B. 1988. Science Teaching: Making the System Work. In This Year in School Science 1988: Papers from the Forum for School Science. Washington, DC: American Association for the Advancement of Science.

Cohen, D.K., M.W. McLaughlin, and J.E. Talbert, eds. 1993. Teaching for Understanding: Challenges for Policy and Practice. San Francisco: Jossey-Bass.

Darling-Hammond, L. 1992. Standards of Practice for Learner Centered Schools. New York: National Center for Restructuring Schools and Learning.

Harlen, W. 1992. The Teaching of Science. London: David Fulton Publishers.

Leinhardt, G. 1993. On Teaching. In Advances in Instructional Psychology, R. Glaser ed., vol.4: 1-54. Hillsdale, NJ: Lawrence Erlbaum and Associates.

Loucks-Horsley, S., J.G. Brooks, M.O. Carlson, P. Kuerbis, D.P. Marsh, M. Padilla, H. Pratt, and K.L. Smith. 1990. Developing and Supporting Teachers for Science Education in the Middle Years. Andover, MA: The National Center for Improving Science Education.

Loucks-Horsley, S., M.O. Carlson, L.H. Brink, P. Horwitz, D.P. Marsh, H. Pratt, K.R. Roy, and K. Worth. 1989. Developing and Supporting Teachers for Elementary School Science Education. Andover, MA: The National Center for Improving Science Education.

McGilly, K., ed. 1994. Classroom Lessons: Integrating Cognitive Theory and Classroom Practice. Cambridge, MA: MIT Press.

NBPTS (National Board for Professional Teaching Standards). 1991. Toward High and Rigorous Standards for the Teaching Profession: Initial Policies and Perspectives of the National Board for Professional Teaching Standards, 3rd ed. Detroit, MI: NBPTS.

NCTM (National Council of Teachers of Mathematics). 1991. Professional Standards for Teaching Mathematics. Reston, VA: NCTM.

NRC (National Research Council). 1994. Learning, Remembering, Believing: Enhancing Human Performance, D. Druckman and R.A. Bjork, eds. Washington, DC: National Academy Press.

NRC (National Research Council). 1990. Fulfilling the Promise: Biology Education in the Nation's Schools. Washington, DC: National Academy Press.

NRC (National Research Council). 1987. Education and Learning to Think, L.B. Resnick, ed. Washington, DC: National Academy Press.

Schoen, D. 1987. Educating the Reflective Practitioner: Toward a New Design for Teaching and Learning in the Professions. San Francisco: Jossey-Bass.

Shulman, L.S. 1987. Knowledge and teaching foundations of the new reform. Harvard Education Review, 57 (1): 1-22.

observe

Learn

Interact

Change

Becoming an effective science teacher is a continuous process that stretches across the life of a teacher, from his or her undergraduate years to the end of a professional career.

Standards for Professional Development for Teachers of Science

The *National Science Education Standards* present a vision of learning and teaching science in which all students have the opportunity to become scientifically literate. In this vision, teachers of science are professionals responsible for their own professional development and for the maintenance of the teaching profession. The standards in this chapter provide criteria for making judgments about the quality of the professional development opportunities that teachers of science will need to implement the *National Science Education Standards.* ▌ Professional development for teachers should be analogous to professional development for other professionals. Becoming an effective science teacher is a continuous process that stretches from preservice experiences in undergraduate years to the end of a professional career. Science has a rapidly changing knowledge base and expanding relevance to societal issues, and teachers will need ongoing opportunities to build their understanding and ability. Teachers also must have opportunities to develop understanding of how students with diverse interests, abilities, and experiences make sense of scientific ideas and what a teacher does to support and guide all students. And teachers require the opportunity to study and engage in research on science teaching and learning, and to share with colleagues what they have learned.

The standards in this chapter are intended to inform everyone with a role in professional development. They are criteria for the science and education faculties of colleges and universities, who have the primary responsibility for the initial preparation of teachers of science; for teachers who select and design

The current reform effort requires a substantive change in how science is taught; an equally substantive change is needed in professional development practices.

activities for personal professional development; and for all others who design and lead professional development activities.

These standards are also criteria for state and national policy makers who determine important policies and practices, such as requirements for teacher certification and the budget for professional development. In this vision of science education, policies must change so that ongoing, effective professional development becomes central in teachers' lives.

The current reform effort in science education requires a substantive change in how science is taught. Implicit in this reform is an equally substantive change in professional development practices at all levels. Much current professional development involves traditional lectures to convey science content and emphasis on technical training about teaching. For example, undergraduate science courses typically communicate science as a body of facts and rules to be memorized, rather than a way of knowing about the natural world; even the science laboratories in most colleges fail to teach science as inquiry. Moreover, teacher-preparation courses and inservice activities in methods of teaching science frequently emphasize technical skills rather than decision making, theory, and reasoning. If reform is to be accomplished, professional development must include experiences that engage prospective and practicing teachers in active learning that builds their knowledge, understanding, and ability. The vision of science and how it is learned as described in the *Standards* will be nearly impossible to convey to students in schools if the teachers themselves have never experienced it. Simply put, preservice programs and professional development activities for practicing teachers must model good science teaching, as described in the teaching standards in Chapter 3.

Four assumptions about the nature of professional development experiences and about the context within which they take place frame the professional development standards:

- **Professional development for a teacher of science is a continuous, lifelong process.**

- **The traditional distinctions between "targets," "sources," and "supporters" of teacher development activities are artificial.**
- **The conventional view of professional development for teachers needs to shift from technical training for specific skills to opportunities for intellectual professional growth.**
- **The process of transforming schools requires that professional development opportunities be clearly and appropriately connected to teachers' work in the context of the school.**

See Professional Development Standard D

PROFESSIONAL DEVELOPMENT FOR A TEACHER OF SCIENCE IS A CONTINUOUS, LIFELONG PROCESS. The understanding and abilities required to be a masterful teacher of science are not static. Science content increases and changes, and a teacher's understanding in science must keep pace. Knowledge about the process of learning is also continually developing, requiring that teachers remain informed. Further, we live in an ever-changing society, which deeply influences events in schools; social changes affect students as they come to school and affect what they need to carry away with them. In addition, teachers must be involved in the development and refinement of new approaches to teaching, assessment, and curriculum.

See Professional Development Standard A

Teachers of science build skills gradually, starting in their undergraduate years, where they engage in science and gain some experience in teaching. They then experience the realities of their first years in the classroom, work with other teachers, take advantage of professional development offerings, and learn from their own efforts and those of

their colleagues. This gradual development has several implications—the transition between the education of prospective and practicing teachers is a case in point. The primary responsibility for the early stages of preservice education rests with colleges and universities, but it must be shared with the practice community as prospective teachers begin their clinical work. For inservice education, the practice community has the major responsibility, drawing upon the resources of higher education, science-rich centers, and the scientific community. Continuous professional development requires a gradual shift from campus to

Science content increases and changes, and a teacher's understanding in science must keep pace.

school, accompanied by collaboration among all those engaged in professional development activities.

Because the following standards assume continuous professional development, they are not divided into standards for the education of prospective teachers and standards for the professional development of practicing teachers. Rather they are applicable to all activities and programs that occur over a teacher's career.

THE TRADITIONAL DISTINCTIONS BETWEEN "TARGETS," "SOURCES," AND "SUPPORTERS" OF TEACHER DEVELOPMENT ACTIVITIES ARE ARTIFICIAL. In the vision of science education described by the *Standards*, practicing teachers—traditionally the targets for professional development—have the opportunity to become sources of their own growth as well as supporters of the growth of others. Prospective teachers must have the opportunity to become active participants in schools through internships, clinical studies, and research. Teachers should have opportunities for structured reflection on their teach-

The challenge of professional development…is to create optimal collaborative learning situations in which the best sources of expertise are linked with the experiences and current needs of the teachers.

ing practice with colleagues, for collaborative curriculum planning, and for active participation in professional teaching and scientific networks. The challenge of professional development for teachers of science is to create optimal collaborative learning situations in which the best sources of expertise are linked with the experiences and current needs of the teachers.

Principals and qualified community members should also participate in professional development activities in order to increase their own understanding of student science learning and of the roles and responsibilities of teachers.

THE CONVENTIONAL VIEW OF PROFESSIONAL DEVELOPMENT FOR TEACHERS NEEDS TO SHIFT FROM TECHNICAL TRAINING FOR SPECIFIC SKILLS TO OPPORTUNITIES FOR INTELLECTUAL PROFESSIONAL GROWTH. This assumption highlights the need for a shift from viewing teaching as a technical

activity to one requiring both theoretical and practical understanding and ability. Professional development occurs in many more ways than delivery of information in the typical university course, institute, or teacher workshop. Another way to learn more about teaching science is to conduct classroom-based research, and a useful way to learn science content is to participate in research at a scientific laboratory. In all instances, professional development activities must be sustained, contextual, and require participation and reflection. The *Standards* assume broad concepts of how, in what formats, and under what conditions professional development can take place.

THE PROCESS OF TRANSFORMING SCHOOLS REQUIRES THAT PROFESSIONAL DEVELOPMENT OPPORTUNITIES BE CLEARLY AND APPROPRIATELY CONNECTED TO TEACHERS' WORK IN THE CONTEXT OF THE SCHOOL. Whenever possible, the professional development of teachers should occur in the contexts where the teachers' understandings and abilities will be used. Although learning science might take place in a science laboratory, learning to teach science needs to take place through interactions with practitioners in places where students are learning science, such as in classrooms and schools.

The Standards

The first three professional development standards can be summarized as learning science, learning to teach science, and learning to learn. Each begins with a description of what is to be learned followed by a description of how the opportunities to learn are best designed. The fourth standard addresses the characteristics of quality professional development programs at all levels.

PROFESSIONAL DEVELOPMENT STANDARD A:
Professional development for teachers of science requires learning essential science content through the perspectives and methods of inquiry. Science learning experiences for teachers must

- Involve teachers in actively investigating phenomena that can be studied scientifically, interpreting results, and making sense of findings consistent with currently accepted scientific understanding.
- Address issues, events, problems, or topics significant in science and of interest to participants.
- Introduce teachers to scientific literature, media, and technological resources that expand their science knowledge and their ability to access further knowledge.
- Build on the teacher's current science understanding, ability, and attitudes.
- Incorporate ongoing reflection on the process and outcomes of understanding science through inquiry.
- Encourage and support teachers in efforts to collaborate.

KNOWLEDGE AND UNDERSTANDING OF SCIENCE

One of the most serious questions in science education is what science a teacher needs to know. What does it mean to know a lot or a little, have a sound foundation, and have in-depth understanding? The criteria of credit

hours that states, professional organizations, and higher education institutions use to prescribe content requirements are inadequate indicators of what is learned in a course. Therefore, the following discussion focuses on the nature of the opportunities to learn science needed by teachers, rather than on credit hours. It is assumed that teachers of science will continue to learn science throughout their careers.

To meet the *Standards*, all teachers of science must have a strong, broad base of scientific knowledge extensive enough for them to

- Understand the nature of scientific inquiry, its central role in science, and how to use the skills and processes of scientific inquiry.
- Understand the fundamental facts and concepts in major science disciplines.
- Be able to make conceptual connections within and across science disciplines, as well as to mathematics, technology, and other school subjects.
- Use scientific understanding and ability when dealing with personal and societal issues.

Beyond the firm foundation provided by the content standards in Chapter 6, how much more science a teacher needs to know for a given level of schooling is an issue of breadth versus depth to be debated and decided locally while respecting the intent of the *Standards*.

Breadth implies a focus on the basic ideas of science and is central to teaching science at all grade levels. Depth refers to knowing and understanding not only the basic ideas within a science discipline, but also some of the supporting experimental and theoretical knowledge. The ways ideas interconnect and

See Content Standards (all grade levels) in Chapter 6

build upon each other within and across content areas are other important aspects of the depth of understanding. The depth of understanding of science content required varies according to the grade level of teaching responsibility.

Teachers of grades K-4 usually are generalists who teach most, if not all, school subjects. A primary task for these teachers is to lay the experiential, conceptual, and attitudinal foundation for future learning in science by guiding students through a range of inquiry activities. To achieve this, elementary teachers of science need to have the opportunity to develop a broad knowledge of science content in addition to some in-depth experiences in at least one science subject. Such in-depth experiences will allow teachers to develop an understanding of inquiry and the structure and production

Prospective and practicing teachers must take science courses in which they learn science through inquiry, having the same opportunities as their students will have to develop understanding.

of science knowledge. That knowledge prepares teachers to guide student inquiries, appraise current student understanding, and further students' understanding of scientific ideas. Although thorough science knowledge in many areas would enhance the work of an elementary teacher, it is more realistic to expect a generalist's knowledge.

Science curricula are organized in many different ways in the middle grades. Science experiences go into greater depth, are more quantitative, require more sophisticated rea-

soning skills, and use more sophisticated apparatus and technology. These requirements of the science courses change the character of the conceptual background required of middle level teachers of science. While maintaining a breadth of science knowledge, they need to develop greater depth of understanding than their colleagues teaching grades K-4. An intensive, thorough study of at least one scientific discipline will help them meet the demands of their teaching and gain appreciation for how scientific knowledge is produced and how disciplines are structured.

At the secondary level, effective teachers of science possess broad knowledge of all disciplines and a deep understanding of the scientific disciplines they teach. This implies being familiar enough with a science discipline to take part in research activities within that discipline.

Teachers must possess the skills necessary to guide inquiries based on students' questions. An important test of the appropriate level of understanding for all teachers of science at all levels is the teacher's ability to determine what students understand about science and to use this data to formulate activities that aid the development of sound scientific ideas by their students.

LEARNING SCIENCE

Prospective and practicing teachers of science acquire much of their formal science knowledge through coursework in colleges and universities. For all teachers, undergraduate science courses are a major factor in defining what science content is learned. Those courses also provide models for how science should be taught. For K-4 teachers

See System Standard B

and 5-8 teachers with general certification, undergraduate introductory science courses often are the only science courses taken. Because of the crucial role of such courses, reform in the content and teaching of undergraduate science is imperative. The courses for practicing teachers—those taught at universities as part of graduate programs as well as those typically included in school-based, inservice programs—also require redesign.

Teachers of science will be the representatives of the science community in their classrooms, and they form much of their image of science through the science courses that they take in college. If that image is to reflect the nature of science as presented in these standards, prospective and practicing teachers must take science courses in which they learn science through inquiry, having the same opportunities as their students will have to develop understanding. College science faculty therefore must design courses that are heavily based on investigations, where current and future teachers have direct contact with phenomena, gather and interpret data using appropriate technology, and are involved in groups working on real, open-ended problems. Those science courses must allow teachers to develop a deep understanding of accepted scientific ideas and the manner in which they were formulated. They must also address problems, issues, events, and topics that are important to science, the community, and teachers.

Learning science through inquiry should also provide opportunities for teachers to use scientific literature, media, and technology to broaden their knowledge beyond the scope of immediate inquiries. Courses in science

should allow teachers to develop understanding of the logical reasoning that is demonstrated in research papers and how a specific piece of research adds to the accumulated knowledge of science. Those courses should also support teachers in using a variety of technological tools, such as computerized databases and specialized laboratory tools.

In the vision described by the *Standards,* all prospective and practicing teachers who

Teachers of science will be the representatives of the science community in their classrooms.

study science participate in guided activities that help them make sense of the new content being learned, whether it comes by lecture, reading, small-group discussion, or laboratory investigation. Courses and other activities include ongoing opportunities for teachers to reflect on the process and the outcomes of their learning. Instructors help teachers understand the nature of learning science as they develop new concepts and skills. Those who teach science must be attentive to the scientific ideas that teachers bring with them, provide time for learning experiences to be shared, and be knowledgeable about strategies that promote and encourage reflection.

Science faculty also need to design courses for prospective and practicing teachers that purposely engage them in the collaborative aspects of scientific inquiry. Some aspects of inquiry are individual efforts, but many are not, and teachers need to experience the value and benefits of cooperative work as well as the struggles and tensions that it can produce.

PROFESSIONAL DEVELOPMENT STANDARD B:

Professional development for teachers of science requires integrating knowledge of science, learning, pedagogy, and students; it also requires applying that knowledge to science teaching. Learning experiences for teachers of science must

- Connect and integrate all pertinent aspects of science and science education.
- Occur in a variety of places where effective science teaching can be illustrated and modeled, permitting teachers to struggle with real situations and expand their knowledge and skills in appropriate contexts.
- Address teachers' needs as learners and build on their current knowledge of science content, teaching, and learning.
- Use inquiry, reflection, interpretation of research, modeling, and guided practice to build understanding and skill in science teaching.

KNOWLEDGE OF SCIENCE TEACHING

Effective science teaching is more than knowing science content and some teaching strategies. Skilled teachers of science have special understandings and abilities that integrate their knowledge of science content, curriculum, learning, teaching, and students. Such knowledge allows teachers to tailor learning situations to the needs of individuals and groups. This special knowledge, called "pedagogical content knowledge," distinguishes the science knowledge of teachers from that of scientists. It is one element that defines a professional teacher of science.

In addition to solid knowledge of science, teachers of science must have a firm grounding in learning theory—understanding how learning occurs and is facilitated. Learning is an active process by which students individually and collaboratively achieve understanding. Effective teaching requires that teachers know what students of certain ages are likely to know, understand, and be able to do; what they will learn quickly; and what will be a struggle. Teachers of science need to anticipate typical misunderstandings and to

See the principle *Learning science is an active process* in Chapter 2

Skilled teachers of science have special understandings and abilities that integrate their knowledge of science content, curriculum, learning, teaching, and students.

judge the appropriateness of concepts for the developmental level of their students. In addition, teachers of science must develop understanding of how students with different backgrounds, experiences, motivations, learning styles, abilities, and interests learn science. Teachers use all of that knowledge to make effective decisions about learning objectives, teaching strategies, assessment tasks, and curriculum materials.

See Teaching Standard B

Effective teachers of science also have a broad repertoire of instructional strategies that engage students in multiple ways. They are familiar with a wide range of curricula. They have the ability to examine critically and select activities to use with their students to promote the understanding of science.

See Program Standard B

Inquiry into practice is essential for effective teaching. Teachers need continuous opportunities to do so. Through collaborations with colleagues, teachers should

Teachers use their knowledge of learning to make effective decisions about learning objectives, teaching strategies, assessment tasks, and curriculum materials.

inquire into their own practice by posing questions such as the following:

How should laboratory journals be structured?

Is this experiment appropriate for the understanding and ability of the students?

What type of research do students need to do to extend their understanding?

Is this curriculum unit appropriate for this group of third-grade students?

Does a particular study allow students sufficient opportunity to devise their own experiments?

Are all students participating equally?

Assessment is an important tool for good inquiry into teaching. In the daily operation of their classrooms, skilled teachers of science are diagnosticians who understand students' ideas, beliefs, and reasoning. Effective teachers are knowledgeable about the various educational purposes for assessment and know how to implement and interpret a variety of assessment strategies.

Skilled teachers of science also know how to create and manage the physical, social, and intellectual environment in a classroom community of science learners.

See Teaching Standard C

See Teaching Standards D and E

LEARNING TO TEACH SCIENCE

Developing pedagogical content knowledge of science requires that teachers of science have the opportunity to bring together the knowledge described above and develop an integrated view of what it means to teach and learn science. The teaching standards in Chapter 3 are designed to guide teachers' decisions about each of the complex activities involved in teaching science. In the vision described by the *Standards*, teachers also develop concepts and language to engage in discourse with their peers about content, curriculum, teaching, learning, assessment, and students.

The development of pedagogical content knowledge by teachers mirrors what we know about learning by students; it can be fully developed only through continuous experience. But experience is not sufficient. Teachers also must have opportunities to engage in analysis of the individual components of pedagogical content knowledge— science, learning, and pedagogy—and make connections between them.

In this vision, people responsible for professional development work together with each other and with teachers as they integrate their knowledge and experiences. For example, higher education science and education faculty must learn to work together: An instructor in a university science course might invite a member of the science education faculty to participate in regular discussion time designed to help students reflect on how they came to learn science concepts. Not only must the departments in higher education institutions work together, but schools and higher education institutions must enter into true collaboration. And

See Professional Development Standard D

Genetics

Ms. J. recently attended a workshop with other teachers at the university where she learned equally from the instructors and the other attendees. She also reads research regularly, reviews resources, and makes judgments about their value for her teaching. Ms. J. engages in an iterative planning process, moving from a broad semester plan to daily details. The students in her high-school class have opportunities to develop mental models, work with instructional technology, use multiple materials, teach one another, and consider the personal, social, and ethical aspects of science. She has the support of the school and district and has the resources she needs. She also relies on resources in the community.

[This example highlights some elements from Teaching Standards A, B, D, and E; Professional Development Standards A, B, and C; 9-12 Content Standards A, C, F, and G; Program Standards C and D; and System Standards D and G.]

Ms. J. is eager to begin the school year, and is particularly looking forward to teaching a semester course on transmission genetics—how traits are inherited from one generation to the next. She taught the course before and read extensively about the difficulties students have with transmission genetics conceptually and as a means of developing problem-solving skills. She also has been learning about new approaches to teaching genetics. From her reading and from a workshop she attended for high-school teachers at the local university, she knows that many people have been experimenting with ways to improve genetics instruction. She also knows that several computer programs are available that simulate genetics events.

Ms. J. is convinced that many important learning goals of the schoolís science program can be met in this course. She wants to provide the students with opportunities to understand the basic principles of transmission genetics. She also wants them to appreciate how using a mental model is useful to understanding. She wants her students to engage in and learn the processes of inquiry as they develop their mental models. Ms. J. also wants students to understand the effect of transmission genetics on their lives and on society; here she wants them to address an issue that includes science and ethics.

Selecting an appropriate computer program is important, because simulation will be key to much of the first quarter of the course. Ms. J. has reviewed several and noted common features. Each simulation allows students to select parental phenotypes and make crosses. Offspring were produced quickly by all the programs; genotypes and phenotypes are distributed stochastically according to the inheritance pattern. With such programs, students will be able to simulate many generations of crosses in a single class period. All the programs are open-ended—no answer books are provided to check answers. All the programs allow students to begin with data and construct a model of the elements and processes of an inheritance pattern. Students will be able to use the model to predict the phenotypes and genotypes of future offspring and check predictions by making the crosses. Ms. J. chooses one of the simulations after reviewing it carefully and considering the budget she has for supplies. Enough computers are available to permit students to work in teams of four.

Students will work in their teams to develop models of inheritance patterns during the first quarter. Ms. J. plans to obtain reprints of Mendel's original article for students to read early in the quarter. It has a nice model for an inheritance pattern, and students will examine it as they identify elements of a mental model. In addition to using the simulations, Ms. J. wants students to work with living organisms. She will need to order the proper yeast strains, fruit flies, and Fast Plants. She has commercially prepared units in genetics using each of these organisms and has adapted the units

to meet the needs of the students. Each organism has advantages and limitations when used to study transmission genetics; students will be working in teams and will share with other teams what they learn from the different organisms.

During the second quarter, students will focus on human genetics. Ms. J. intends to contact the local university to arrange for a particular speaker from the clinical genetics department. The speaker and Ms. J. have worked together before, and she knows how well the speaker presents information on classes of inherited human disorders, human pedigree analysis, new research in genetic susceptibility to common illnesses, and the many careers associated with human genetics. Someone from the state laboratory also will come and demonstrate

karyotyping and leave some photographs so students can try sorting chromosomes to get a feel for the skill required to do this. Having students perform a karyotype will give new meaning to a phrase in the text: "the chromosome images are sorted by type."

Each student will become an "expert" in one inherited human disorder, learning about the mode of inheritance, symptoms, frequency, effect on individuals and family, care, and such. Students will present their reports to the class. They will also work in pairs to solve an ethical case study associated with an inherited disorder. Drawing on several articles about teaching ethical issues to children, Ms. J. has created one of her own, and with the help of colleagues and the staff at the clinical genetics center, she has developed several case studies from which the students will develop their ethical issue papers. Part of the case study will require students to draw a pedigree. Ms. J. is gathering print matter: fliers from the March of Dimes, textbooks on clinical genetics, some novels and short stories about people with inherited disorders, and articles from popular magazines. This is an ongoing effort—she has been collecting material for some years now. She also has posters and pictures from service organizations she will put up around the room, but some wall space needs to be saved for student data charts.

Having reviewed the goals and structure of the course, Ms. J.'s next planning step is to map tasks by week. She has a good idea of how long different activities will take from her previous experience teaching this course. Planning for each week helps ensure that the live materials and the speakers are coordinated for the right time. But Ms. J. knows that it is likely that she will need to adjust scheduling. Ms. J. and the students will set routines and procedures during the first week; then students will do much of the class work in their teams.

Finally, Ms. J. begins to map out the days of the first week. On the first day of class, the students will share why they chose this course and what their hopes and expectations are. They might also describe what they already know about genetics and what questions they bring to class.

science-rich centers, industry, and other organizations must participate in professional development activities with teachers.

See Program Standard D and System Standard D

Some of the most powerful connections between science teaching and learning are made through thoughtful practice in field experiences, team teaching, collaborative research, or peer coaching. Field experience starts early in the preservice program and continues throughout a teaching career. Whenever possible, the context for learning to teach science should involve actual students, real student work, and outstanding curriculum materials. Trial and error in teaching situations, continual thoughtful reflection, interaction with peers, and much repetition of teaching science content combine to develop the kind of integrated understanding that characterizes expert teachers of science.

New forms of collaboration that foster integrated professional development for teachers must be developed. One promising possibility is the reorganization of teacher education institutions into a professional development school model, where practitioners and theoreticians are involved in teacher education activities in a collegial relationship. Another is extensive collaboration among schools, colleges, local industry, and other science-rich centers.

Many teachers come to learning activities with preconceptions about teaching science. At a minimum, their own science learning experiences have defined teaching for them. More accomplished teachers have their own teaching styles and strategies and their own views of learning and teaching. When teachers have the time and opportunity to describe their own views about learning and

teaching, to conduct research on their own teaching, and to compare, contrast, and revise their views, they come to understand the nature of exemplary science teaching.

Learning experiences for prospective and practicing teachers must include inquiries into the questions and difficulties teachers have. Assessment is an example. Teachers must have opportunities to observe practitioners of good classroom assessment and to

When teachers have the time and opportunity to describe their own views about learning and teaching, to conduct research on their own teaching, and to compare, contrast, and revise their views, they come to understand the nature of exemplary science teaching.

review critically assessment instruments and their use. They need to have structured opportunities in aligning curriculum and assessment, in selecting and developing appropriate assessment tasks, and in analyzing and interpreting the gathered information. Teachers also need to have opportunities to collaborate with other teachers to evaluate student work—developing, refining, and applying criteria for evaluation. Practicing teachers will benefit from opportunities to participate in organized sessions for scoring open-ended assessments.

See *Assessments Conducted by Classroom Teachers* in Chapter 5

Professional development activities create opportunities for teachers to confront new and different ways of thinking; to participate in demonstrations of new and different ways of acting; to discuss, examine, critique, explore, argue, and struggle with new ideas;

to try out new approaches in different situations and get feedback on the use of new ideas, skills, tools, and behaviors; to reflect on the experiments and experiences of teaching science, and then to revise and try again.

Teacher learning is analogous to student learning: Learning to teach science requires that the teacher articulate questions, pursue answers to those questions, interpret information gathered, propose applications, and fit the new learning into the larger picture of science teaching.

These suggestions for preservice and inservice professional development do not dictate a certain structure. They could be met in a college course, a sustained inservice workshop or institute, a residency in a science-rich center, a seminar for new teachers, a teacher study or action research group, or a teacher network. It is the nature of the learning situation that is important, not the structure.

PROFESSIONAL DEVELOPMENT STANDARD C:
Professional development for teachers of science requires building understanding and ability for lifelong learning. Professional development activities must

- Provide regular, frequent opportunities for individual and collegial examination and reflection on classroom and institutional practice.
- Provide opportunities for teachers to receive feedback about their teaching and to understand, analyze, and apply that feedback to improve their practice.
- Provide opportunities for teachers to learn and use various tools and techniques for self-reflection and collegial reflection, such as peer coaching, portfolios, and journals.
- Support the sharing of teacher expertise by preparing and using mentors, teacher advisers, coaches, lead teachers, and resource teachers to provide professional development opportunities.
- Provide opportunities to know and have access to existing research and experiential knowledge.
- Provide opportunities to learn and use the skills of research to generate new knowledge about science and the teaching and learning of science.

The primary job of a teacher is to promote learning, and it follows that teachers themselves are dedicated learners. Lifelong learning by teachers is essential for several reasons. One obvious reason is to keep current in science. Teachers do not leave preservice programs with complete understanding of all the science they will need in their teaching careers, and they need to continue to clarify and deepen their understanding of the science content that is part of their teaching responsibility.

Another reason teachers must have the opportunity to continue to learn is made clear by the observation that tomorrow's students will have markedly different needs from today's students; even today's employers require employees who can frame problems and design their own tasks, think critically, and work together.

Teaching itself is complex, requiring constant learning and continual reflection. New knowledge, skills, and strategies for teaching come from a variety of sources—research, new materials and tools, descriptions of best

See Professional Development Standard A

See Professional Development Standard B

practice, colleagues, supervisors, self-reflection on teaching, and reflection on the learning of students in the classroom. Teachers continually consider and contribute to the advances in the knowledge base of teaching and learning.

KNOWLEDGE FOR LIFELONG LEARNING

From their first days considering teaching as a profession through their entire careers, teachers of science develop the skills to analyze their learning needs and styles through self-reflection and active solicitation of feedback from others. They must have the skills to use tools and techniques for self-assessment (such as journal writing, study groups, and portfolios) and collaborative reflection strategies (such as peer coaching, mentoring, and peer consulting). Teachers of science should be able to use the *Standards* and district expectations to set personal goals and take responsibility for their own professional development.

Learning is a developmental process that takes time and often is hard work. As does any professional, teachers of science will stumble, wrestle, and ponder, while realizing that failure is a natural part of developing new skills and understanding. However, effective teachers know how to access research-based resources and, when faced with a learning need, pursue new knowledge and skills that are based on research or effective practice. Teachers of science need to develop the skills to conduct research in their classrooms on science teaching and learning and be able to share their results with others.

LEARNING SKILLS FOR LIFELONG LEARNING

The integrated knowledge needed to teach science well is developed over time. Thus, the acquisition of the skills for continuous learning should be an explicit component of all learning experiences.

As lifelong learners, teachers need to reflect on their experiences and have techniques and the time to do so. Preservice courses must allocate time to teach prospective teachers techniques for reflection, and practicing teachers must be given opportunities to develop these skills as well. Many techniques for reflection on practice are available, and their use is becoming more widespread. Self-reflection tools such as journals, audiotapes or videotapes, and portfolios allow teachers to capture their teaching, track their development over time, analyze their progress, and identify needs for further learning. Other techniques include peer observation, coaching, and mentoring beginning teachers in either structured or unstructured settings. Teachers also need opportunities to form study groups or hold less-formal sharing sessions.

Continuous learning is an active process that will require different norms from those that are presently operative in colleges and in schools: norms of experimentation and risk-taking, of trust and collegial support, and, most relevant to science, of careful and dedicated inquiry. Schools in which risk-taking is encouraged will provide learning communities for adults as well as for students. Other learning environments that can provide such conditions are professional networks—collegial groups where teachers find help, support, ideas, strategies, and solutions to their problems. Examples include professional science-teaching associations, state and local organizations, and telecommunications networks. Those types of groups provide safe and rich learning environments in which teachers can share resources, ask and address hard questions, and continue to learn.

See Program Standard D and System Standard D

Being a lifelong learner also requires that teachers have the resources for professional development and the time to use them. Such resources include access to formal and informal courses that allow them to keep abreast of current science, access to research on curriculum, teaching, and assessment found in journals and at professional meetings; media and technology to access databases and to analyze teaching; and opportunities to observe other teachers. Conducting formal and informal classroom-based research is a powerful means to improve practice. This research includes asking questions about how students learn science, trying new approaches to teaching, and evaluating the results in student achievement from these approaches. Conducting such research requires time and resources.

PROFESSIONAL DEVELOPMENT STANDARD D:
Professional development programs for teachers of science must be coherent and integrated. Quality preservice and inservice programs are characterized by
- Clear, shared goals based on a vision of science learning, teaching, and teacher development congruent with the *National Science Education Standards*.

- Integration and coordination of the program components so that understanding and ability can be built over time, reinforced continuously, and practiced in a variety of situations.
- Options that recognize the developmental nature of teacher professional growth and individual and group interests, as well as the needs of teachers who have varying degrees of experience, professional expertise, and proficiency.
- Collaboration among the people involved in programs, including teachers, teacher educators, teacher unions, scientists, administrators, policy makers, members of professional and scientific organizations, parents, and business people, with clear respect for the perspectives and expertise of each.
- Recognition of the history, culture, and organization of the school environment.
- Continuous program assessment that captures the perspectives of all those involved, uses a variety of strategies, focuses on the process and effects of the program, and feeds directly into program improvement and evaluation.

See Program Standard A

The professional development of teachers is complicated: there is much for teachers of science to know and be able to do; materials need to be critiqued and questions need to be researched; a variety of information and expertise needs to be tapped; and many individuals and institutions claim responsibility for professional development. However, for an individual teacher, prospective or practicing, professional development too often is a random combination of courses, conferences, research experiences, workshops, networking opportunities, internships, and mentoring relationships. More coherence is sorely needed.

Professional development programs and practices require a focus on the vision of science education presented by the *Standards*. Attention must be paid at the state, district, and college and school levels to fitting the various pieces of professional development programs together to achieve a common set of goals. Preservice program coordination requires mechanisms and strategies for connecting and integrating science courses, pedagogy courses, and clinical experiences (i.e., experiences in schools and classrooms). Such coordination also is needed for programs for practicing teachers, who often face myriad offerings by school districts, individual schools, professional associations, unions, business and industry, regional service centers, publishing companies, local universities, nearby research laboratories, museums, and federal and state agencies.

See System Standards A and B

Professional development opportunities for teachers must account for differing degrees and forms of expertise represented in any group, and they must recognize the nature of quality experiences as described in standards A and B. Programs must be designed not just to impart technical skills, but to deepen and enrich understanding and ability. Professional development activities must extend over long periods and include a range of strategies to provide opportunities for teachers to refine their knowledge, understanding, and abilities continually.

Individual teachers of science should have the opportunity to put together programs for professional development, as should groups of teachers, whether formally constituted or informally connected through common

needs and interests. The many providers of teacher professional development activities will continue to design programs. However, the strongest programs result from collaborations among teachers, developers (such as university faculty, science coordinators, and teachers), and other stakeholders (including community agencies, science-rich centers, scientists, school administrators, and business and industry). Such collaborations increase coherence, and they bring a wide variety of expertise and resources to bear on a set of common goals that are directly connected to the needs of teachers.

The success of professional development for practicing teachers is heavily dependent on the organizational dynamics of schooling, such as a climate that permits change and risk-taking, good relationships among school personnel, communication structures, and an appropriate distribution of authority. Professional development programs therefore must involve administrators and other school staff. All must be committed to ensuring that prospective teachers, new teachers, and practicing teachers who wish to implement new ideas as part of their professional development are supported and integrated into the ongoing life of the school.

Finally, those who plan and conduct professional development programs must continually evaluate the attainments of teachers and the opportunities provided them to ensure that their programs are maximally useful for teachers.

CHANGING EMPHASES

The *National Science Education Standards* envision change throughout the system. The professional development standards encompass the following changes in emphases:

LESS EMPHASIS ON	MORE EMPHASIS ON
Transmission of teaching knowledge and skills by lectures	Inquiry into teaching and learning
Learning science by lecture and reading	Learning science through investigation and inquiry
Separation of science and teaching knowledge	Integration of science and teaching knowledge
Separation of theory and practice	Integration of theory and practice in school settings
Individual learning	Collegial and collaborative learning
Fragmented, one-shot sessions	Long-term coherent plans
Courses and workshops	A variety of professional development activities
Reliance on external expertise	Mix of internal and external expertise
Staff developers as educators	Staff developers as facilitators, consultants, and planners
Teacher as technician	Teacher as intellectual, reflective practitioner
Teacher as consumer of knowledge about teaching	Teacher as producer of knowledge about teaching
Teacher as follower	Teacher as leader
Teacher as an individual based in a classroom	Teacher as a member of a collegial professional community
Teacher as target of change	Teacher as source and facilitator of change

References for Further Reading

AAAS (American Association for the Advancement of Science). 1990. The Liberal Art of Science: Agenda for Action: The Report of the Project on Liberal Education and the Sciences. Washington, DC: AAAS

Darling-Hammond, L. 1993. Reframing the school reform agenda: Developing capacity for school transformation. Phi Delta Kappan, 74 (10): 752-761.

Feiman-Nemser, S. 1989. Teacher Preparation: Structural and Conceptual Alternatives. East Lansing, MI: National Center for Research on Teaching.

Goodlad, J.I. 1994. Educational Renewal: Better Teachers, Better Schools. San Francisco: Jossey-Bass.

Hargreaves, A., and M.G. Fullan, eds. 1992. Understanding Teacher Development. New York: Teachers College Press.

Holmes Group. 1986. Tomorrow's Teachers: A Report of the Holmes Group. East Lansing, MI: Holmes Group.

Joyce, B., ed. 1990. Changing School Culture Through Staff Development: 1990 Yearbook of The Association for Supervision and Curriculum Development. Alexandria, VA: Association for Supervision and Curriculum Development.

Kahle, J.B. 1993. Teaching science for excellence and equity. In This Year in School Science 1993, A.E. Haley-Oliphant and S. Rogg, eds. Washington, DC: American Association for the Advancement of Science.

Lieberman, A., and L. Miller, eds. 1991. Staff Development for Education in the '90s: New Demands, New Realities, New Perspectives, 2nd ed. New York: Teachers College Press.

Little, J.W. 1993. Teachers' professional development in a climate of educational reform. Educational Evaluation and Policy Analysis, 15 (2): 129-151.

McDermott, L.C. 1990. A perspective in teacher preparation in physics and other sciences: the need for special science courses for teachers. American Journal of Physics, 58(1990).

NRC (National Research Council). 1996. The Role of Scientists in the Professional Development of Science Teachers. Washington, DC: National Academy Press.

NRC (National Research Council). 1990. Fulfilling the Promise: Biology Education in the Nation's Schools. Washington, DC: National Academy Press.

Raizen, S.A., and A.M. Michelsohn, eds.. 1994. The Future of Science in Elementary Schools: Educating Prospective Teachers. San Francisco: Jossey-Bass.

Shulman, L.S. 1990. Reconnecting foundations to the substance of teacher education. Teachers College Record, 91 (3): 301-310.

Stevenson, H.W., and J.W. Stigler. 1992. The Learning Gap: Why Our Schools Are Failing and What We Can Learn from Japanese and Chinese Education. New York: Summit Books.

Tyson, H. 1994. Who Will Teach the Children? Progress and Resistance in Teacher Education. San Francisco: Jossey-Bass.

observe

Learn

Change

Interact

Student achievement can be interpreted only in light of the quality of the programs they have experienced.

Assessment in Science Education

The assessment standards provide criteria to judge progress toward the science education vision of scientific literacy for all. The standards describe the quality of assessment practices used by teachers and state and federal agencies to measure student achievement and the opportunity provided students to learn science. By identifying essential characteristics of exemplary assessment practices, the standards serve as guides for developing assessment tasks, practices, and policies. These standards can be applied equally to the assessment of students, teachers, and programs; to summative and formative assessment practices; and to classroom assessments as well as large-scale, external assessments. ▮ This chapter begins with an introduction that describes the components of the assessment process and a contemporary view of measurement theory and practice. This introduction is followed by the assessment standards and then by discussions of some ways teachers use assessments and some characteristics of assessments conducted at the district, state, and national levels. The chapter closes with

The assessment process is an effective tool for communicating the expectations of the science education system to all concerned with science education.

two sample assessment tasks, one to probe students' understanding of the natural world and another to probe their ability to inquire.

In the vision described by the *National Science Education Standards*, assessment is a primary feedback mechanism in the science education system. For example, assessment data provide students with feedback on how well they are meeting the expectations of their teachers and parents, teachers with feedback on how well their students are learning, districts with feedback on the effectiveness of their teachers and programs, and policy makers with feedback on how well policies are working. Feedback leads to changes in the science education system by stimulating changes in policy, guiding teacher professional development, and encouraging students to improve their understanding of science.

The assessment process is an effective tool for communicating the expectations of the science education system to all concerned with science education. Assessment practices and policies provide operational definitions of what is important. For example, the use of an extended inquiry for an assessment task signals what students are to learn, how

teachers are to teach, and where resources are to be allocated.

Assessment is a systematic, multistep process involving the collection and interpretation of educational data. The four components of the assessment process are detailed in Figure 5.1.

As science educators are changing the way they think about good science education, educational measurement specialists are acknowledging change as well. Recognition of the importance of assessment to contemporary educational reform has catalyzed research, development, and implementation of new methods of data collection along with new ways of judging data quality. These changes in measurement theory and practice are reflected in the assessment standards.

In this new view, assessment and learning are two sides of the same coin. The methods used to collect educational data define in measurable terms what teachers should teach and what students should learn. And when students engage in an assessment exercise, they should learn from it.

This view of assessment places greater confidence in the results of assessment procedures that sample an assortment of variables using diverse data-collection methods, rather than the more traditional sampling of one variable by a single method. Thus, all aspects of science achievement—ability to inquire, scientific understanding of the natural world, understanding of the nature and utility of science—are measured using multiple methods such as performances and portfolios, as well as conventional paper-and-pencil tests.

The assessment standards include increased emphasis on the measurement of

See Assessment Standard B

FIGURE 5.1. COMPONENTS OF THE ASSESSMENT PROCESS

The four components can be combined in numerous ways. For example, teachers use student achievement data to plan and modify teaching practices, and business leaders use per capita educational expenditures to locate businesses. The variety of uses, users, methods, and data contributes to the complexity and importance of the assessment process.

DATA USE	DATA COLLECTION	METHODS TO COLLECT DATA	USERS OF DATA
▮ Plan teaching	To describe and quantify:	▮ Paper and pencil testing	▮ Teachers
▮ Guide learning		▮ Performance testing	▮ Students
▮ Calculate grades	▮ Student achievement and attitude	▮ Interviews	▮ Educational administrators
▮ Make comparisons		▮ Portfolios	▮ Parents
▮ Credential and license	▮ Teacher preparation and quality	▮ Performances	▮ Public
▮ Determine access to special or advanced education	▮ Program characteristics	▮ Observing programs, students, and teachers in classroom	▮ Policymakers
▮ Develop education theory	▮ Resource allocation	▮ Transcript analysis	▮ Institutions of higher education
▮ Inform policy formulation	▮ Policy instruments	▮ Expert reviews of educational materials	▮ Business and industry
▮ Monitor effects of policies			▮ Government
▮ Allocate resources			
▮ Evaluate quality of curricula, programs, and teaching practices			

⟨·····⟩   ⟨·····⟩   ⟨·····⟩

DECISIONS AND ACTION BASED ON DATA

opportunity to learn. Student achievement can be interpreted only in light of the quality of the programs they have experienced.

Another important shift is toward "authentic assessment." This movement calls for exercises that closely approximate the intended outcomes of science education. Authentic assessment exercises require students to apply scientific knowledge and reasoning to situations similar to those they will encounter in the world outside the classroom, as well as to situations that approximate how scientists do their work.

Another conceptual shift within the educational measurement area that has significant implications for science assessment involves validity. Validity must be concerned not only with the technical quality of educational data, but also with the social and educational consequences of data interpretation.

An important assumption underlying the assessment standards is that states and local districts can develop mechanisms to measure students' achievement as specified in the content standards and to measure the opportunities for learning science as specified in the program and system standards. If the principles in the assessment standards are followed, the information resulting from new modes of assessment applied locally can have common meaning and value in terms of the national standards, despite the use of different assessment procedures and instruments in different locales. This contrasts with the traditional view of educational measurement that allows for comparisons only when they are based on parallel forms of the same test.

The Standards

ASSESSMENT STANDARD A: Assessments must be consistent with the decisions they are designed to inform.

- Assessments are deliberately designed.
- Assessments have explicitly stated purposes.
- The relationship between the decisions and the data is clear.
- Assessment procedures are internally consistent.

The essential characteristic of well-designed assessments is that the processes used to collect and interpret data are consistent with the purpose of the assessment. That match of purpose and process is achieved through thoughtful planning that is available for public review.

ASSESSMENTS ARE DELIBERATELY DESIGNED. Educational data profoundly influence the lives of students, as well as the people and institutions responsible for science education. People who must use the results of assessments to make decisions and take actions, as well as those who are affected by the decisions and actions, deserve assurance that assessments are carefully conceptualized. Evidence of careful conceptualization is found in written plans for assessments that contain

- Statements about the purposes that the assessment will serve.
- Descriptions of the substance and technical quality of the data to be collected.
- Specifications of the number of students or schools from which data will be obtained.

- Descriptions of the data-collection method.
- Descriptions of the method of data interpretation.
- Descriptions of the decisions to be made, including who will make the decisions and by what procedures.

ASSESSMENTS HAVE EXPLICITLY STATED PURPOSES. Conducting assessments is a resource-intensive activity. Routine assessments in the classroom place considerable demands on the time and intellectual resources of teachers and students. Large-scale assessments, such as those conducted by districts, states, and the federal government, require tremendous human and fiscal expenditures. Such resources should be expended only with the assurance that the decisions and actions that follow will increase the scientific literacy of the students—an assurance that can be made only if the purpose of the assessment is clear.

THE RELATIONSHIP BETWEEN THE DECISIONS AND THE DATA IS CLEAR. Assessments test assumptions about relationships among educational variables. For example, if the purpose is to decide if a school district's management system should be continued, assessment data might be collected about student achievement. This choice of assessment would be based on the following assumed relationship: the management system gives teachers responsibility for selecting the science programs, teachers have an incentive to implement effectively the programs they select, and effective implementation improves science achievement. The relationship between the decision to be made and the data to be collected is specified.

See Teaching Standard F

ASSESSMENT PROCEDURES NEED TO BE INTERNALLY CONSISTENT. For an assessment to be internally consistent, each component must be consistent with all others. A link of inferences must be established and reasonable alternative explanations eliminated. For example, in the district management example above, the relationship between the management system and student achievement is not adequately tested if student achievement is the only variable measured. The extent to which the management system increased teacher responsibility and led to changes in the science programs that could influence science achievement must also be measured.

ASSESSMENT STANDARD B: Achievement and opportunity to learn science must be assessed.

- Achievement data collected focus on the science content that is most important for students to learn.
- Opportunity-to-learn data collected focus on the most powerful indicators.
- Equal attention must be given to the assessment of opportunity to learn and to the assessment of student achievement.

ACHIEVEMENT DATA COLLECTED FOCUS ON THE SCIENCE CONTENT THAT IS MOST IMPORTANT FOR STUDENTS TO LEARN. The content standards define the science all students will come to understand. They portray the outcomes of science education as rich and varied, encompassing

- The ability to inquire.
- Knowing and understanding scientific facts, concepts, principles, laws, and theories.

The Insect and the Spider

Titles in this example emphasize some of the components of the assessment process. In the vision of science education described in the Standards, teaching often cannot be distinguished from assessment. In this example, Ms. M. uses information from observations of student work and discussion to change classroom practice to improve student understanding of complex ideas. She has a repertoire of analogies, questions, and examples that she has developed and uses when needed. The students develop answers to questions about an analogy using written and diagrammatic representations. The administrator recognizes that teachers make plans but adapt them and provided Ms. M. with an opportunity to explain the reasoning supporting her decision.

[This example highlights some elements of Teaching Standard A and B; Assessment Standard A, 5-8 Content Standard B, and Program Standard F.]

SCIENCE CONTENT: The 5-8 Physical Science Content Standard includes an understanding of motions and forces. One of the supporting ideas is that the motion of an object can be described by the change in its position with time.

ASSESSMENT ACTIVITY: Students respond to questions about frames of reference with extended written responses and diagrams.

ASSESSMENT TYPE: This is an individual extended response exercise embedded in teaching.

ASSESSMENT PURPOSE: The teacher uses the information from this activity to improve the lesson.

DATA: Students' written responses. Teacher's observations.

CONTEXT: A seventh-grade class is studying the motion of objects. One student, describing his idea about motion and forces, points to a book on the desk and says "right now the book is not moving." A second student interrupts, "Oh, yes it is. The book is on the desk, the desk is on the floor, the floor is a part of the building, the building is sitting on the Earth, the Earth is rotating on its axis and revolving around the Sun, and the whole solar system is moving through the Milky Way." The second student sits back with a self-satisfied smile on her face. All discussion ceases.

Ms. M. signals time and poses the following questions to the class. Imagine an insect and a spider on a lily pad floating down a stream. The spider is walking around the edge of lily pad. The insect is sitting in the middle of the pad watching the spider. How would the insect describe its own motion? How would the insect describe the spider's motion? How would a bird sitting on the edge of the stream describe the motion of the insect and the spider? After setting the class to work discussing the questions, the teacher walks around the room listening to the discussions. Ms. M. asks the students to write answers to the questions she posed; she suggests that the students use diagrams as a part of the responses.

The school principal had been observing Ms. M. during this class and asked her to explain why she had not followed her original lesson plan. Ms. M. explained that the girl had made a similar statement to the class twice before. Ms. M. realized that the girl was not being disruptive but was making a legitimate point that the other members of the class were not grasping. So Ms. M. decided that continuing with the discussion of motions and forces would not be fruitful until the class had developed a better concept of frame of reference. Her questions were designed to help the students realize that motion is described in terms of some point of reference. The insect in the middle of lily pad would describe its motion and the motion of the spider in terms of its reference frame, the lily pad. In contrast, the bird watching from the edge of the stream would describe the motion of the lily pad and its passengers in terms of its reference frame, namely the ground on which it was standing. Someone on the ground observing the bird would say that the bird was not in motion, but an observer on the moon would have a different answer.

- The ability to reason scientifically.
- The ability to use science to make personal decisions and to take positions on societal issues.
- The ability to communicate effectively about science.

This assessment standard highlights the complexity of the content standards while addressing the importance of collecting data on all aspects of student science achievement.

See Content Standards B, C, and D (all grade levels)

Educational measurement theory and practice have been well developed primarily to measure student knowledge about subject matter; therefore, many educators and policy analysts have more confidence in instruments designed to measure a student's command of information about science than in instruments designed to measure students' understanding of the natural world or their ability

See the principal *Learning science is an active process* in Chapter 2

to inquire. Many current science achievement tests measure "inert" knowledge—discrete, isolated bits of knowledge—rather than "active" knowledge—knowledge that is rich and well-structured. Assessment processes that include all outcomes for student achievement must probe the extent and organization of a student's knowledge. Rather than checking whether students have memorized certain items of information, assessments need to probe for students' understanding, reasoning, and the utilization of knowledge. Assessment and learning are so closely related that if all the outcomes are not assessed, teachers and students likely will redefine their expectations for learning science only to the outcomes that are assessed.

OPPORTUNITY-TO-LEARN DATA COLLECTED FOCUS ON THE MOST POWERFUL INDICATORS. The system, program, teaching, and professional development standards portray the conditions that must exist throughout the science education system if all students are to have the opportunity to learn science.

At the classroom level, some of the most powerful indicators of opportunity to learn are teachers' professional knowledge, including content knowledge, pedagogical knowledge, and understanding of students; the extent to which content, teaching, professional development, and assessment are coordinated; the time available for teachers to teach and students to learn science; the availability of resources for student inquiry; and the quality of educational materials available. The teaching and program standards define in greater detail these and other indicators of opportunity to learn.

Some indicators of opportunity to learn have their origins at the federal, state, and district levels and are discussed in greater detail in the systems standards. Other powerful indicators of opportunity to learn beyond the classroom include per-capita educational expenditures, state science requirements for graduation, and federal allocation of funds to states.

Compelling indicators of opportunity to learn are continually being identified, and ways to collect data about them are being designed. Measuring such indicators presents many technical, theoretical, economic, and social challenges, but those challenges do not obviate the responsibility of moving forward on implementing and assessing opportunity to learn. The assessment standards call for a policy-level commitment of the resources necessary for research and development related to assessing opportunity to learn. That commitment includes the development of the technical skills to assess opportunity to learn among science education professionals, including teachers, supervisors, administrators, and curriculum developers.

EQUAL ATTENTION MUST BE GIVEN TO THE ASSESSMENT OF OPPORTUNITY TO LEARN AND TO THE ASSESSMENT OF STUDENT ACHIEVEMENT. Students cannot be held accountable for achievement unless they are given adequate opportunity to learn science. Therefore, achievement and opportunity to learn science must be assessed equally.

See Program Standard E and System Standard E

ASSESSMENT STANDARD C:
The technical quality of the data collected is well matched to the decisions and actions taken on the basis of their interpretation.

- The feature that is claimed to be measured is actually measured.
- Assessment tasks are authentic.
- An individual student's performance is similar on two or more tasks that claim to measure the same aspect of student achievement.
- Students have adequate opportunity to demonstrate their achievements.
- Assessment tasks and methods of presenting them provide data that are sufficiently stable to lead to the same decisions if used at different times.

Standard C addresses the degree to which the data collected warrant the decisions and actions that will be based on them. The quality of the decisions and the appropriateness of resulting action are limited by the quality of the data. The more serious the consequences for students or teachers, the greater confidence those making the decisions must have in the technical quality of the data. Confidence is gauged by the quality of the assessment process and the consistency of the measurement over alternative assessment processes. Judgments about confidence are based on several different indicators, some of which are discussed below.

THE FEATURE THAT IS CLAIMED TO BE MEASURED IS ACTUALLY MEASURED. The content and form of an assessment task must be congruent with what is supposed to be measured. This is "validity." For instance, if an assessment claims to measure students' ability to frame questions for conducting scientific inquiry and to design an inquiry to address the questions, a short-answer format would not be an appropriate task. Requiring students to pose questions and design inquiries to address them would be an appropriate task. However, if the purpose of

The content and form of an assessment task must be congruent with what is supposed to be measured.

an assessment task is to measure students' knowledge of the characteristics that distinguish groups of minerals, a multiple-choice format might be suitable as well as efficient.

ASSESSMENT TASKS ARE AUTHENTIC. When students are engaged in assessment tasks that are similar in form to tasks in which they will engage in their lives outside the classroom or are similar to the activities of scientists, great confidence can be attached to the data collected. Such assessment tasks are authentic.

Classroom assessments can take many forms, including observations of student performance during instructional activities; interviews; formal performance tasks; portfolios; investigative projects; written reports; and multiple choice, short-answer, and essay examinations. The relationship of some of those forms of assessment tasks to the goals of science education are not as obvious as others. For instance, a student's ability to obtain and evaluate scientific information might be measured using a short-answer test to identify the sources of high-quality scientific information about toxic waste. An alternative and more authentic method is to ask the student to locate such information and develop an annotated bibliography and a judgment about the scientific quality of the information.

AN INDIVIDUAL STUDENT'S PERFORMANCE IS SIMILAR ON TWO OR MORE TASKS THAT CLAIM TO MEASURE THE SAME ASPECT OF STUDENT ACHIEVEMENT. This is one aspect of reliability. Suppose that the purpose of an assessment is to measure a student's ability to pose appropriate questions. A student might be asked to pose questions in a situation set in the physical sciences. The student's performance and the task are consistent if the performance is the same when the task is set in the context of the life sciences, assuming the student has had equal opportunities to learn physical and life sciences.

STUDENTS HAVE ADEQUATE OPPORTUNITIES TO DEMONSTRATE THEIR ACHIEVEMENTS. For decision makers to have confidence in assessment data, they need assurance that students have had the opportunity to demonstrate their full understanding and ability. Assessment tasks must be developmentally appropriate, must be set in contexts that are familiar to the students, must not require reading skills or vocabulary that are inappropriate to the students' grade level, and must be as free from bias as possible.

ASSESSMENT TASKS AND THE METHODS OF PRESENTING THEM PROVIDE DATA THAT ARE SUFFICIENTLY STABLE TO LEAD TO THE SAME DECISIONS IF USED AT DIFFERENT TIMES. This is another aspect of reliability, and is especially important for large-scale assessments, where changes in performance of groups is of interest. Only with stable measures can valid inferences about changes in group performance be made.

Although the confidence indicators discussed above focus on student achievement data, an analogous set of confidence indicators can be generated for opportunity to

Assessment tasks must be developmentally appropriate, must be set in contexts that are familiar to the students, must not require reading skills or vocabulary that are inappropriate to the students' grade level, and must be as free from bias as possible.

learn. For instance, teacher quality is an indicator of opportunity to learn. Authenticity is obtained if teacher quality is measured by systematic observation of teaching performance by qualified observers. Confidence in the measure is

See Teaching Standard C

achieved when the number of observations is large enough for a teacher to exhibit a full range of teaching knowledge and skill. Consistency of performance is also established through repeated observations.

Data-collection methods can take many forms. Each has advantages and disadvantages. The choice among them is usually

The choice of assessment form should be consistent with what one wants to measure and to infer.

constrained by tradeoffs between the type, quality, and amount of information gained, and the time and resources each requires. However, to serve the intended purpose, the choice of assessment form should be consistent with what one wants to measure and to infer. It is critical that the data and their method of collection yield information with confidence levels consistent with the consequences of its use. Public confidence in educational data and their use is related to technical quality. This public confidence is influenced by the extent to which technical quality has been considered by educators and policy makers and the skill with which they communicate with the public about it.

ASSESSMENT STANDARD D: Assessment practices must be fair.

- Assessment tasks must be reviewed for the use of stereotypes, for assumptions that reflect the perspectives or experiences of a particular group, for language that might be offensive to a particular group, and for other features that might distract students from the intended task.

- Large-scale assessments must use statistical techniques to identify potential bias among subgroups.
- Assessment tasks must be appropriately modified to accommodate the needs of students with physical disabilities, learning disabilities, or limited English proficiency.
- Assessment tasks must be set in a variety of contexts, be engaging to students with different interests and experiences, and must not assume the perspective or experience of a particular gender, racial, or ethnic group.

A premise of the *National Science Education Standards* is that all students should have access to quality science education and should be expected to achieve scientific literacy as defined by the content standards. It follows that the processes used to assess student achievement must be fair to all students. This is not only an ethical requirement but also a measurement requirement. If assessment results are more closely related to gender or ethnicity than to the preparation received or the science understanding and ability being assessed, the validity of the assessment process is questionable.

See Program Standard E and System Standard E

ASSESSMENT TASKS MUST BE REVIEWED FOR THE USE OF STEREOTYPES, FOR ASSUMPTIONS THAT REFLECT THE PERSPECTIVES OR EXPERIENCES OF A PARTICULAR GROUP, FOR LANGUAGE THAT MIGHT BE OFFENSIVE TO A PARTICULAR GROUP, AND FOR OTHER FEATURES THAT MIGHT DISTRACT STUDENTS FROM THE INTENDED TASK. Those who plan and implement science assessments must pay deliberate attention to issues of fairness.

The concern for fairness is reflected in the procedures used to develop assessment tasks, in the content and language of the assessment tasks, in the processes by which students are assessed, and in the analyses of assessment results.

LARGE-SCALE ASSESSMENTS MUST USE STATISTICAL TECHNIQUES TO IDENTIFY POTENTIAL BIAS AMONG SUBGROUPS. Statistical techniques require that both sexes and different racial and ethnic backgrounds be included in the development of large-scale assessments. Bias can be determined with some certainty through the combination of statistical evidence and expert judgment. For instance, if an exercise to assess understanding of inertia using a flywheel results in differential performance between females and males, a judgment that the exercise is biased might be plausible based on the assumption that males and females have different experiences with flywheels.

ASSESSMENT TASKS MUST BE MODIFIED APPROPRIATELY TO ACCOMMODATE THE NEEDS OF STUDENTS WITH PHYSICAL DISABILITIES, LEARNING DISABILITIES, OR LIMITED ENGLISH PROFICIENCY. Whether assessments are large scale or teacher conducted, the principle of fairness requires that data-collection methods allow students with physical disabilities, learning disabilities, or limited English proficiency to demonstrate the full extent of their science knowledge and skills.

ASSESSMENT TASKS MUST BE SET IN A VARIETY OF CONTEXTS, BE ENGAGING TO STUDENTS WITH DIFFERENT INTERESTS AND EXPERIENCES, AND MUST NOT ASSUME THE PERSPECTIVE OR EXPERIENCE OF A PARTICULAR GENDER, RACIAL, OR ETHNIC GROUP. The requirement that assessment exercises be authentic and thus in context increases the likelihood that all tasks have some degree of bias for some population of students. Some contexts will have more appeal to males and others to females. If, however, assessments employ a variety of tasks, the collection will be "equally unfair" to all. This is one way in which the deleterious effects of bias can be avoided.

ASSESSMENT STANDARD E:
The inferences made from assessments about student achievement and opportunity to learn must be sound.

- **When making inferences from assessment data about student achievement and opportunity to learn science, explicit reference needs to be made to the assumptions on which the inferences are based.**

Even when assessments are well planned and the quality of the resulting data high, the interpretations of the empirical evidence can result in quite different conclusions. Making inferences involves looking at empirical data through the lenses of theory, personal beliefs, and personal experience. Making objective inferences is extremely difficult, partly because individuals are not always aware of their assumptions. Consequently, confidence in the validity of inferences requires explicit reference to the assumptions on which those inferences are based.

For example, if the science achievement on a large-scale assessment of a sample of students from a certain population is high, several conclusions are possible. Students from the population might be highly motivated; or because of excellent instruction, students from the population might have greater opportunity to learn science; or the test might be biased in some way in favor of the students. Little confidence can be placed in any of these conclusions without clear statements about the assumptions and a developed line of reasoning from the evidence to the conclusion. The level of confidence in conclusions is raised when those conducting assessments have been well trained in the process of making inferences from educational assessment data. Even then, the general public, as well as professionals, should demand open and understandable descriptions of how the inferences were made.

Assessments Conducted by Classroom Teachers

Teachers are in the best position to put assessment data to powerful use. In the vision of science education described by the *Standards*, teachers use the assessment data in many ways. Some of the ways teachers might use these data are presented in this section.

IMPROVING CLASSROOM PRACTICE

See Teaching Standard C

Teachers collect information about students' understanding almost continuously and make adjustments to their teaching on the basis of their interpretation of that information. They observe critical incidents in the classroom, formulate hypotheses about the causes of those incidents, question students to test their hypotheses, interpret student's responses, and adjust their teaching plans.

PLANNING CURRICULA

Teachers use assessment data to plan curricula. Some data teachers have collected themselves; other data come from external sources. The data are used to select content, activities, and examples that will be incorporated into a course of study, a module, a unit, or a lesson. Teachers use the assessment data to make judgments about

- The developmental appropriateness of the science content.
- Student interest in the content.
- The effectiveness of activities in producing the desired learning outcomes.
- The effectiveness of the selected examples.
- The understanding and abilities students must have to benefit from the selected activities and examples.

Planning for assessment is integral to instruction. Assessments embedded in the curriculum serve at least three purposes: to determine the students' initial understandings and abilities, to monitor student progress, and to collect information to grade student achievement. Assessment tasks used for those purposes reflect what students are expected to learn; elicit the full extent of students' understanding; are set in a variety of contexts; have practical, aesthetic, and heuristic value; and have meaning outside the classroom. Assessment tasks also provide important clues to students about what is important to learn.

DEVELOPING SELF-DIRECTED LEARNERS

Students need the opportunity to evaluate and reflect on their own scientific understanding and ability. Before students can do this, they need to understand the goals for learning science. The ability to self-assess understanding is an essential tool for self-directed learning. Through self-reflection, students clarify ideas of what they are supposed to learn. They

When teachers treat students as serious learners and serve as coaches rather than judges, students come to understand and apply standards of good scientific practice.

begin to internalize the expectation that they can learn science. Developing self-assessment skills is an ongoing process throughout a student's school career, becoming increasingly more sophisticated and self-initiated as a student progresses.

Conversations among a teacher and students about assessment tasks and the teacher's evaluation of performance provide students with necessary information to assess their own work. In concert with opportunities to apply it to individual work and to the work of peers, that information contributes to the development of students' self-assessment skills. By developing these skills, students become able to take responsibility for their own learning.

Teachers have communicated their assessment practices, their standards for performance, and criteria for evaluation to students when students are able to

- Select a piece of their own work to provide evidence of understanding of a scientific concept, principle, or law—or their ability to conduct scientific inquiry.
- Explain orally, in writing, or through illustration how a work sample provides evidence of understanding.
- Critique a sample of their own work using the teacher's standards and criteria for quality.
- Critique the work of other students in constructive ways.

Involving students in the assessment process increases the responsibilities of the teacher. Teachers of science are the representatives of the scientific community in their classrooms; they represent a culture and a way of thinking that might be quite unfamiliar to students. As representatives, teachers are expected to model reflection, fostering a learning environment where students review each others' work, offer suggestions, and challenge mistakes in investigative processes, faulty reasoning, or poorly supported conclusions.

A teacher's formal and informal evaluations of student work should exemplify scientific practice in making judgments. The standards for judging the significance, soundness, and creativity of work in professional scientific work are complex, but they are not arbitrary. In the work of classroom learning and investigation, teachers represent the standards of practice of the scientific community. When teachers treat students as serious learners and serve as coaches rather than judges, students come to understand and apply standards of good scientific practice.

REPORTING STUDENT PROGRESS

An essential responsibility of teachers is to report on student progress and achievement

See Teaching Standard C

to the students themselves, to their colleagues, to parents and to policy makers. Progress reports provide information about

- The teacher's performance standards and criteria for evaluation.
- A student's progress from marking period to marking period and from year to year.
- A student's progress in mastering the science curriculum.
- A student's achievement measured against standards-based criteria.

See System Standards A and B

Each of these issues requires a different kind of information and a different mode of assessment.

Especially challenging for teachers is communicating to parents and policy makers the new methods of gathering information that are gaining acceptance in schools. Parents and policy makers need to be reassured that the newer methods are not only as good as, but better than, those used when they were in school. Thus, in developing plans for assessment strategies to compile evidence of student achievement, teachers demonstrate that alternative forms of data collection and methods of interpreting them are as valid and reliable as the familiar short-answer test.

The purported objectivity of short-answer tests is so highly valued that newer modes of assessment such as portfolios, performances, and essays that rely on apparently more subjective scoring methods are less trusted by people who are not professional educators. Overcoming this lack of trust requires that teachers use assessment plans for monitoring student progress and for grading. Clearly relating assessment tasks and products of student work to the valued goals of science education is integral to

assessment plans. Equally important is that the plans have explicit criteria for judging the quality of students' work that policy makers and parents can understand.

RESEARCHING TEACHING PRACTICES

Master teachers engage in practical inquiry of their own teaching to identify conditions that promote student learning and to understand why certain practices are effective. The teacher as a researcher engages in assessment activities that are similar to scientific inquiries when collecting data to answer questions about effective teaching practices. Engaging in classroom research means that teachers develop assessment plans that involve collecting data about students' opportunities to learn as well as their achievement.

See Professional Development Standards B and C

Assessments Conducted at the District, State, and National Levels

Science assessments conducted by district, state, and national authorities serve similar purposes and are distinguished primarily by scale—that is, by the number of students, teachers, or schools on which data are collected.

Assessments may be conducted by authorities external to the classroom for the purposes of

- Formulating policy.
- Monitoring the effects of policies.
- Enforcing compliance with policies.

See System Standards A and B

- Demonstrating accountability.
- Making comparisons.
- Monitoring progress toward goals.

See Program
Standard A

In addition to those purposes, assessments are conducted by school districts to make judgments about the effectiveness of specific programs, schools, and teachers and to report to taxpayers on the district's accomplishments.

The high cost of external assessments and their influence on science teaching practices demand careful planning and implementation. Well-planned, large-scale assessments include teachers during planning and implementation. In addition, all data collected are analyzed, sample sizes are well rationalized, and the sample is representative of the population of interest. This section discusses the characteristics of large-scale assessments.

DATA ANALYSIS

Far too often, more educational data are collected than are analyzed or used to make decisions or take action. Large-scale assessment planners should be able to describe how the data they plan to collect will be used to improve science education.

TEACHER INVOLVEMENT

See Teaching
Standard F

The development and interpretation of externally designed assessments for monitoring the educational system should include the active participation of teachers. Teachers' experiences with students make them indispensable participants in the design, development, and interpretation of assessments prepared beyond the classroom. Their involvement helps to ensure congruence of the classroom practice of science education and external assessment practices. Whether at the district, state, or national level, teachers of science need to work with others who make contributions to the assessment process, such as educational researchers, educational measurement specialists, curriculum specialists, and educational policy analysts.

SAMPLE SIZE

The size of the sample on which data are collected depends on the purpose of the assessment and the number of students, teachers, schools, districts, or states that the assessment plan addresses. If, for instance, a state conducts an assessment to learn about student science achievement in comparison with students in another state, it is sufficient to obtain data from a scientifically defined sample of the students in the state. If, however, the purpose of the assessment is to give state-level credit to individual students for science courses, then data must be collected for every student.

REPRESENTATIVE SAMPLE

For all large-scale assessments, even those at the district level, the information should be collected in ways that minimize the time demands on individual students. For many accountability purposes, a sampling design can be employed that has different representative samples of students receiving different sets of tasks. This permits many different dimensions of the science education system to be monitored. Policy makers and taxpayers can make valid inferences about student achievement and opportunity to learn across the nation, state, or district without requiring extensive time commitments from every student in the sample.

Sample Assessments of Student Science Achievement

To illustrate the assessment standards, two examples are provided below. The content standards are stated in terms of understandings and abilities; therefore, the first example is about understanding the natural world. This example requires a body of scientific knowledge and the competence to reason with that information to make predictions, to develop explanations, and to act in scientifically rational ways. The example focuses on predictions and justifying those predictions. The second example is about the ability to inquire, which also requires a body of scientific information and the competence to reason with it to conceptualize, plan, and perform investigations. (These assessment tasks and the content standards do not have a one-to-one correspondence.)

ASSESSING UNDERSTANDING OF THE NATURAL WORLD

The content standards call for scientific understanding of the natural world. Such understanding requires knowing concepts, principles, laws, and theories of the physical, life, and earth sciences, as well as ideas that are common across the natural sciences. That understanding includes the capacity to reason with knowledge. Discerning what a student knows or how the student reasons is not possible without communication, either verbal or representational, a third essential component of understanding.

Inferences about students' understanding can be based on the analysis of their performances in the science classroom and their work products. Types of performances include making class or public presentations, discussing science matters with peers or teachers, and conducting laboratory work. Products of student work include examina-

Clearly relating assessment tasks and products of student work to the valued goals of science education is integral to assessment plans.

tions, journal notes, written reports, diagrams, data sets, physical and mathematical models, and collections of natural objects. Communication is fundamental to both performance and product-based assessments.

Understanding takes different perspectives and is displayed at different levels of sophistication. A physicist's understanding of respiration might be quite different from that of a chemist, just as a cell biologist's understanding of respiration is quite different from that of a physician. The physicist, the chemist, the biologist, and the physician all have a highly sophisticated understanding of respiration. They bring many of the same scientific principles to bear on the concept. However, each is likely to give greater emphasis to concepts that have special significance in their particular discipline. A physicist's emphasis might be on energetics, with little emphasis on the organisms in which respiration takes place. The physician, on the other hand, might emphasize respiration as it specifically applies to humans. The context of application also contributes to differences in perspective. The cell biologist's understanding might focus on the mechanisms by which respiration occurs in the cell; the physician's understanding might focus on human respiratory disorders and physical and pathological causes.

An ordinary citizen's understanding of respiration will be much less sophisticated

Eliciting and analyzing explanations are useful ways of assessing science achievement.

than that of a practicing scientist. However, even the citizen's understanding will have different perspectives, reflecting differences in experience and exposure to science.

Legitimate differences in perspectives and sophistication of understanding also will be evident in each student's scientific understanding of the natural world. A challenge to teachers and others responsible for assessing understanding is to decide how such variability is translated into judgments about the degree to which individual students or groups of them understand the natural world. The example that follows illustrates how explanations of the natural world can be a rich source of information about how students understand it.

Because explanation is central to the scientific enterprise, eliciting and analyzing explanations are useful ways of assessing science achievement. The example illustrates how thoughtfully designed assessment exercises requiring explanations provide students with the opportunity to demonstrate the full range of their scientific understanding. Exercises of this sort are not designed to

learn whether a student knows a particular fact or concept, but rather to tap the depth and breadth of the student's understanding. Exercises of this sort are difficult to design and are a challenge to score. The example that follows illustrates these challenges.

THE PROMPT. The assessment task begins with a prompt that includes a description of the task and directions. The prompt reads

Some moist soil is placed inside a clear glass jar. A healthy green plant is planted in the soil. The cover is screwed on tightly. The jar is located in a window where it receives sunlight. Its temperature is maintained between 60° and 80°F. How long do you predict the plant will live? Write a justification supporting your prediction. Use relevant ideas from the life, physical, and earth sciences to make a prediction and justification. If you are unsure of a prediction, your justification should state that, and tell what information you would need to make a better prediction. You should know that there is not a single correct prediction.

Many attributes make the "plant in a jar" a good exercise for assessing understanding. The situation, a plant in a closed jar, can be described to students verbally, with a diagram, or with the actual materials, thus eliminating reading as a barrier to a student response. The situation can be understood by students of all ages, minimizing students' prior knowledge of the situation as a factor in ability to respond. The explanation for the prediction can be developed at many different levels of complexity, it can be qualitative or quantitative. It can be based on experience or theory, and it uses ideas from the physical, life, and earth sciences, as well as cross-disciplinary ideas, thus allowing students to demonstrate the full range of

See Teaching Standard B

their understanding of science at various levels of their study of science.

DEVELOPING SCORING RUBRICS. The process of scoring student-generated explanations requires the development of a scoring rubric. The rubric is a standard of performance for a defined population. Typically, scoring rubrics are developed by the teachers of the students in the target population. The performance standard is developed through a consensus process called "social moderation." The steps in designing a scoring rubric involve defining the performance standard for the scientifically literate adult and then deciding which elements of that standard are appropriate for students in the target population. The draft performance standard is refined by subsequent use with student performance and work. Finally, student performances with respect to the rubric are differentiated. Performances are rated satisfactory, exemplary, or inadequate. Differences in opinions about the rubric and judgments about the quality of students' responses are moderated by a group of teachers until consensus is reached for the rubric.

Because a target population has not been identified, and rubrics need to function in the communities that develop them, this section does not define a rubric. Rather the steps in developing a rubric are described.

THE PERFORMANCE OF A SCIENTIFI-CALLY LITERATE ADULT. Developing a scoring rubric begins with a description of the performance standard for scientifically literate adults. That performance standard is developed by a rubric development team. Members of the team write individual responses to the exercise that reflect how each believes a scientifically literate adult should respond. They also seek responses from other adults. Based on the individual responses, the team negotiates a team response that serves as the initial standard.

The team's standard is analyzed into the components of the response. In the plant-in-a-jar exercise, the components are the predictions, the information used to justify the predictions, the reasoning used to justify predictions, and the quality of the communication.

Examples of predictions from a scientifically literate adult about how long the plant can live in the jar might include (1) insufficient information to make a prediction, (2) the plant can live indefinitely, or (3) insects or disease might kill the plant. Whatever the prediction, it should be justified. For example, if the assertion is made that the information provided in the prompt is insufficient to make a prediction, then the explanation should describe what information is needed to make a prediction and how that information would be used.

Scientifically literate adults will rely on a range of knowledge to justify their predictions. The standard response developed by the team of teachers will include concepts from the physical, life, and earth sciences, as well as unifying concepts in science. All are applicable to making and justifying a prediction about the life of a plant in a jar, but because of the differences in emphasis, no one person would be expected to use all of them. Some concepts, such as evaporation, condensation, energy (including heat, light, chemical), energy conversions, energy transmission, chemical interactions, catalysis, conservation of mass, and dynamic equilib-

See Content Standards B, C, and D (all grade levels)

rium, are from physical science. Other concepts are from life sciences, such as plant physiology, plant growth, photosynthesis, respiration, plant diseases, and plant and insect interaction. Still other concepts are from the earth sciences, such as soil types, composition of the atmosphere, water cycle, solar energy, and mineral cycle. Finally, unifying concepts might be used to predict and justify a prediction about the plant in the jar. Those might include closed, open, and isolated systems; physical models; patterns of change; conservation; and equilibrium.

See Unifying
Concepts and
Processes in
Chapter 6

The knowledge required to predict the life of a plant in a jar is not be limited to single concepts. A deeper understanding of

A well-crafted justification . . . demonstrates reasoning characterized by a succession of statements that follow one another logically without gaps from statement to statement.

the phenomena could be implied by a justification that includes knowledge of chemical species and energy. Keeping track of energy, of $C_6H_{12}O_6$ (sugar), CO_2 (carbon dioxide), H_2O (water), and O_2 (oxygen), and of minerals requires knowing about the changes they undergo in the jar and about equilibria among zones in the jar (soil and atmosphere). The jar and its contents form a closed system with respect to matter but an open system with respect to energy. The analysis of the life expectancy of the plant in the jar also requires knowing that the matter in the jar changes form, but the mass remains constant. In addition, knowing that gases from the atmosphere and minerals in

the soil become a part of the plant is important to the explanation.

A deeper understanding of science might be inferred from a prediction and justification that included knowledge of the physical chemistry of photosynthesis and respiration. Photosynthesis is a process in which radiant energy of visible light is converted into chemical bond energy in the form of special carrier molecules, such as ATP, which in turn are used to store chemical bond energy in carbohydrates. The process begins with light absorption by chlorophyll, a pigment that gives plants their green color. In photosynthesis, light energy is used to drive the reaction:

Carbon dioxide + water → *sugar + oxygen.*

Respiration is a process in which energy is released when chemical compounds react with oxygen. In respiration, sugars are broken down to produce useful chemical energy for the plant in the reaction:

Sugar + oxygen → *water + carbon dioxide.*

Photosynthesis and respiration are complementary processes, because photosynthesis results in the storage of energy, and respiration releases it. Photosynthesis removes CO_2 from the atmosphere; respiration adds CO_2 to the atmosphere.

A justification for a prediction about the life of the plant in the jar might include knowledge of dynamic equilibrium. Equilibrium exists between the liquid and vapor states of water. The liquid water evaporates continuously. In the closed container, at constant temperature, the rate of condensation equals the rate of evaporation. The water is in a state of dynamic equilibrium.

Another attribute of a well-crafted justification relates to assumptions. The justification should be explicit about the assumptions that underlie it and even contain some speculation concerning the implications of making alternative assumptions.

Finally, a well-crafted justification for any prediction about the plant in the jar demonstrates reasoning characterized by a succession of statements that follow one another logically without gaps from statement to statement.

SCORING RUBRICS FOR DIFFERENT POPULATIONS OF STUDENTS. The plant-in-a-jar assessment exercise is an appropriate prompt for understanding plants at any grade level. Development of the scoring rubrics for students at different grade levels requires consideration of the science experiences and developmental level of the students. For instance, the justifications of students in elementary school could be expected to be based primarily on experiences with plants. Student justifications would contain little, if any, scientific terminology. A fourth-grade student might respond to the exercise in the following way:

The plant could live. It has water and sunlight. It could die if it got frozen or a bug eats it. We planted seeds in third grade. Some kids forgot to water them and they died. Eddie got scared that his seeds would not grow. He hid them in his desk. They did. The leaves were yellow. After Eddie put it in the sun it got green. The plants in our terrarium live all year long.

Expectations for justifications constructed by students in grades 5-8 are different. These should contain more generalized knowledge and use more sophisticated language and scientific concepts such as light, heat, oxygen, carbon dioxide, energy, and photosynthesis.

By grade 12, the level of sophistication should be much higher. Ideally, the 12th grader would see the plant in a jar as a physical model of the Earth's ecosystem, and view photosynthesis and respiration as complementary processes.

Setting a performance standard for a population of students depends on the population's developmental level and their experiences with science. Considerations to be made in using student responses for developing a rubric can be illustrated by discussing two justifications constructed by students who have just completed high-school biology. Student E has constructed an exemplary justification for her prediction about the plant in the jar. Student S has constructed a less satisfactory response but has not completely missed the point.

STUDENT E: *If there are no insects in the jar or microorganisms that might cause some plant disease, the plant might grow a bit and live for quite a while. I know that when I was in elementary school we did this experiment. My plant died—it got covered with black mold. But some of the plants other kids had got bigger and lived for more than a year.*

The plant can live because it gets energy from the sunlight. When light shines on the leaves, photosynthesis takes place. Carbon dioxide and water form carbohydrates and oxygen. This reaction transforms energy from the sun into chemical energy. Plants can do this because they have chlorophyll.

The plant needs carbohydrates for life processes like growing and moving. It uses the carbohydrates and oxygen to produce energy for life processes like growth and motion. Carbon dioxide is produced too.

After some time the plant probably will stop growing. I think that happens when all the minerals in the soil are used up. For the plant to grow it needs minerals from the soil. When parts of the plant die, the plant material rots and minerals go back into the soil. So that's why I think that how much the plant will grow will depend on the minerals in the soil.

The gases, oxygen, carbon dioxide and water vapor just keep getting used over and over. What I'm not sure about is if the gases get used up. Can the plant live if there is no carbon dioxide left for photosynthesis? If there is no carbon dioxide, will the plant respire and keep living?

I'm pretty sure a plant can live for a long time sealed up in a jar, but I'm not sure how long or exactly what would make it die.

STUDENT S: *I believe that putting a small plant in a closed mayonnaise jar at 60-80°F is murder. I believe that this plant will not last past a week (3 days). This is so for many reasons. Contained in a jar with constant sunlight at 80°F the moisture in the soil will most likely start to evaporate almost immediately. This will leave the soil dry while the air is humid. Since we are in a closed container no water can be restored to the soil (condensation). This in turn will cause no nutrients from the soil to reach the upper plant, no root pressure!*

Besides this, with photosynthesis occurring in the leaves, at least for a short time while water supplies last, the CO_2 in the air is being used up and O_2 is replacing it. With no CO_2 and no H_2O, no light reaction and/or dark reaction can occur and the plant can't make carbohydrates. The carbohydrates are needed for energy.

In conclusion, in a jar closed from CO_2 and water, plants use up their resources quickly, preventing the equation $CO_2 + H_2O \rightarrow C_6H_{12}O_6$ and O_2 and, therefore, energy from carbohydrates.

This jar also works as a catalyst to speed up the process by causing evaporation of H_2O through incomplete vaporization. This would shut down the root hair pressure in the plant which allows water (if any) + nutrients to reach the leaves. All

in all the plant will not live long (3 days at the most then downhill).

Judging the quality of information contained in a justification requires consensus on the information contained in it and then using certain standards to compare that information with the information in the rubric. Standards that might be applied include the scientific accuracy of the information in the justification, the appropriateness of the knowledge to the student's age and experience, the sophistication of the knowledge, and the appropriateness of the application of the knowledge to the situation.

Foremost, judgments about the quality of the information contained in the justification should take into account the accuracy of the information the student used in crafting the response. Student S's justification contains some misinformation about the water evaporation-condensation cycle and about dynamic equilibrium in closed systems. The statements in which this inference is made are "the moisture in the soil will most likely start to evaporate almost immediately. This will leave the soil dry while the air is humid. Since we are in a closed container no water can be restored to the soil (condensation)." The student's statement that "soil in the container will be dry while the air is humid," suggests lack of knowledge about equilibrium in a closed system. In contrast with Student S's misinformation, Student E's justification contains information that is neither unusually sophisticated when viewed against the content of most high-school biology texts, nor erroneous.

Judgments about the appropriateness of the information are more difficult to make. A person familiar with the biology course the student took might assert that the information in the student's response is not as sophisticated as what was taught in the course. In that case, the content of the biology course is being used as the standard for rating the quality of the responses. Alternatively, the standard for rating the appropriateness of the information might be the scientific ideas in the content standards.

Student E's response is rated higher than Student S's on the basis of the quality of information. Student S's justification provides some information about what the student does and does not know and provides some evidence for making inferences about the structure of the student's knowledge. For example, the student did not consider the complementary relationship of photosynthesis and respiration in crafting the justification. Perhaps the student does not know about respiration or that the processes are complementary. Alternatively, the two concepts may be stored in memory in a way that did not facilitate bringing both to bear on the exercise. Testing the plausibility of the inferences about the student's knowledge structure would require having a conversation with the student. To learn if the student knows about respiration, one simply has to ask. If the student knows about it and did not apply it in making the prediction, this is evidence that respiration is not understood in the context of the life processes of plants.

Student E's response is well structured and consistent with the prediction. The statements form a connected progression. The prediction is tentative and the justification indicates it is tentative due to the lack of information in the prompt and the stu-

dent's uncertainty about the quantitative details of the condition under which photosynthesis and respiration occur. The student is explicit about certain assumptions, for instance, the relationship of minerals in the soil and plant growth. The questions the student poses in the justification can be interpreted as evidence that alternative assumptions have been considered.

In contrast, Student S's prediction is stated with unwarranted assurance and justified without consideration of anything more than the availability of sufficient water. Furthermore, the justification does not proceed in a sequential way, proceeding from general principles or empirical evidence to a justification for the prediction.

Student S's response highlights an important point that justifies separating the scoring of information from the scoring of reasoning. A student can compose a well-reasoned justification using incorrect information. For instance, had the student posed the following justification, the reasoning would be adequate even if the conclusion that the soil is dry were not correct. The reasoning would be rated higher had the student communicated that

Plants need energy to live. Plants get energy from sunlight through a process of photosynthesis. Plants need water to photosynthesize. Because the soil is dry, water can't get to the leaves, the plant can't photosynthesize and will die from lack of energy.

Developing scoring rubrics through moderation requires highly informed teachers experienced in the process. Even when teachers are adequately prepared, the moderation process takes time. The content standards call for knowledge with understanding.

Considerable resources must therefore be devoted to preparing teachers and others in the science education system to design and rate assessments that require students to display understanding, such as just described.

ASSESSING THE ABILITY TO INQUIRE

The second assessment example focuses on inquiry. The content standards call for understanding scientific inquiry and developing the ability to inquire. As in understanding the natural world, understanding and doing inquiry are contingent on knowing concepts, principles, laws, and theories of the physical, life, and earth sciences. Inquiry also requires reasoning capabilities and skills in manipulating laboratory or field equipment.

As in understanding the natural world, inferences about students' ability to inquire

Understanding and doing inquiry are contingent on knowing concepts, principles, laws, and theories of the physical, life, and earth sciences.

and their understanding of the process can be based on the analysis of performance in the science classroom and work products.

The example that follows describes twelfth grade students' participation in an extended inquiry. The exercise serves two purposes. It provides the teacher with information about how well students have met the inquiry standards. Equally important, it serves as a capstone experience for the school science program. The extended inquiry is introduced early in the school

year. It involves students working as individuals and in small groups investigating a question of their choice.

IDENTIFYING A WORTHWHILE AND RESEARCHABLE QUESTION.

Throughout the school science program, students have been encouraged to identify questions that interest them and are amenable to investigation. These questions are recorded in student research notebooks. Early in the senior year of high school, students prepare draft statements of the question they propose to investigate and discuss why that question is a reasonable one. Those drafts are circulated to all members of the class. Students prepare written reviews of their classmate's proposals, commenting on the quality of the research question and the rationale for investigating it. Students then revise their research question based on peer feedback. Finally, students present and defend their revised questions to the class.

PLANNING THE INVESTIGATION.
The teacher encourages but does not require students to work together in research groups of two to four students. After presenting research questions to the class, students form the research groups, which come to agreement on a question to investigate and begin developing a preliminary plan for conducting the investigation. Each individual in the group is required to keep extensive records of the group's work, especially documenting the evolution of their final research question from the several questions originally proposed. As plans for investigations evolve, the research questions are sharpened and modified to meet the practical constraints of time and resources avail-

able to the class. Each student maintains journal notes on this process. When a group is satisfied that their plan has progressed to the point where work can begin, the plan is presented to classmates. Written copies of the plan are distributed for written review, followed by a class seminar to discuss each research plan. On the basis of peer feedback, each group revises its research plan, recognizing that as the plan is implemented, it will require still further revisions. Each student in the class is responsible for reviewing the research plan of every group, including a written critique and recommendations for modifying the plan.

EXECUTING THE RESEARCH PLAN. During this phase of the extended investigation, students engage in an iterative process involving assembling and testing apparatus; designing and testing forms of data collection; developing and testing a data collection schedule; and collecting, organizing, and interpreting data.

DRAFTING THE RESEARCH REPORT. Based on the notes of individuals, the group prepares a written report, describing the research. That report also includes data that have been collected and preliminary analysis. Based on peer feedback, the groups modify their procedures and continue data collection. When a group is convinced that the data-collection method is working and the data are reasonably consistent, they analyze the data and draw conclusions.

After a seminar at which the research group presents its data, the analysis, and conclusions, the group prepares a first draft of the research report. This draft is circulated to classmates for preparation of individual critiques. This feedback is used by the group to prepare its final report.

ASSESSING INDIVIDUAL STUDENT ACHIEVEMENT. While the class is engaged in the extended investigation, the teacher observes each student's performance as the student makes presentations to the class, interacts with peers, and uses computers and laboratory apparatus. In addition, the teacher has products of the individual student's work, as well as group work, including draft research questions, critiques of other student work, and the individual student's research notebook. Those observations of student performance and work products are a rich source of data from which the teacher can make inferences about each student's understanding of scientific ideas and the nature of scientific inquiry. For instance, in the context of planning the inquiry, students pose questions for investigation. Their justifications for why the question is a scientific one provide evidence from which to infer the extent and quality of their understanding of the nature of science, understanding of the natural world, understanding of the life, physical, and earth sciences, as well as the quality and extent of their scientific knowledge and their capacity to reason scientifically.

Evidence for the quality of a student's ability to reason scientifically comes from the rationale for the student's own research question and from the line of reasoning used to progress from patterns in the collected data to the conclusions. In the first instance, the student distills a research question from an understanding of scientific

ideas associated with some natural phenomenon. In the second instance, the student generates scientific information based on data. In either case, the quality of the reasoning can be inferred from how well connected the chain of reasoning is, how explicit the student is about the assumptions made, and the extent to which speculations on the implications of having made alternative assumptions are made.

The writing and speaking requirements of this extended investigation provide ample evidence for assessing the ability of the student to communicate scientific ideas.

CHANGING EMPHASES

The *National Science Education Standards* envision change throughout the system. The assessment standards encompass the following changes in emphases:

LESS EMPHASIS ON	MORE EMPHASIS ON
Assessing what is easily measured	Assessing what is most highly valued
Assessing discrete knowledge	Assessing rich, well-structured knowledge
Assessing scientific knowledge	Assessing scientific understanding and reasoning
Assessing to learn what students do not know	Assessing to learn what students do understand
Assessing only achievement	Assessing achievement and opportunity to learn
End of term assessments by teachers	Students engaged in ongoing assessment of their work and that of others
Development of external assessments by measurement experts alone	Teachers involved in the development of external assessments

References for Further Reading

Baron, J.B. 1992. SEA Usage of Alternative Assessment: The Connecticut Experience. In Focus on Evaluation and Measurement, vol. 1 and 2. Proceedings of the National Research Symposium on Limited English Proficient Student Issues.. Washington, DC.

Baxter, G.P., R.J. Shavelson, and J. Pine. 1992. Evaluation of procedure-based scoring for hands-on science assessment. Journal of Educational Measurement, 29 (1): 1-17.

Champagne, A.B., and S.T. Newell. 1992. Directions for Research and Development: Alternative Methods of Assessing Scientific Literacy. Journal of Research in Science Teaching 29 (8): 841-860.

Glaser, R. 1992. Cognitive Theory as the Basis for Design of Innovative Assessment: Design Characteristics of Science Assessments. Los Angeles, CA: National Center for Research on Evaluation, Standards, and Student Testing.

Koretz, D., B. Stecher, S. Klein, and D. McCaffrey. 1994. The Vermont Portfolio Assessment Program: Findings and Implications. Educational Measurement: Issues and Practice, 13 (3): 5-16.

Loucks-Horsley, S., R. Kapitan, M.O. Carlson, P.J. Kuerbis, R.C. Clark, G.M. Nelle, T.P. Sachse, and E. Walton. 1993. Elementary School Science for the '90s. Andover, MA: The Network, Inc.

Messick, S. 1994. The interplay of evidence and consequences in the validation of performance assessments. Educational Researcher, 23 (2): 13-23.

Moss, P.A. 1994. Can there be validity without reliability? Educational Researcher, 23 (2): 13-23.

NRC (National Research Council). 1991. Improving Instruction and Assessment in Early Childhood Education: Summary of a Workshop Series. Washington, DC: National Academy Press.

NRC (National Research Council). 1989. Fairness in Employment Testing: Validity Generalization, Minority Issues, and the General Aptitude Test Battery. J.A. Hartigan, and A.K. Wigdor, eds. Washington, DC: National Academy Press.

Oakes, J., T. Ormseth, R. Bell, and P. Camp. 1990. Multiplying Inequalities: The Effect of Race, Social Class, and Tracking on Students' Opportunities to Learn Mathematics and Science. Santa Monica, CA: RAND Corporation.

Raizen, S.A., J.B. Baron, A.B. Champagne, E. Haertel, I.V. Mullis, and J. Oakes. 1990. Assessment in Science Education: The Middle Years. Washington, DC: National Center for Improving Science Education.

Raizen, S.A., J.B. Baron, A.B. Champagne, E. Haertel, I.V. Mullis, and J. Oakes. 1989. Assessment in Elementary School Science Education. Washington, DC: National Center for Improving Science Education.

Ruiz-Primo, M.A., G.P. Baxter, and R.J. Shavelson. 1993. On the stability of performance assessments. Journal of Educational Measurement, 30 (1): 41-53.

Shavelson, R.J. 1991. Performance assessment in science. Applied Measurement in Education, 4 (4): 347-62.

Shavelson, R.J., G. Baxter, and J. Pine. 1992. Performance assessments: Political rhetoric and measurement reality. Educational Researcher, 21 (4): 22-27.

observe

Learn

Interact

Change

Students need
knowledge and
understanding in
physical, life, and earth
and space science to
apply science.

Science Content Standards

The content standards presented in this chapter outline what students should know, understand, and be able to do in natural science. The content standards are a complete set of outcomes for students; they do not prescribe a curriculum. These standards were designed and developed as one component of the comprehensive vision of science education presented in the *National Science Education Standards* and will be most effective when used in conjunction with all of the standards described in this book. Furthermore, implementation of the content standards cannot be successful if only a subset of the content standards is used (such as implementing only the subject matter standards for physical, life, and earth science). ▐ This introduction sets the framework for the content standards by describing the categories of the content standards with a rationale for each category, the form of the standards, the criteria used to select the standards, and some advice for using the science content standards.

Rationale

The eight categories of content standards are

- **Unifying concepts and processes in science.**
- **Science as inquiry.**
- **Physical science.**
- **Life science.**
- **Earth and space science.**
- **Science and technology.**
- **Science in personal and social perspectives.**
- **History and nature of science.**

The standard for unifying concepts and processes is presented for grades K-12, because the understanding and abilities associated with major conceptual and procedural schemes need to be developed over an entire education, and the unifying concepts and processes transcend disciplinary boundaries. The next seven categories are clustered for grades K-4, 5-8, and 9-12. Those clusters were selected based on a combination of factors, including cognitive development theory, the classroom experience of teachers, organization of schools, and the frameworks of other disciplinary-based standards. References for additional reading for all the content standards are presented at the end of Chapter 6.

The sequence of the seven grade-level content standards is not arbitrary: Each standard subsumes the knowledge and skills of other standards. Students' understandings and abilities are grounded in the experience of inquiry, and inquiry is the foundation for the development of understandings and abilities of the other content standards. The personal and social aspects of science are emphasized increasingly in the progression from science as inquiry standards to the history and nature of science standards. Students need solid knowledge and understanding in physical, life, and earth and space science if they are to apply science.

Multidisciplinary perspectives also increase from the subject-matter standards to the standard on the history and nature of science, providing many opportunities for integrated approaches to science teaching.

UNIFYING CONCEPTS AND PROCESSES STANDARD

Conceptual and procedural schemes unify science disciplines and provide students with powerful ideas to help them understand the natural world. Because of the underlying principles embodied in this standard, the understandings and abilities described here are repeated in the other content standards. Unifying concepts and processes include

- **Systems, order, and organization.**
- **Evidence, models, and explanation.**
- **Change, constancy, and measurement.**
- **Evolution and equilibrium.**
- **Form and function.**

This standard describes some of the integrative schemes that can bring together students' many experiences in science education across grades K-12. The unifying concepts and processes standard can be the focus of instruction at any grade level but should always be closely linked to outcomes aligned with other content standards. In the early grades, instruction should establish the meaning and use of unifying concepts and processes—for example, what it means to measure and how to use measurement tools. At the upper grades, the standard should facilitate and enhance the learning of scientific concepts and principles by providing students with a big picture of scientific ideas—for example, how measurement is important in all scientific endeavors.

SCIENCE AS INQUIRY STANDARDS

In the vision presented by the *Standards*, inquiry is a step beyond "science as a process," in which students learn skills, such as observation, inference, and experimentation. The new vision includes the "processes of science" and requires that students combine processes and scientific knowledge as they use scientific reasoning and critical thinking to develop their understanding of science. Engaging students in inquiry helps students develop

- Understanding of scientific concepts.
- An appreciation of "how we know" what we know in science.
- Understanding of the nature of science.

- Skills necessary to become independent inquirers about the natural world.
- The dispositions to use the skills, abilities, and attitudes associated with science.

Science as inquiry is basic to science education and a controlling principle in the ultimate organization and selection of students' activities. The standards on inquiry highlight the ability to conduct inquiry and develop understanding about scientific inquiry. Students at all grade levels and in every domain of science should have the opportunity to use scientific inquiry and develop the ability to think and act in ways associated with inquiry, including asking questions, planning and conducting investigations, using appropriate tools and techniques to gather data, thinking critically and logically about relationships between evidence and explanations, constructing and analyzing alternative explanations, and communicating scientific arguments. Table 6.1 shows the standards for inquiry. The science as inquiry standards are described in terms of activities resulting in student development of certain abilities and in terms of student understanding of inquiry.

TABLE 6.1. SCIENCE AS INQUIRY STANDARDS

LEVELS K-4	LEVELS 5-8	LEVELS 9-12
Abilities necessary to do scientific inquiry	Abilities necessary to do scientific inquiry	Abilities necessary to do scientific inquiry
Understanding about scientific inquiry	Understanding about scientific inquiry	Understanding about scientific inquiry

PHYSICAL SCIENCE, LIFE SCIENCE, AND EARTH AND SPACE SCIENCE STANDARDS

The standards for physical science, life science, and earth and space science describe the subject matter of science using three widely accepted divisions of the domain of science. Science subject matter focuses on the science facts, concepts, principles, theories, and models that are important for all students to know, understand, and use. Tables 6.2, 6.3, and 6.4 are the standards for physical science, life science, and earth and space science, respectively.

SCIENCE AND TECHNOLOGY STANDARDS

The science and technology standards in Table 6.5 establish connections between the natural and designed worlds and provide students with opportunities to develop decision-making abilities. They are not standards for technology education; rather, these standards emphasize abilities associated with the process of design and fundamental understandings about the enterprise of science and its various linkages with technology.

As a complement to the abilities developed in the science as inquiry standards,

TABLE 6.2. PHYSICAL SCIENCE STANDARDS

LEVELS K-4	LEVELS 5-8	LEVELS 9-12
Properties of objects and materials	Properties and changes of properties in matter	Structure of atoms
Position and motion of objects	Motions and forces	Structure and properties of matter
Light, heat, electricity, and magnetism	Transfer of energy	Chemical reactions
		Motions and forces
		Conservation of energy and increase in disorder
		Interactions of energy and matter

TABLE 6.3. LIFE SCIENCE STANDARDS

LEVELS K-4	LEVELS 5-8	LEVELS 9-12
Characteristics of organisms	Structure and function in living systems	The cell
Life cycles of organisms	Reproduction and heredity	Molecular basis of heredity
Organisms and environments	Regulation and behavior	Biological evolution
	Populations and ecosystems	Interdependence of organisms
	Diversity and adaptations of organisms	Matter, energy, and organization in living systems
		Behavior of organisms

these standards call for students to develop abilities to identify and state a problem, design a solution—including a cost and risk-and-benefit analysis—implement a solution, and evaluate the solution.

Science as inquiry is parallel to technology as design. Both standards emphasize student development of abilities and understanding. Connections to other domains, such as mathematics, are clarified in Chapter 7, *Program Standards.*

SCIENCE IN PERSONAL AND SOCIAL PERSPECTIVES STANDARDS

An important purpose of science education is to give students a means to understand and act on personal and social issues. The science in personal and social perspec-

tives standards help students develop decision-making skills. Understandings associated with the concepts in Table 6.6 give students a foundation on which to base decisions they will face as citizens.

HISTORY AND NATURE OF SCIENCE STANDARDS

In learning science, students need to understand that science reflects its history and is an ongoing, changing enterprise. The standards for the history and nature of science recommend the use of history in school science programs to clarify different aspects of scientific inquiry, the human aspects of science, and the role that science has played in the development of various cultures. Table 6.7 provides an overview of this standard.

TABLE 6.4. EARTH AND SPACE SCIENCE STANDARDS		
LEVELS K-4	**LEVELS 5-8**	**LEVELS 9-12**
Properties of earth materials	Structure of the earth system	Energy in the earth system
Objects in the sky	Earth's history	Geochemical cycles
Changes in earth and sky	Earth in the solar system	Origin and evolution of the earth system
		Origin and evolution of the universe

TABLE 6.5. SCIENCE AND TECHNOLOGY STANDARDS		
LEVELS K-4	**LEVELS 5-8**	**LEVELS 9-12**
Abilities to distinguish between natural objects and objects made by humans	Abilities of technological design	Abilities of technological design
Abilities of technological design	Understanding about science and technology	Understanding about science and technology
Understanding about science and technology		

TABLE 6.6. SCIENCE IN PERSONAL AND SOCIAL PERSPECTIVES

LEVELS K-4	LEVELS 5-8	LEVELS 9-12
Personal health	Personal health	Personal and community health
Characteristics and changes in populations	Populations, resources, and environments	Population growth
Types of resources	Natural hazards	Natural resources
Changes in environments	Risks and benefits	Environmental quality
Science and technology in local challenges	Science and technology in society	Natural and human-induced hazards
		Science and technology in local, national, and global challenges

TABLE 6.7. HISTORY AND NATURE OF SCIENCE STANDARDS

LEVELS K-4	LEVELS 5-8	LEVELS 9-12
Science as a human endeavor	Science as a human endeavor	Science as a human endeavor
	Nature of science	Nature of scientific knowledge
	History of science	Historical perspectives

Form of the Content Standards

Below is an example of a content standard. Each content standard states that, as the result of activities provided for all students in the grade level discussed, the content of the standard is to be understood or the abilities are to be developed.

PHYSICAL SCIENCE (EXAMPLE)

CONTENT STANDARD B:
As a result of the activities in grades K-4, all students should develop an understanding of
- Properties of objects and materials
- Position and motion of objects
- Light, heat, electricity, and magnetism

After each content standard is a section entitled, **Developing Student Understanding** (or abilities and understanding, when appropriate), which elaborates upon issues associated with opportunities to learn the content. This section describes linkages among student learning, teaching, and classroom situations. This discussion on developing student understanding, including the remarks on the selection of content for grade levels, is based in part on educational research. It also incorporates the experiences of many thoughtful people, including teachers, teacher educators, curriculum developers, and educational researchers. (Some references to research on student understanding and abilities are located at the end of the chapter.)

The next section of each standard is a **Guide to the Content Standard**, which describes the fundamental ideas that underlie the standard. Content is fundamental if it

- Represents a central event or phenomenon in the natural world.
- Represents a central scientific idea and organizing principle.
- Has rich explanatory power.
- Guides fruitful investigations.
- Applies to situations and contexts common to everyday experiences.
- Can be linked to meaningful learning experiences.
- Is developmentally appropriate for students at the grade level specified.

Criteria for the Content Standards

Three criteria influence the selection of science content. The first is an obligation to the domain of science. The subject matter in the physical, life, and earth and space science standards is central to science education and must be accurate. The presentation in national standards also must accommodate the needs of many individuals who will implement the standards in school science programs. The standards represent science

TABLE 6.8. CONTENT STANDARDS, GRADES K-4

UNIFYING CONCEPTS AND PROCESSES	SCIENCE AS INQUIRY	PHYSICAL SCIENCE	LIFE SCIENCE
Systems, order, and organization	Abilities necessary to do scientific inquiry	Properties of objects and materials	Characteristics of organisms
Evidence, models, and explanation	Understandings about scientific inquiry	Position and motion of objects	Life cycles of organisms
Change, constancy, and measurement		Light, heat, electricity, and magnetism	Organisms and environments
Evolution and equilibrium			
Form and function			

EARTH AND SPACE SCIENCE	SCIENCE AND TECHNOLOGY	SCIENCE IN PERSONAL AND SOCIAL PERSPECTIVES	HISTORY AND NATURE OF SCIENCE
Properties of earth materials	Abilities of technological design	Personal health	Science as a human endeavor
Objects in the sky	Understandings about science and technology	Characteristics and changes in populations	
Changes in earth and sky	Abilities to distinguish between natural objects and objects made by humans	Types of resources	
		Changes in environments	
		Science and technology in local challenges	

content accurately and appropriately at all grades, with increasing precision and more scientific nomenclature from kindergarten to grade 12.

The second criterion is an obligation to develop content standards that appropriately represent the developmental and learning abilities of students. Organizing principles were selected that express meaningful links to direct student observations of the natural world. The content is aligned with students' ages and stages of development. This criterion includes increasing emphasis on abstract and conceptual understandings as students progress from kindergarten to grade 12.

Tables 6.8, 6.9, and 6.10 display the standards grouped according to grade levels K-4, 5-8, and 9-12, respectively. These tables provide an overview of the standards for elementary-, middle-, and high-school science programs.

The third criterion is an obligation to present standards in a usable form for those who must implement the standards, e.g., curriculum developers, science supervisors, teachers, and other school personnel. The standards need to provide enough breadth of content to define the domains of science, and they need to provide enough depth of content to direct the design of science curricula. The descriptions also need to be understandable by school personnel and to accommodate the structures of elementary, middle, and high schools, as well as the grade levels used in national standards for other disciplines.

TABLE 6.9. CONTENT STANDARDS, GRADES 5-8

UNIFYING CONCEPTS AND PROCESSES	SCIENCE AS INQUIRY	PHYSICAL SCIENCE	LIFE SCIENCE
Systems, order, and organization	Abilities necessary to do scientific inquiry	Properties and changes of properties in matter	Structure and function in living systems
Evidence, models, and explanation	Understandings about scientific inquiry	Motions and forces	Reproduction and heredity
Change, constancy, and measurement		Transfer of energy	Regulation and behavior
Evolution and equilibrium			Populations and ecosystems
Form and function			Diversity and adaptations of organisms

EARTH AND SPACE SCIENCE	SCIENCE AND TECHNOLOGY	SCIENCE IN PERSONAL AND SOCIAL PERSPECTIVES	HISTORY AND NATURE OF SCIENCE
Structure of the earth system	Abilities of technological design	Personal health	Science as a human endeavor
Earth's history	Understandings about science and technology	Populations, resources, and environments	Nature of science
Earth in the solar system		Natural hazards	History of science
		Risks and benefits	
		Science and technology in society	

TABLE 6.10. CONTENT STANDARDS, GRADES 9-12

UNIFYING CONCEPTS AND PROCESSES	SCIENCE AS INQUIRY	PHYSICAL SCIENCE	LIFE SCIENCE
Systems, order, and organization	Abilities necessary to do scientific inquiry	Structure of atoms	The cell
Evidence, models, and explanation	Understandings about scientific inquiry	Structure and properties of matter	Molecular basis of heredity
Change, constancy, and measurement		Chemical reactions	Biological evolution
Evolution and equilibrium		Motions and forces	Interdependence of organisms
Form and function		Conservation of energy and increase in disorder	Matter, energy, and organization in living systems
		Interactions of energy and matter	Behavior of organisms

EARTH AND SPACE SCIENCE	SCIENCE AND TECHNOLOGY	SCIENCE IN PERSONAL AND SOCIAL PERSPECTIVES	HISTORY AND NATURE OF SCIENCE
Energy in the earth system	Abilities of technological design	Personal and community health	Science as a human endeavor
Geochemical cycles	Understandings about science and techology	Population growth	Nature of scientific knowledge
Origin and evolution of the earth system		Natural resources	Historical perspectives
Origin and evolution of the universe		Environmental quality	
		Natural and human-induced hazards	
		Science and technology in local, national, and global challenges	

Use of the Content Standards

Many different individuals and groups will use the content standards for a variety of purposes. *All users and reviewers are reminded that the content described is not a science curriculum.* Content is what students should learn. Curriculum is the way content is organized and emphasized; it includes structure, organization, balance, and presentation of the content in the classroom. Although the structure for the content standards organizes the understanding and abilities to be acquired by all students K-12, that structure does not imply any particular organization for science curricula.

Persons responsible for science curricula, teaching, assessment and policy who use the *Standards* should note the following

■ None of the eight categories of content

standards should be eliminated. For instance, students should have opportunities to learn science in personal and social perspectives and to learn about the history and nature of science, as well as to learn subject matter, in the school science program.

- No standards should be eliminated from a category. For instance, "biological evolution" cannot be eliminated from the life science standards.

- Science content can be added. The connections, depth, detail, and selection of topics can be enriched and varied as appropriate for individual students and school science programs. However, addition of content must not prevent the learning of fundamental concepts by all students.

- The content standards must be used in the context of the standards on teaching and assessment. Using the standards with traditional teaching and assessment strategies defeats the intentions of the *National Science Education Standards*.

As science advances, the content standards might change, but the conceptual organization will continue to provide students with knowledge, understanding, and abilities that will improve their scientific literacy.

CHANGING EMPHASES

The *National Science Education Standards* envision change throughout the system. The science content standards encompass the following changes in emphases:

LESS EMPHASIS ON	MORE EMPHASIS ON
Knowing scientific facts and information	Understanding scientific concepts and developing abilities of inquiry
Studying subject matter disciplines (physical, life, earth sciences) for their own sake	Learning subject matter disciplines in the context of inquiry, technology, science in personal and social perspectives, and history and nature of science
Separating science knowledge and science process	Integrating all aspects of science content
Covering many science topics	Studying a few fundamental science concepts
Implementing inquiry as a set of processes	Implementing inquiry as instructional strategies, abilities, and ideas to be learned

CHANGING EMPHASES TO PROMOTE INQUIRY

LESS EMPHASIS ON	MORE EMPHASIS ON
Activities that demonstrate and verify science content	Activities that investigate and analyze science questions
Investigations confined to one class period	Investigations over extended periods of time
Process skills out of context	Process skills in context
Emphasis on individual process skills such as observation or inference	Using multiple process skills—manipulation, cognitive, procedural
Getting an answer	Using evidence and strategies for developing or revising an explanation
Science as exploration and experiment	Science as argument and explanation
Providing answers to questions about science content	Communicating science explanations
Individuals and groups of students analyzing and synthesizing data without defending a conclusion	Groups of students often analyzing and synthesizing data after defending conclusions
Doing few investigations in order to leave time to cover large amounts of content	Doing more investigations in order to develop understanding, ability, values of inquiry and knowledge of science content
Concluding inquiries with the result of the experiment	Applying the results of experiments to scientific arguments and explanations
Management of materials and equipment	Management of ideas and information
Private communication of student ideas and conclusions to teacher	Public communication of student ideas and work to classmates

observe

Learn

Interact

Change

Lifelong scientific
literacy begins
with attitudes
and values
established in the
earliest years

Content Standard: K–12

Unifying Concepts and Processes

STANDARD: As a result of activities in grades K-12, all students should develop understanding and abilities aligned with the following concepts and processes:

- Systems, order, and organization
- Evidence, models, and explanation
- Constancy, change, and measurement
- Evolution and equilibrium
- Form and function

DEVELOPING STUDENT UNDERSTANDING

This standard presents broad unifying concepts and processes that complement the analytic, more discipline-based perspectives presented in the other content standards. The conceptual and procedural schemes in this standard provide students with productive and insightful ways of thinking about and integrating a range of basic ideas that explain the natural and designed world.

The unifying concepts and processes in this standard are a subset of the many unifying ideas in science and technology. Some of the criteria used in the selection and organization of this standard are

- The concepts and processes provide connections between and among traditional scientific disciplines.
- The concepts and processes are fundamental and comprehensive.
- The concepts and processes are understandable and usable by people who will implement science programs.
- The concepts and processes can be expressed and experienced in a developmentally appropriate manner during K-12 science education.

Each of the concepts and processes of this standard has a continuum of complexity that lends itself to the K-4, 5-8, and 9-12 grade-level clusters used in the other content standards. In this standard, however, the boundaries of disciplines and grade-level divisions are not distinct—teachers should develop students' understandings continuously across grades K-12.

Systems and subsystems, the nature of models, and conservation are fundamental concepts and processes included in this standard. Young students tend to interpret phenomena separately rather than in terms of a system. Force, for example, is perceived as a property of an object rather than the result of interacting bodies. Students do not recognize the differences between parts and whole systems, but view them as similar. Therefore, teachers of science need to help students recognize the properties of objects, as emphasized in grade-level content standards, while helping them to understand systems.

As another example, students in middle school and high school view models as physical copies of reality and not as conceptual representations. Teachers should help students understand that models are developed and tested by comparing the model with observations of reality.

Teachers in elementary grades should recognize that students' reports of changes in such things as volume, mass, and space can represent errors common to well-recognized developmental stages of children.

GUIDE TO THE CONTENT STANDARD
Some of the fundamental concepts that underlie this standard are

SYSTEMS, ORDER, AND ORGANIZATION   The natural and designed world is complex; it is too large and complicated to investigate and comprehend all at once. Scientists and students learn to define small portions for the convenience of investigation. The units of investigation can be referred to as "systems." A system is an organized group of related objects or components that form a whole. Systems can consist, for example, of organisms, machines, fundamental particles, galaxies, ideas, numbers, transportation, and education. Systems have boundaries, components, resources flow (input and output), and feedback.

The goal of this standard is to think and analyze in terms of systems. Thinking and analyzing in terms of systems will help students keep track of mass, energy, objects, organisms, and events referred to in the other content standards. The idea of simple systems encompasses subsystems as well as identifying the structure and function of systems, feedback and equilibrium, and the distinction between open and closed systems.

Science assumes that the behavior of the universe is not capricious, that nature is the same everywhere, and that it is understandable and predictable. Students can develop an understanding of regularities in systems, and by extension, the universe; they then can develop understanding of basic laws, theories, and models that explain the world.

Newton's laws of force and motion, Kepler's laws of planetary motion, conservation laws, Darwin's laws of natural selection, and chaos theory all exemplify the idea of order and regularity. An assumption of order establishes the basis for cause-effect relationships and predictability.

Prediction is the use of knowledge to identify and explain observations, or changes, in advance. The use of mathematics, especially

See Program Standard C

probability, allows for greater or lesser certainty of predictions.

Order—the behavior of units of matter, objects, organisms, or events in the universe—can be described statistically. Probability is the relative certainty (or uncertainty) that individuals can assign to selected events happening (or not happening) in a specified space or time. In science, reduction of uncertainty occurs through such processes as the development of knowledge about factors influencing objects, organisms, systems, or events; better and more observations; and better explanatory models.

Types and levels of organization provide useful ways of thinking about the world. Types of organization include the periodic table of elements and the classification of organisms. Physical systems can be described at different levels of organization—such as fundamental particles, atoms, and molecules. Living systems also have different levels of organization—for example, cells, tissues, organs, organisms, populations, and communities. The complexity and number of fundamental units change in extended hierarchies of organization. Within these systems, interactions between components occur. Further, systems at different levels of organization can manifest different properties and functions.

EVIDENCE, MODELS, AND EXPLANATION
Evidence consists of observations and data on which to base scientific explanations. Using evidence to understand interactions allows individuals to predict changes in natural and designed systems.

Models are tentative schemes or structures that correspond to real objects, events, or classes of events, and that have explana-

See Content Standard A (all grade levels)

tory power. Models help scientists and engineers understand how things work. Models take many forms, including physical objects, plans, mental constructs, mathematical equations, and computer simulations.

Scientific explanations incorporate existing scientific knowledge and new evidence

As students develop and…understand more science concepts and processes, their explanations should become more sophisticated…frequently reflecting a rich scientific knowledge base, evidence of logic, higher levels of analysis, and greater tolerance of criticism and uncertainty.

from observations, experiments, or models into internally consistent, logical statements. Different terms, such as "hypothesis," "model," "law," "principle," "theory," and "paradigm" are used to describe various types of scientific explanations. As students develop and as they understand more science concepts and processes, their explanations should become more sophisticated. That is, their scientific explanations should more frequently include a rich scientific knowledge base, evidence of logic, higher levels of analysis, greater tolerance of criticism and uncertainty, and a clearer demonstration of the relationship between logic, evidence, and current knowledge.

CONSTANCY, CHANGE, AND MEASUREMENT
Although most things are in the process of becoming different—changing—some properties of objects and processes are characterized by constancy, including the speed

See Content Standard B (grades 9-12)

of light, the charge of an electron, and the total mass plus energy in the universe. Changes might occur, for example, in properties of materials, position of objects, motion, and form and function of systems. Interactions within and among systems result in change. Changes vary in rate, scale, and pattern, including trends and cycles.

Energy can be transferred and matter can be changed. Nevertheless, when measured, the sum of energy and matter in systems, and by extension in the universe, remains the same.

Changes in systems can be quantified. Evidence for interactions and subsequent change and the formulation of scientific explanations are often clarified through quantitative distinctions—measurement. Mathematics is essential for accurately measuring change.

Different systems of measurement are used for different purposes. Scientists usually use the metric system. An important part of measurement is knowing when to use which system. For example, a meteorologist might use degrees Fahrenheit when reporting the weather to the public, but in writing scientific reports, the meteorologist would use degrees Celsius.

Scale includes understanding that different characteristics, properties, or relationships within a system might change as its dimensions are increased or decreased.

Rate involves comparing one measured quantity with another measured quantity, for example, 60 meters per second. Rate is also a measure of change for a part relative to the whole, for example, change in birth rate as part of population growth.

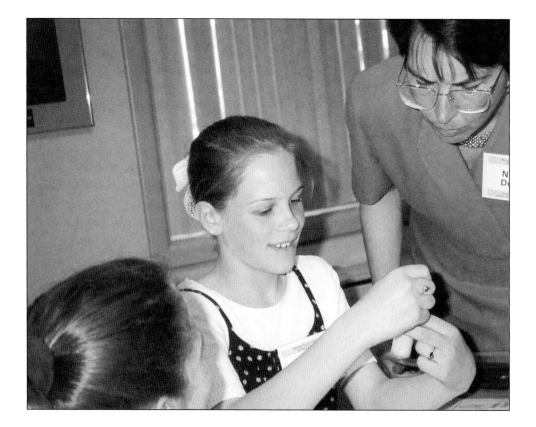

EVOLUTION AND EQUILIBRIUM

See Content Standard C (grades 9-12)

Evolution is a series of changes, some gradual and some sporadic, that accounts for the present form and function of objects, organisms, and natural and designed systems. The general idea of evolution is that the present arises from materials and forms of the past. Although evolution is most commonly associated with the biological theory explaining the process of descent with modification of organisms from common ancestors, evolution also describes changes in the universe.

Equilibrium is a physical state in which forces and changes occur in opposite and off-setting directions: for example, opposite forces are of the same magnitude, or off-setting changes occur at equal rates. Steady state, balance, and homeostasis also describe equilibrium states. Interacting units of matter tend toward equilibrium states in which the energy is distributed as randomly and uniformly as possible.

See Content Standard C (grades 5-8)

FORM AND FUNCTION Form and function are complementary aspects of objects, organisms, and systems in the natural and designed world. The form or shape of an object or system is frequently related to use, operation, or function. Function frequently relies on form. Understanding of form and function applies to different levels of organization. Students should be able to explain function by referring to form and explain form by referring to function.

observe
Learn
Interact
Change

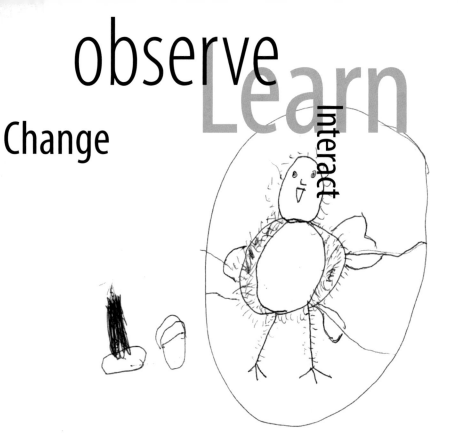

I drew a chick. It needs I don't know.

I drew an alligator. It needs water and sunshine and food.

In elementary grades, students begin to develop the physical and intellectual abilities of scientific inquiry.

Content Standards: K-4

Science as Inquiry

As a result of activities in grades K-4, all students should develop

- Abilities necessary to do scientific inquiry
- Understanding about scientific inquiry

DEVELOPING STUDENT ABILITIES AND UNDERSTANDING

From the earliest grades, students should experience science in a form that engages them in the active construction of ideas and explanations and enhances their opportunities to develop the abilities of doing science. Teaching science as inquiry provides teachers with the opportunity to develop student abilities and to enrich student understanding of science. Students should do science in ways that are within their developmental capabilities. This standard sets forth some abilities of scientific inquiry appropriate for students in grades K-4.

In the early years of school, students can investigate earth materials, organisms, and properties of common objects. Although children develop concepts and vocabulary from such experiences, they also should develop inquiry skills. As students focus on the processes of doing investigations, they develop the ability to ask scientific questions, investigate aspects of the world around them, and use their observations to construct reasonable explanations for the questions posed. Guided by teachers, students continually develop their science knowledge. Students should also learn through the inquiry process how to communicate about their own and their peers' investigations and explanations.

There is logic is behind the abilities outlined in the inquiry standard, but a step-by-step sequence or scientific method is not implied. In practice, student questions might arise from previous investigations, planned classroom activities, or questions students ask each other. For instance, if children ask each other how animals are similar and different, an investigation might arise into characteristics of organisms they can observe.

Full inquiry involves asking a simple question, completing an investigation, answering the question, and presenting the results to others. In elementary grades, students begin to develop the physical and intellectual abilities of scientific inquiry. They can design investigations to try things to see what happens—they tend to focus on concrete results of tests and will entertain the idea of a "fair" test (a test in which only one variable at a time is changed). However, children in K–4 have difficulty with experimentation as a process of testing ideas and the logic of using evidence to formulate explanations.

GUIDE TO THE CONTENT STANDARD
Fundamental abilities and concepts that underlie this standard include

ABILITIES NECESSARY TO DO SCIENTIFIC INQUIRY

ASK A QUESTION ABOUT OBJECTS, ORGANISMS, AND EVENTS IN THE ENVIRONMENT. This aspect of the standard emphasizes students asking questions that they can answer with scientific knowledge, combined with their own observations. Students should answer their questions by seeking information from reliable sources of scientific information and from their own observations and investigations.

PLAN AND CONDUCT A SIMPLE INVESTIGATION. In the earliest years, investigations are largely based on systematic observations. As students develop, they may design and conduct simple experiments to answer questions. The idea of a fair test is

possible for many students to consider by fourth grade.

EMPLOY SIMPLE EQUIPMENT AND TOOLS TO GATHER DATA AND EXTEND THE SENSES. In early years, students develop simple skills, such as how to observe, measure, cut, connect, switch, turn on and off, pour, hold, tie, and hook. Beginning with simple instruments, students can use rulers to measure the length, height, and depth of objects and materials; thermometers to measure temperature; watches to measure time; beam balances and spring scales to measure weight and force; magnifiers to observe objects and organisms; and microscopes to observe the finer details of plants, animals, rocks, and other materials. Children also develop skills in the use of computers and calculators for conducting investigations.

USE DATA TO CONSTRUCT A REASONABLE EXPLANATION. This aspect of the standard emphasizes the students' thinking as they use data to formulate explanations. Even at the earliest grade levels, students should learn what constitutes evidence and judge the merits or strength of the data and information that will be used to make explanations. After students propose an explanation, they will appeal to the knowledge and evidence they obtained to support their explanations. Students should check their explanations against scientific knowledge, experiences, and observations of others.

COMMUNICATE INVESTIGATIONS AND EXPLANATIONS. Students should begin developing the abilities to communicate, critique, and analyze their work and the work of other students. This communica-

See Teaching
Standard B

tion might be spoken or drawn as well as written.

See Content Standard G (grades K-4)

UNDERSTANDINGS ABOUT SCIENTIFIC INQUIRY

- Scientific investigations involve asking and answering a question and comparing the answer with what scientists already know about the world.

- Scientists use different kinds of investigations depending on the questions they are trying to answer. Types of investigations include describing objects, events, and organisms; classifying them; and doing a fair test (experimenting).

See Program Standard C

- Simple instruments, such as magnifiers, thermometers, and rulers, provide more information than scientists obtain using only their senses.

- Scientists develop explanations using observations (evidence) and what they already know about the world (scientific knowledge). Good explanations are based on evidence from investigations.

- Scientists make the results of their investigations public; they describe the investigations in ways that enable others to repeat the investigations.

- Scientists review and ask questions about the results of other scientists' work.

Physical Science

CONTENT STANDARD B:

As a result of the activities in grades K-4, all students should develop an understanding of

- Properties of objects and materials
- Position and motion of objects
- Light, heat, electricity, and magnetism

DEVELOPING STUDENT UNDERSTANDING

During their early years, children's natural curiosity leads them to explore the world by observing and manipulating common objects and materials in their environment. Children compare, describe, and sort as they begin to form explanations of the world. Developing a subject-matter knowledge base to explain and

Full inquiry involves asking a simple question, completing an investigation, answering the question, and presenting the results to others.

predict the world requires many experiences over a long period. Young children bring experiences, understanding, and ideas to school; teachers provide opportunities to continue children's explorations in focused settings with other children using simple tools, such as magnifiers and measuring devices.

Physical science in grades K-4 includes topics that give students a chance to increase their understanding of the characteristics of objects and materials that they encounter daily. Through the observation, manipulation, and classification of common objects, children reflect on the similarities and differences of the objects. As a result, their initial sketches and single-word descriptions lead to increasingly more detailed drawings and richer verbal descriptions. Describing, grouping, and sorting solid objects and materials is possible early in this grade range. By grade 4, distinctions between the properties of objects and materials can be understood in specific contexts, such as a set of rocks or living materials.

Willie the Hamster

Ms. W. encourages students to engage in an investigation initiated by a question that signals student interest. The context for the investigation is one familiar to the students—a pet in the classroom. She teaches some of the important aspects of inquiry by asking the students to consider alternative explanations, to look at the evidence, and to design a simple investigation to test a hypothesis. Ms. W. has planned the science classes carefully, but changes her plans to respond to student interests, knowing the goals for the school science program and shaping the activities to be consistent with those goals. She understands what is developmentally appropriate for students of this age—she chooses not to launch into an abstract explanation of evaporation. She has a classroom with the resources she needs for the students to engage in an inquiry activity.

[This example highlights some elements of Teaching Standards A, B, D, E, and F; K-4 Content Standards A and B; Program Standards A, C, and D; and System Standard D.]

George is annoyed. There was plenty of water in the watering can when he left it on the windowsill on Friday. Now the can is almost empty, and he won't have time to go the restroom and fill it so that he can water the plants before science class starts. As soon as Ms. W. begins science class, George raises his hand to complain about the disappearance of the water. "Who used the water?" he asks. "Did someone drink it? Did someone spill it?" None of the students in the class touched the watering can, and Ms. W asks what the students think happened to the water.

Marie has an idea. If none of the children took the water, then it must be that Willie, their pet hamster, is leaving his cage at night and drinking the water. The class decides to test Marie's idea by covering the watering can so that Willie cannot drink the water. The children implement their investigation, and the next morning observe that the water level has not dropped. The children now have proof that their explanation is correct. Ms. W. asks the class to consider alternative explanations consistent with their observations. Are they sure that Willie is getting out of his cage at night? The children are quite certain that he is.

"How can you be sure?" asks Ms. W. The children devise an ingenious plan to convince her that Willie is getting out of the cage. They place his cage in the middle of the sand table and smooth the sand. After several days and nights, the children observe that no footprints have appeared in the sand, and the water level has not changed. The children now conclude that Willie is not getting out of his cage at night.

"But wait." says Kahena, "Why should Willie get out of his cage? Willie can see that the watering can is covered." So the class decides to leave the cage in the middle of the sand table and take the cover off the watering can. The water level begins to drop again, yet there are no footprints in the sand. Now the children dismiss the original idea about the disappearance of the water, and Ms. W. takes the opportunity to give the class more experiences with the disappearance of water.

At Ms. W.'s suggestion, a container of water with a wide top is placed on the windowsill and the class measures and records changes in the water level each day using strips of paper to represent the height of the

water. These strips are dated and pasted on a large sheet of paper to create a bar graph. After a few days, the students discern a pattern: The level of water fell steadily but did not decrease the same amount each day. After considerable discussion about the differences, Patrick observes that when his mother dries the family's clothes, she puts them in the dryer. Patrick notes that the clothes are heated inside the dryer and that when his mother does not set the dial on the dryer to heat, the clothes just spin around and do not dry as quickly. Patrick suggests that water might disappear faster when it is warmer.

Based on their experience using strips of paper to measure changes in the level of water and in identifying patterns of change, the students and Ms. W. plan an investigation to learn whether water disappears faster when it is warmer.

The children's experiences with the disappearance of water continue with an investigation about how the size (area) of the uncovered portion of the container influences how fast the water disappears and another where the children investigate whether using a fan to blow air over the surface of a container of water makes the water disappear faster.

Young children begin their study of matter by examining and qualitatively describing objects and their behavior. The important but abstract ideas of science, such as atomic structure of matter and the conservation of energy, all begin with observing and keeping track of the way the world behaves. When carefully observed, described, and measured, the properties of objects, changes in properties over time, and the changes that occur when materials interact provide the necessary precursors to the later introduction of more abstract ideas in the upper grade levels.

Students are familiar with the change of state between water and ice, but the idea of liquids having a set of properties is more nebulous and requires more instructional effort than working with solids. Most students will have difficulty with the generalization that many substances can exist as either a liquid or a solid. K-4 students do not understand that water exists as a gas when it boils or evaporates; they are more likely to think that water disappears or goes into the sky. Despite that limitation, students can conduct simple investigations with heating and evaporation that develop inquiry skills and familiarize them with the phenomena.

When students describe and manipulate objects by pushing, pulling, throwing, dropping, and rolling, they also begin to focus on the position and movement of objects: describing location as up, down, in front, or behind, and discovering the various kinds of motion and forces required to control it. By experimenting with light, heat, electricity, magnetism, and sound, students begin to understand that phenomena can be observed, measured, and controlled in various ways. The children cannot understand a complex concept such as energy. Nonetheless, they have intuitive notions of energy—for example, energy is needed to get things done; humans get energy from food. Teachers can build on the intuitive notions of students without requiring them to memorize technical definitions.

Sounds are not intuitively associated with the characteristics of their source by younger K-4 students, but that association can be developed by investigating a variety of concrete phenomena toward the end of the K-4 level. In most children's minds, electricity begins at a source and goes to a target. This mental model can be seen in students' first attempts to light a bulb using a battery and wire by attaching one wire to a bulb. Repeated activities will help students develop an idea of a circuit late in this grade range and begin to grasp the effect of more than one battery. Children cannot distinguish between heat and temperature at this age; therefore, investigating heat necessarily must focus on changes in temperature.

As children develop facility with language, their descriptions become richer and include more detail. Initially no tools need to be used, but children eventually learn that they can add to their descriptions by measuring objects—first with measuring devices they create and then by using conventional measuring instruments, such as rulers, balances, and thermometers. By recording data and making graphs and charts, older children can search for patterns and order in their work and that of their peers. For example, they can determine the speed of an object as fast, faster, or fastest in the earliest grades. As students get older, they can represent motion on simple grids and graphs and describe speed as the distance traveled in a given unit of time.

GUIDE TO THE CONTENT STANDARD
Fundamental concepts and principles that underlie this standard include

PROPERTIES OF OBJECTS AND MATERIALS

- Objects have many observable properties, including size, weight, shape, color, temperature, and the ability to react with other substances. Those properties can be measured using tools, such as rulers, balances, and thermometers.
- Objects are made of one or more materials, such as paper, wood, and metal. Objects can be described by the properties of the materials from which they are made, and those properties can be used to separate or sort a group of objects or materials.
- Materials can exist in different states—solid, liquid, and gas. Some common materials, such as water, can be changed from one state to another by heating or cooling.

POSITION AND MOTION OF OBJECTS

- The position of an object can be described by locating it relative to another object or the background.
- An object's motion can be described by tracing and measuring its position over time.
- The position and motion of objects can be changed by pushing or pulling. The size of the change is related to the strength of the push or pull.

- Sound is produced by vibrating objects. The pitch of the sound can be varied by changing the rate of vibration.

LIGHT, HEAT, ELECTRICITY, AND MAGNETISM

- Light travels in a straight line until it strikes an object. Light can be reflected by a mirror, refracted by a lens, or absorbed by the object.
- Heat can be produced in many ways, such as burning, rubbing, or mixing one substance with another. Heat can move from one object to another by conduction.
- Electricity in circuits can produce light, heat, sound, and magnetic effects. Electrical circuits require a complete loop through which an electrical current can pass.
- Magnets attract and repel each other and certain kinds of other materials.

Life Science

CONTENT STANDARD C:
As a result of activities in grades K-4, all students should develop understanding of
- **The characteristics of organisms**
- **Life cycles of organisms**
- **Organisms and environments**

DEVELOPING STUDENT UNDERSTANDING

During the elementary grades, children build understanding of biological concepts through direct experience with living things, their life cycles, and their habitats. These experiences emerge from the sense of wonder and natural interests of children who ask questions such as: "How do plants get food? How many different animals are there? Why do some animals eat other animals? What is the largest plant? Where did the dinosaurs go?" An understanding of the characteristics of organisms, life cycles of organisms, and of the complex interactions among all components of the natural environment begins with questions such as these and an understanding of how individual organisms maintain and continue life. Making sense of the way organisms live in their environments will develop some understanding of the diversity of life and how all living organisms depend on the living and nonliving environment for survival. Because the child's world at grades K-4 is closely associated with the home, school, and immediate environment, the study of organisms should include observations and interactions within the natural world of the child. The experiences and activities in grades K-4 provide a concrete foundation for the progressive development in the later grades of major biological concepts, such as evolution, heredity, the cell, the biosphere, interdependence, the behavior of organisms, and matter and energy in living systems.

Children's ideas about the characteristics of organisms develop from basic concepts of living and nonliving. Piaget noted, for instance, that young children give anthropomorphic explanations to organisms. In lower elementary grades, many children associate "life" with any objects that are active in any way. This view of life develops into one in which movement becomes the defining characteristic. Eventually children incorporate other concepts, such as eating, breathing, and

reproducing to define life. As students have a variety of experiences with organisms, and subsequently develop a knowledge base in the life sciences, their anthropomorphic attributions should decline.

In classroom activities such as classification, younger elementary students generally use mutually exclusive rather than hierarchical categories. Young children, for example, will use two groups, but older children will use several groups at the same time. Students do not consistently use classification schemes similar to those used by biologists until the upper elementary grades.

As students investigate the life cycles of organisms, teachers might observe that young children do not understand the continuity of life from, for example, seed to seedling or larvae to pupae to adult. But teachers will notice that by second grade, most students know that children resemble their parents. Students can also differentiate learned from inherited characteristics. However, students might hold some naive thoughts about inheritance, including the belief that traits are inherited from only one parent, that certain traits are inherited exclusively from one parent or the other, or that all traits are simply a blend of characteristics from each parent.

Young children think concretely about individual organisms. For example, animals are associated with pets or with animals kept in a zoo. The idea that organisms depend on their environment (including other organisms in some cases) is not well developed in young children. In grades K-4, the focus should be on establishing the primary association of organisms with their environments and the secondary ideas of dependence on various aspects of the environment and of behaviors that help various animals survive. Lower elementary students can understand the food link between two organisms.

GUIDE TO THE CONTENT STANDARD
Fundamental concepts and principles that underlie this standard include

THE CHARACTERISTICS OF ORGANISMS

- Organisms have basic needs. For example, animals need air, water, and food; plants require air, water, nutrients, and light. Organisms can survive only in environments in which their needs can be met. The world has many different environments, and distinct environments support the life of different types of organisms.
- Each plant or animal has different structures that serve different functions in growth, survival, and reproduction. For example, humans have distinct body structures for walking, holding, seeing, and talking.
- The behavior of individual organisms is influenced by internal cues (such as hunger) and by external cues (such as a change in the environment). Humans and other organisms have senses that help them detect internal and external cues.

LIFE CYCLES OF ORGANISMS

- Plants and animals have life cycles that include being born, developing into adults, reproducing, and eventually dying. The details of this life cycle are different for different organisms.
- Plants and animals closely resemble their parents.

- Many characteristics of an organism are inherited from the parents of the organism, but other characteristics result from an individual's interactions with the environment. Inherited characteristics include the color of flowers and the number of limbs of an animal. Other features, such as the ability to ride a bicycle, are learned through interactions with the environment and cannot be passed on to the next generation.

ORGANISMS AND THEIR ENVIRONMENTS

- All animals depend on plants. Some animals eat plants for food. Other animals eat animals that eat the plants.
- An organism's patterns of behavior are related to the nature of that organism's environment, including the kinds and numbers of other organisms present, the availability of food and resources, and the physical characteristics of the environment. When the environment changes, some plants and animals survive and reproduce, and others die or move to new locations.
- All organisms cause changes in the environment where they live. Some of these changes are detrimental to the organism or other organisms, whereas others are beneficial.
- Humans depend on their natural and constructed environments. Humans change environments in ways that can be either beneficial or detrimental for themselves and other organisms.

See Content Standard F (grades K-4)

Earth and Space Science

DEVELOPING STUDENT UNDERSTANDING

Young children are naturally interested in everything they see around them—soil, rocks, streams, rain, snow, clouds, rainbows, sun, moon, and stars. During the first years of school, they should be encouraged to observe closely the objects and materials in their environment, note their properties, distinguish one from another and develop their own explanations of how things become the way they are. As children become more familiar with their world, they can be guided to observe changes, including cyclic changes, such as night and day and the seasons; predictable trends, such as growth and decay, and less consistent changes, such as weather or the appearance of meteors. Children should have opportunities to observe rapid changes, such as the movement of water in a stream, as well as gradual changes, such as the erosion of soil and the change of the seasons.

Children come to school aware that earth's surface is composed of rocks, soils, water, and living organisms, but a closer look will help them identify many additional properties of earth materials. By carefully observing and describing the properties of many rocks, children will begin to see that some rocks are made of a single substance, but most are made of several substances. In later grades, the substances can be identified as minerals. Understanding rocks and minerals should not be extended to the study of the source of the rocks, such as sedimentary, igneous, and metamorphic, because the origin of rocks and minerals has little meaning to young children.

Playgrounds and nearby vacant lots and parks are convenient study sites to observe a variety of earth materials. As students collect rocks and observe vegetation, they will become aware that soil varies from place to place in its color, texture, and reaction to water. By planting seeds in a variety of soil samples, they can compare the effect of different soils on plant growth. If they revisit study sites regularly, children will develop an understanding that earth's surface is constantly changing. They also can simulate some changes, such as erosion, in a small tray of soil or a stream table and compare their observations with photographs of similar, but larger scale, changes.

By observing the day and night sky regularly, children in grades K-4 will learn to identify sequences of changes and to look for patterns in these changes. As they observe changes, such as the movement of an object's shadow during the course of a day, and the positions of the sun and the moon, they will find the patterns in these movements. They can draw the moon's shape for each evening on a calendar and then determine the pattern in the shapes over several weeks. These understandings should be confined to observations,

Weather

Mr. H. plans a year-long science activity integral to the entire school science program. The students are to observe and record information about the daily weather. Mr. H. begins the activity by assessing what students know, but realizes that students might use terms without understanding. He focuses on the aspects of weather that his teaching experience and knowledge from research on student abilities lead him to believe are developmentally appropriate, and he keeps a record of terms to help him modify his plans as the activity progresses. Students design instruments for measuring weather that are within the range of their skills and a parent provides expertise. They make measurements using their mathematical knowledge and skills; they organize data in a meaningful way and communicate the data to other students. There is an ebb and flow of teacher-directed, whole-class discussions and small-group work sessions.

[This example highlights some elements of Teaching Standards A, B, D, and E; Professional Development Standard C; the Content Standard on Unifying Concepts and Processes; K-4 Content Standards A, D, E, and F; and Program Standards A, C, and D.]

Mr. H.'s fourth grade class was in charge of the school weather station as part of the schoolwide science program. In planning for the weather station, Mr. H. reviewed the objectives he and his colleagues had defined for the activity. Because of their age, the students would not be studying the causes of weather change such as air pressure, the worldwide air currents, or the effects of land and sea masses. Rather, over the course of the year, they would identify and observe the elements of weather; devise and use measurement and data collection strategies;

build measurement instruments; analyze data to find patterns and relationships within the data; and communicate their work to the entire school.

Mr. H. introduced the weather station to the students soon after school opened. After a discussion of students' experiences with and ideas about weather, Mr. H. asked the class what kinds of information they thought would be important to collect and how they might go about collecting it. The children quickly identified the need to record whether the day was sunny or cloudy, presence of precipitation, and the temperature. Mr. H. asked some questions, and the list became more complicated: What kinds of clouds were evident? How much precipitation accumulated? How did temperature change during the day? What was the wind speed and direction? One student said that he had heard on the weather report that there was a high-pressure front moving in. What is a front, he asked, and is it important? At the end of the discussion, someone mentioned humidity and recalled the muggy heat wave of the summer.

When Mr. H. thought about the lesson and reviewed what he was going to do next, he realized that much of what the students had said was predictable. He wondered about the last two items—humidity and air pressure. Those concepts were well beyond the students' ability to fully understand, yet they were familiar with the words. Mr. H. decided to continue, as he had planned, focusing on the most observable weather conditions and see whether the children's interests in humidity and air pressure were maintained.

The class spent time the next week discussing and planning how they were going to measure weather conditions, what tools would they need, and how they would collect and organize their data. Groups worked in the classroom and in the library; each group chose one aspect of weather for its focus. Mr. H. spent some time with each group supporting their ideas, pushing them further, and providing specific guidance when needed. He encouraged the groups to get together and compare notes. Twice during the week, the whole class came together and groups shared their work while students critiqued and offered ideas.

Several weeks later, the weather station of the fourth grade was in operation. After much work, including some trial and error, library research, and the helpful input of a parent who was a skilled mechanic, the students were recording data twice a day for wind direction and speed, using a class-made anemometer and wind vane; tempera-ture, using a commercial thermometer (the students did make a thermometer following the directions in a book but decided that they would get better data with a commercial one); precipitation, using a rain gauge; and cloud formation. Design of the anemometer was extremely difficult. It was easy to build something that would turn in the wind, but the students needed help in figuring how to measure the speed. The children were also measuring air pressure with a homemade barometer that a parent had helped one group construct. Mr. H. supported this, although the children's ability to understand the concept was limited. The interest of the student and her parent and the class' familiarity with the term seemed reason enough.

The students recorded their data on charts in the classroom for 2 months. Then it was time to analyze the data, write the

first report for the class weather book, and make a report to the school. Again, the work began with a discussion. What were some of the ideas that the students had about the weather after all this measuring and recording? Were any patterns observed? Many students thought the temperature was getting lower; several noted that if it was windy one day, it rained the next day. As ideas were presented, other students agreed or challenged what was said. Mr. H. listened and wrote the ideas on a chart as the students spoke. When the discussion quieted, he turned the students' attention to the list and asked them to think about which of the ideas on the board they might actually be able to confirm by reviewing the data. They listed several and agreed on the following list for a starting place: Is the temperature getting lower? What is the relationship between the direction of the wind and the weather the next day? What happened when the pressure went down or up? Was it colder when it was cloudy?

Mr. H. reminded the students of some ways they might represent the data to help them in the analysis; he then assigned tasks, and the students returned to their groups. Several days later, the work was well under way. One group was working on a bar graph showing the total number of sunny, cloudy, and rainy days; another had made a temperature graph that showed the daily fluctuations and showed the weather definitely was getting colder; an interesting table illustrated that when the pressure dropped the weather usually seemed to get worse. The next challenge was to prepare an interesting report for the school, highlighting all that had been learned.

The weather class continued to operate the weather station all year. The students became quite independent and efficient in collecting data. The data were analyzed approximately every 2 months. Some new questions were considered, and the basic ones continued. Midyear Mr. H. was satisfied that the students understood the use of charts and graphs, and he introduced a simple computer program that the students could use to log their data.

Not only did students learn to ask questions and collect, organize, and present data, they learned how to describe daily weather changes in terms of temperature, windspeed and direction, precipitation, and humidity.

descriptions, and finding patterns. Attempting to extend this understanding into explanations using models will be limited by the inability of young children to understand that earth is approximately spherical. They also have little understanding of gravity and usually have misconceptions about the properties of light that allow us to see objects such as the moon. (Although children will say that they live on a ball, probing questions will reveal that their thinking may be very different.)

Students can discover patterns of weather changes during the year by keeping a journal. Younger students can draw a daily weather picture based on what they see out a window or at recess; older students can make simple charts and graphs from data they collect at a simple school weather station.

Emphasis in grades K-4 should be on developing observation and description skills and the explanations based on observations. Younger children should be encouraged to talk about and draw what they see and think. Older students can keep journals, use instruments, and record their observations and measurements.

GUIDE TO THE CONTENT STANDARD
Fundamental concepts and principles that underlie this standard include

PROPERTIES OF EARTH MATERIALS
- Earth materials are solid rocks and soils, water, and the gases of the atmosphere. The varied materials have different physical and chemical properties, which make them useful in different ways, for example, as building materials, as sources of fuel, or for growing the plants we use as food. Earth materials provide many of the resources that humans use.
- Soils have properties of color and texture, capacity to retain water, and ability to support the growth of many kinds of plants, including those in our food supply.
- Fossils provide evidence about the plants and animals that lived long ago and the nature of the environment at that time.

OBJECTS IN THE SKY
- The sun, moon, stars, clouds, birds, and airplanes all have properties, locations, and movements that can be observed and described.
- The sun provides the light and heat necessary to maintain the temperature of the earth.

CHANGES IN THE EARTH AND SKY
- The surface of the earth changes. Some changes are due to slow processes, such as erosion and weathering, and some changes are due to rapid processes, such as landslides, volcanic eruptions, and earthquakes.
- Weather changes from day to day and over the seasons. Weather can be described by measurable quantities, such as temperature, wind direction and speed, and precipitation.
- Objects in the sky have patterns of movement. The sun, for example, appears to move across the sky in the same way every day, but its path changes slowly over the seasons. The moon moves across the sky on a daily basis much like the sun. The observable shape of the moon changes from day to day in a cycle that lasts about a month.

Science and Technology

CONTENT STANDARD E:

As a result of activities in grades K-4, all students should develop

- Abilities of technological design
- Understanding about science and technology
- Abilities to distinguish between natural objects and objects made by humans

DEVELOPING STUDENT ABILITIES AND UNDERSTANDING

The science and technology standards connect students to the designed world, offer them experience in making models of useful things, and introduce them to laws of nature through their understanding of how technological objects and systems work.

This standard emphasizes developing the ability to design a solution to a problem and understanding the relationship of science and technology and the way people are involved in both. This standard helps establish design as the technological parallel to inquiry in science. Like the science as inquiry standard, this standard begins the understanding of the design process, as well as the ability to solve simple design problems.

Children in grades K-4 understand and can carry out design activities earlier than they can inquiry activities, but they cannot easily tell the difference between the two, nor is it important whether they can. In grades K-4, children should have a variety of educational experiences that involve science and technology, sometimes in the same activity and other times separately. When the activities are informal and open, such as building a balance and comparing the weight of objects on it, it is difficult to separate inquiry from technological design. At other times, the distinction might be clear to adults but not to children.

Children's abilities in technological problem solving can be developed by firsthand experience in tackling tasks with a technological purpose. They also can study technological products and systems in their world—zippers, coat hooks, can openers, bridges, and automobiles. Children can engage in projects that are appropriately challenging for their developmental level—ones in which they must design a way to fasten, move, or communicate. They can study existing products to determine function and try to identify problems solved, materials used, and how well a product does what it is supposed to do. An old technological device, such as an apple peeler, can be used as a mystery object for students to investigate and figure out what it does, how it helps people, and what problems it might solve and cause. Such activities provide excellent opportunities to direct attention to specific technology—the tools and instruments used in science.

Suitable tasks for children at this age should have clearly defined purposes and be related with the other content standards. Tasks should be conducted within immediately familiar contexts of the home and school. They should be straightforward; there should be only one or two well-defined ways to solve the problem, and there should be a single, well-defined criterion for success. Any construction of objects should

Weather Instruments

Titles in this example emphasize some important components of the assessment process. Superficially, this assessment task is a simple matching task, but the teacher's professional judgment is still key. For example, is the term "wind gauge" most appropriate or should the more technical term "anemometer" be used? The teacher needs to decide if the use of either term places some students at a disadvantage. Teacher planning includes collecting pictures of weather instruments and ensuring that all students have equal opportunity to study them. A teacher who uses this assessment task recognizes that all assessments have strengths and weaknesses; this task is appropriate for one purpose, and other modes of assessment are appropriate for other purposes. This assessment task presupposes that students have developed some understanding of weather, technology, changing patterns in the environment, and the roles science and technology have in society. The teacher examines the patterns in the responses to evaluate the individual student responses.

[This example highlights some elements of Teaching Standards A, C, and D; Assessment Standards A, B, and D; and K-4 Content Standards D, E, and F.]

SCIENCE CONTENT: The K-4 content standard for earth science is supported by the fundamental concept that weather can be described in measurable quantities.

ASSESSMENT ACTIVITY: Students match pictures of instruments used to measure weather conditions with the condition the instrument measures.

ASSESSMENT TYPE: Individual, short-answer responses to matching item format.

DATA: Students' responses.

ASSESSMENT PURPOSE: When used in conjunction with other data, this assessment activity provides information to be used in assigning a grade.

CONTEXT: This assessment activity is appropriate at the end of a unit on the weather in grades 3 or 4.

ASSESSMENT EXERCISE:

Match pictures of the following weather instruments with the weather condition they measure:

1. Thermometers of various types, including liquid-expansion thermometers, metal-expansion thermometers and digital-electronic thermometers—used to measure temperature.
2. Barometers of various types, including aneroid and mercury types—used to measure air pressure.
3. Weather vanes—used to measure wind direction.
4. Wind gauges of various sorts—instruments to measure windspeed or velocity.
5. Hygrometers of various sorts—to measure moisture in the air.
6. Rain gauges of various sorts—used to measure depth of precipitation.

EVALUATING STUDENT PERFORMANCE:

EXEMPLARY PERFORMANCE: Student matches all instruments with their use.

AVERAGE PERFORMANCE: Student matches familiar forms of measuring instruments with their uses. A student might mistakenly say that the thermometer measures heat or might not understand the concepts of air pressure or humidity. Students at this age cannot be expected to develop sophisticated understanding of the concepts of air pressure, humidity, heat, temperature, speed, or velocity.

require developmentally appropriate manipulative skills used in elementary school and should not require time-consuming preparation and assembly.

Over the course of grades K-4, student investigations and design problems should incorporate more than one material and several contexts in science and technology. A suitable collection of tasks might include making a device to shade eyes from the sun, making yogurt and discussing how it is made, comparing two types of string to see which is best for lifting different objects, exploring how small potted plants can be made to grow as quickly as possible, designing a simple system to hold two objects together, testing the strength of different materials, using simple tools, testing different designs, and constructing a simple structure. It is important also to include design problems that require application of ideas, use of communications, and implementation of procedures—for instance, improving hall traffic at lunch and cleaning the classroom after scientific investigations.

Experiences should be complemented by study of familiar and simple objects through which students can develop observation and analysis skills. By comparing one or two obvious properties, such as cost and strength of two types of adhesive tape, for example, students can develop the abilities to judge a product's worth against its ability to solve a problem. During the K-4 years, an appropriate balance of products could come from the categories of clothing, food, and common domestic and school hardware.

A sequence of five stages—stating the problem, designing an approach, implementing a solution, evaluating the solution, and communicating the problem, design, and solution—provides a framework for planning and for specifying learning outcomes. However, not every activity will involve all of those stages, nor must any particular sequence of stages be followed. For example, some activities might begin by identifying a need and progressing through the stages; other activities might involve only evaluating existing products.

GUIDE TO THE CONTENT STANDARD
Fundamental abilities and concepts that underlie this standard include

ABILITIES OF TECHNOLOGICAL DESIGN

IDENTIFY A SIMPLE PROBLEM. In problem identification, children should develop the ability to explain a problem in their own words and identify a specific task and solution related to the problem.

See Content Standard A (grades K-4)

PROPOSE A SOLUTION. Students should make proposals to build something or get something to work better; they should be able to describe and communicate their ideas. Students should recognize that designing a solution might have constraints, such as cost, materials, time, space, or safety.

IMPLEMENTING PROPOSED SOLUTIONS. Children should develop abilities to work individually and collaboratively and to use suitable tools, techniques, and quantitative measurements when appropriate. Students should demonstrate the ability to balance simple constraints in problem solving.

EVALUATE A PRODUCT OR DESIGN. Students should evaluate their own results or solutions to problems, as well as those of other children, by considering how well a product or design met the challenge to solve a problem. When possible, students should use measurements and include constraints and other criteria in their evaluations. They should modify designs based on the results of evaluations.

COMMUNICATE A PROBLEM, DESIGN, AND SOLUTION. Student abilities should include oral, written, and pictorial communication of the design process and product. The communication might be show and tell, group discussions, short written reports, or pictures, depending on the students' abilities and the design project.

UNDERSTANDING ABOUT SCIENCE AND TECHNOLOGY

- People have always had questions about their world. Science is one way of answering questions and explaining the natural world.
- People have always had problems and invented tools and techniques (ways of doing something) to solve problems. Trying to determine the effects of solutions helps people avoid some new problems.
- Scientists and engineers often work in teams with different individuals doing different things that contribute to the results. This understanding focuses primarily on teams working together and secondarily, on the combination of scientist and engineer teams.
- Women and men of all ages, backgrounds, and groups engage in a variety of scientific and technological work.
- Tools help scientists make better observations, measurements, and equipment for investigations. They help scientists see,

measure, and do things that they could not otherwise see, measure, and do.

ABILITIES TO DISTINGUISH BETWEEN NATURAL OBJECTS AND OBJECTS MADE BY HUMANS

- Some objects occur in nature; others have been designed and made by people to solve human problems and enhance the quality of life.
- Objects can be categorized into two groups, natural and designed.

Science in Personal and Social Perspectives

CONTENT STANDARD F:
As a result of activities in grades K-4, all students should develop understanding of
- **Personal health**
- **Characteristics and changes in populations**
- **Types of resources**
- **Changes in environments**
- **Science and technology in local challenges**

DEVELOPING STUDENT UNDERSTANDING

Students in elementary school should have a variety of experiences that provide initial understandings for various science-related personal and societal challenges. Central ideas related to health, populations, resources, and environments provide the foundations for students' eventual understandings and actions as citizens. Although the emphasis in grades K-4 should be on initial understandings, students can engage in some personal actions in local challenges related to science and technology.

Teachers should be aware of the concepts that elementary school students have about health. Most children use the word "germs" for all microbes; they do not generally use the words "virus" or "bacteria," and when they do, they do not understand the difference between the two. Children generally attribute all illnesses to germs without distinction between contagious and noncontagious diseases and without understanding of organic, functional, or dietary diseases. Teachers can expect students to exhibit little understanding of ideas, such as different origins of disease, resistance to infection, and prevention and cure of disease.

Children link eating with growth, health, strength, and energy, but they do not understand these ideas in detail. They understand connections between diet and health and that some foods are nutritionally better than others, but they do not necessarily know the reasons for these conclusions.

By grades 3 and 4, students regard pollution as something sensed by people and know that it might have bad effects on people and animals. Children at this age usually do not consider harm to plants as part of environmental problems; however, recent media attention might have increased students awareness of the importance of trees in the environment. In most cases, students recognize pollution as an environmental issue, scarcity as a resource issue, and crowded classrooms or schools as population problems. Most young students conceive of these

problems as isolated issues that can be solved by dealing with them individually. For example, pollution can be solved by cleaning up the environment and producing less waste, scarcity can be solved by using less, and

Central ideas related to health, populations, resources, and environments provide the foundations for students' eventual understandings and actions as citizens.

crowding can be solved by having fewer students in class or school. However, understanding the interrelationships is not the priority in elementary school.

As students expand their conceptual horizons across grades K-12, they will eventually develop a view that is not centered exclusively on humans and begin to recognize that individual actions accumulate into societal actions. Eventually, students must recognize that society cannot afford to deal only with symptoms: The causes of the problems must be the focus of personal and societal actions.

GUIDE TO THE CONTENT STANDARD
Fundamental concepts and principles that underlie this standard include

PERSONAL HEALTH

- Safety and security are basic needs of humans. Safety involves freedom from danger, risk, or injury. Security involves feelings of confidence and lack of anxiety and fear. Student understandings include following safety rules for home and school, preventing abuse and neglect, avoiding injury, knowing whom to ask for help, and when and how to say no.

See Content Standard C (grades K-4)

- Individuals have some responsibility for their own health. Students should engage in personal care—dental hygiene, cleanliness, and exercise—that will maintain and improve health. Understandings include how communicable diseases, such as colds, are transmitted and some of the body's defense mechanisms that prevent or overcome illness.

- Nutrition is essential to health. Students should understand how the body uses food and how various foods contribute to health. Recommendations for good nutrition include eating a variety of foods, eating less sugar, and eating less fat.

- Different substances can damage the body and how it functions. Such substances include tobacco, alcohol, over-the-counter medicines, and illicit drugs. Students should understand that some substances, such as prescription drugs, can be beneficial, but that any substance can be harmful if used inappropriately.

CHARACTERISTICS AND CHANGES IN POPULATIONS

- Human populations include groups of individuals living in a particular location. One important characteristic of a human population is the population density—the number of individuals of a particular population that lives in a given amount of space.

- The size of a human population can increase or decrease. Populations will increase unless other factors such as disease or famine decrease the population.

TYPES OF RESOURCES

- Resources are things that we get from the living and nonliving environment to meet the needs and wants of a population.

- Some resources are basic materials, such as air, water, and soil; some are produced from basic resources, such as food, fuel, and building materials; and some resources are nonmaterial, such as quiet places, beauty, security, and safety.

- The supply of many resources is limited. If used, resources can be extended through recycling and decreased use.

See Content Standard D (grades K-4)

CHANGES IN ENVIRONMENTS

- Environments are the space, conditions, and factors that affect an individual's and a population's ability to survive and their quality of life.

- Changes in environments can be natural or influenced by humans. Some changes are good, some are bad, and some are neither good nor bad. Pollution is a change in the environment that can influence the health, survival, or activities of organisms, including humans.

- Some environmental changes occur slowly, and others occur rapidly. Students should understand the different consequences of changing environments in small increments over long periods as compared with changing environments in large increments over short periods.

See Content Standard C (grades K-4)

SCIENCE AND TECHNOLOGY IN LOCAL CHALLENGES

- People continue inventing new ways of doing things, solving problems, and getting work done. New ideas and inventions often affect other people; sometimes the effects are good and sometimes they are bad. It is helpful to try to determine in advance how ideas and inventions will affect other people.

See Content Standard E (grades K-4)

- Science and technology have greatly improved food quality and quantity, transportation, health, sanitation, and communication. These benefits of science and technology are not available to all of the people in the world.

History and Nature of Science

CONTENT STANDARD G:

As a result of activities in grades K-4, all students should develop understanding of

- Science as a human endeavor

DEVELOPING STUDENT UNDERSTANDING

Beginning in grades K-4, teachers should build on students' natural inclinations to ask questions and investigate their world. Groups of students can conduct investigations that begin with a question and progress toward communicating an answer to the question. For students in the early grades, teachers should emphasize the experiences of investigating and thinking about explanations and not overemphasize memorization of scientific terms and information. Students can learn some things about scientific inquiry and significant people from history, which will provide a foundation for the development of sophisticated ideas related to the history and nature of science that will be developed in later years. Through the use of short stories, films, videos, and other examples, elementary teachers can introduce interesting historical examples of

women and men (including minorities and people with disabilities) who have made contributions to science. The stories can highlight how these scientists worked—that is, the questions, procedures, and contributions of diverse individuals to science and technology. In upper elementary grades, students can read and share stories that express the theme of this standard—science is a human endeavor.

GUIDE TO THE CONTENT STANDARD

Fundamental concepts and principles that underlie this standard include

SCIENCE AS A HUMAN ENDEAVOR

- Science and technology have been practiced by people for a long time.
- Men and women have made a variety of contributions throughout the history of science and technology.
- Although men and women using scientific inquiry have learned much about the objects, events, and phenomena in nature, much more remains to be understood. Science will never be finished.
- Many people choose science as a career and devote their entire lives to studying it. Many people derive great pleasure from doing science.

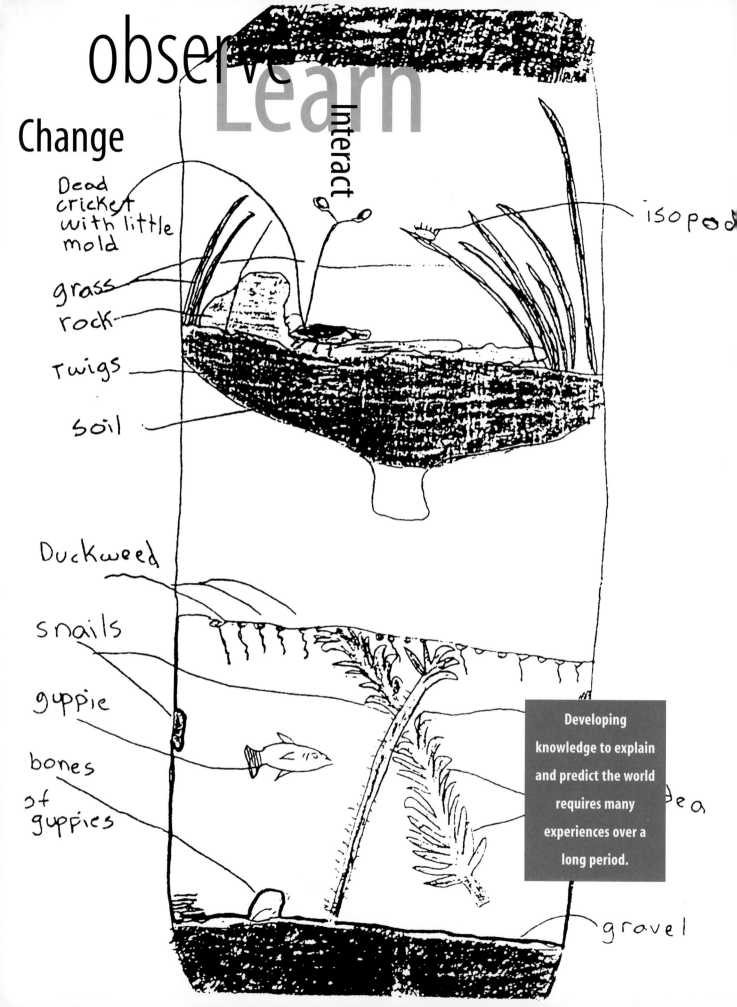

obser*Learn*

Interact

Change

Dead cricket with little mold

grass

rock

Twigs

soil

isopod

Duckweed

snails

guppie

bones of guppies

Developing knowledge to explain and predict the world requires many experiences over a long period.

idea

gravel

Content Standards: 5-8

Science as Inquiry

CONTENT STANDARD A:

As a result of activities in grades 5-8, all students should develop

- Abilities necessary to do scientific inquiry
- Understandings about scientific inquiry

DEVELOPING STUDENT ABILITIES AND UNDERSTANDING

Students in grades 5-8 should be provided opportunities to engage in full and in partial inquiries. In a full inquiry students begin with a question, design an investigation, gather evidence, formulate an answer to the original question, and communicate the investigative process and results. In partial inquiries, they develop abilities and understanding of selected aspects of the inquiry process. Students might, for instance, describe how they would design an investigation, develop explanations based on scientific information and evidence provided through a classroom activity, or recognize and analyze several alternative explanations for a natural phenomenon presented in a teacher-led demonstration.

Students in grades 5-8 can begin to recognize the relationship between explanation and evidence. They can understand that background knowledge and theories guide the design of investigations, the types of observations made, and the interpretations of data. In turn, the experiments and investigations students conduct become experiences that shape and modify their background knowledge.

With an appropriate curriculum and adequate instruction, middle-school students can develop the skills of investigation and the understanding that scientific inquiry is guided by knowledge, observations, ideas, and questions. Middle-school students might have trouble identifying variables and controlling more than one variable in an experiment. Students also might have difficulties understanding the influence of different variables in an experiment—

for example, variables that have no effect, marginal effect, or opposite effects on an outcome.

Teachers of science for middle-school students should note that students tend to center on evidence that confirms their current beliefs and concepts (i.e., personal explanations), and ignore or fail to perceive evidence that does not agree with their current concepts. It is important for teachers of science to challenge current beliefs and concepts and provide scientific explanations as alternatives.

Several factors of this standard should be highlighted. The instructional activities of a scientific inquiry should engage students in identifying and shaping an understanding of the question under inquiry. Students should know what the question is asking, what

Students in grades 5-8 can begin to recognize the relationship between explanation and evidence.

background knowledge is being used to frame the question, and what they will have to do to answer the question. The students' questions should be relevant and meaningful for them. To help focus investigations, students should frame questions, such as "What do we want to find out about . . .?", "How can we make the most accurate observations?", "Is this the best way to answer our questions?" and "If we do this, then what do we expect will happen?"

The instructional activities of a scientific inquiry should involve students in establishing and refining the methods, materials, and data they will collect. As students conduct investigations and make observations, they

should consider questions such as "What data will answer the question?" and "What are the best observations or measurements to make?" Students should be encouraged to repeat data-collection procedures and to share data among groups.

In middle schools, students produce oral or written reports that present the results of their inquiries. Such reports and discussions should be a frequent occurrence in science programs. Students' discussions should center on questions, such as "How should we organize the data to present the clearest answer to our question?" or "How should we organize the evidence to present the strongest explanation?" Out of the discussions about the range of ideas, the background knowledge claims, and the data, the opportunity arises for learners to shape their experiences about the practice of science and the rules of scientific thinking and knowing.

The language and practices evident in the classroom are an important element of doing inquiries. Students need opportunities to present their abilities and understanding and to use the knowledge and language of science to communicate scientific explanations and ideas. Writing, labeling drawings, completing concept maps, developing spreadsheets, and designing computer graphics should be a part of the science education. These should be presented in a way that allows students to receive constructive feedback on the quality of thought and expression and the accuracy of scientific explanations.

This standard should not be interpreted as advocating a "scientific method." The conceptual and procedural abilities suggest a logical progression, but they do not imply a rigid approach to scientific inquiry. On the contrary, they imply codevelopment of the skills of students in acquiring science knowledge, in using high-level reasoning, in applying their existing understanding of scientific ideas, and in communicating scientific information. This standard cannot be met by having the students memorize the abilities and understandings. It can be met only when students frequently engage in active inquiries.

GUIDE TO THE CONTENT STANDARD
Fundamental abilities and concepts that underlie this standard include

ABILITIES NECESSARY TO DO SCIENTIFIC INQUIRY

IDENTIFY QUESTIONS THAT CAN BE ANSWERED THROUGH SCIENTIFIC INVESTIGATIONS. Students should develop the ability to refine and refocus broad and ill-defined questions. An important aspect of this ability consists of students' ability to clarify questions and inquiries and direct them toward objects and phenomena that can be described, explained, or predicted by scientific investigations. Students should develop the ability to identify their questions with scientific ideas, concepts, and quantitative relationships that guide investigation.

DESIGN AND CONDUCT A SCIENTIFIC INVESTIGATION. Students should develop general abilities, such as systematic observation, making accurate measurements, and identifying and controlling variables. They should also develop the ability to clarify their ideas that are influencing and guiding the inquiry, and to understand how those ideas compare with current scientific knowledge. Students can learn to formulate questions, design investigations, execute investigations,

interpret data, use evidence to generate explanations, propose alternative explanations, and critique explanations and procedures.

USE APPROPRIATE TOOLS AND TECHNIQUES TO GATHER, ANALYZE, AND INTERPRET DATA. The use of tools and techniques, including mathematics, will be guided by the question asked and the investigations students design. The use of computers for the collection, summary, and display of evidence is part of this standard. Students should be able to access, gather, store, retrieve, and organize data, using hardware and software designed for these purposes.

DEVELOP DESCRIPTIONS, EXPLANATIONS, PREDICTIONS, AND MODELS USING EVIDENCE. Students should base their explanation on what they observed, and as they develop cognitive skills, they should be able to differentiate explanation from description—providing causes for effects and establishing relationships based on evidence and logical argument. This standard requires a subject matter knowledge base so the students can effectively conduct investigations, because developing explanations establishes connections between the content of science and the contexts within which students develop new knowledge.

THINK CRITICALLY AND LOGICALLY TO MAKE THE RELATIONSHIPS BETWEEN EVIDENCE AND EXPLANATIONS. Thinking critically about evidence includes deciding what evidence should be used and accounting for anomalous data. Specifically, students should be able to review data from a simple experiment, summarize the data, and form a logical argument about the cause-and-effect relationships in the experiment.

Pendulums

Ms. D. wants to focus on inquiry. She wants students to develop an understanding of variables in inquiry and how and why to change one variable at a time. This inquiry process skill is imparted in the context of physical science subject matter. The activity is purposeful, planned, and requires teacher guidance. Ms. D. does not tell students that the number of swings depends on the length of the pendulum, but creates an activity that awakens students' interest and encourages them to ask questions and seek answers. Ms. D. encourages students to look for applications of the science knowledge beyond the classroom. Students keep records of the science activities, and Ms. D. helps them understand that there are different ways to keep records of events. The activity requires mathematical knowledge and skills.. The assessment, constructing a pendulum that swings at six swings per second, is embedded in the activity.

[This example highlights some elements of Teaching Standards B, C, and D; Assessment Standard B; 5-8 Content Standards A and B; and Program Standard C.]

The students in Ms. D.'s fifth grade class are studying motion, direction, and speed. One experiment in this study is designed to enable the students to understand how and why to change one variable at a time. Ms. D. has the students form groups of four; each student has an assigned role. One student—the materials manager—goes to the supply table to pick up a length of string, scissors, tape, and washers of various sizes and weights. Each group is directed to use these materials to 1) construct a pendulum, 2) hang the pendulum so that it swings freely from a pencil taped to the surface of the desk, and 3) count the number of swings of the pendulum in 15 seconds.

The notetaker in each group records the result in a class chart. Ms. D. asks the students to examine the class data. Because the number of swings recorded by each group is different, a lively discussion begins about why this happened. The students decide to repeat the experiment to make sure that they have measured the time and counted the swings correctly. When the second set of

data are entered on the class data table, the results make it clear that the differences are not because students did not count swings or measure time correctly. Again the class discusses why the results are different. Some of the suggestions include the length of the string, the weight of the washer, the diameter of the washer, and how high the student starting the pendulum held the washer to begin the swing.

As each suggestion is made, Ms. D. writes it on the board. The class is then asked to design experiments that could determine which suggestion is correct. Each group chooses to do an experiment to test one of the suggestions, but before the group work continues, Ms. D. collects the pendulums that were used to generate the first and second sets of data. As the groups resume work, one group keeps the string the same length but attaches washers of different diameters and tries to start the swing at exactly the same place. Another group uses one piece of string and one washer, but starts the swing at higher and higher places on an arc. A third group cuts pieces of string of different lengths, but uses one washer and starts the swing at the same place each time. Discussion is animated as students set up their pendulums and the class quiets as they count the swings. Finally, each group shares with the rest of the class what they did and the data they collected. The class concludes that the difference in the number of swings that the pendulum makes is due to the different lengths of string.

The next day, students notice that Ms. D. has constructed a board for the pendulums at the front of the room. Across the top are pegs from which to hang pendulums, and across the bottom are consecutive numbers.

The notetaker from each group is directed to hang the group's original pendulum on the peg corresponding to its number of swings in a fixed time. When all of the pendulums are hung on the peg board, the class is asked to interpret the results. After considerable discussion, the students conclude that the number of swings in a fixed time increases in a regular manner as the length of the string gets shorter.

Ms. D. notes that pendulums were constructed with five and seven swings per 15 seconds on the peg board, but no pendulum with six; she asks each group to construct a pendulum with six swings per 15 seconds. After much measuring and counting and measuring again, and serious discussion on what counts as a "swing," every group declares success. Ms. D. then asks how they can keep the information on the relationship between the length of the string and the number of swings in a form that is more convenient than the peg board and directs the students to make a drawing in their science journals to keep that data. Most students draw the pegboard with the pendulums of different lengths, but some students draw charts and a few make graphs. Ms. D. challenges students to find examples of pendulums at home and in their neighborhoods.

The next science class is spent discussing graphing as students move from their pictures of the string lengths, to lines, to points on a graph, and to a complete graph. Finally, each student is asked to use his or her graph to make a pendulum that will swing an exact number of times.

Students have described, explained, and predicted a natural phenomenon and learned about position and motion and about gathering, analyzing, and presenting data.

Students should begin to state some explanations in terms of the relationship between two or more variables.

RECOGNIZE AND ANALYZE ALTERNATIVE EXPLANATIONS AND PREDICTIONS. Students should develop the ability to listen to and respect the explanations proposed by other students. They should remain open to and acknowledge different ideas and explanations, be able to accept the skepticism of others, and consider alternative explanations.

See Teaching Standard B

COMMUNICATE SCIENTIFIC PROCEDURES AND EXPLANATIONS. With practice, students should become competent at communicating experimental methods, following instructions, describing observations, summarizing the results of other groups, and telling other students about investigations and explanations.

See Program Standard C

USE MATHEMATICS IN ALL ASPECTS OF SCIENTIFIC INQUIRY. Mathematics is essential to asking and answering questions about the natural world. Mathematics can be used to ask questions; to gather, organize, and present data; and to structure convincing explanations.

UNDERSTANDINGS ABOUT SCIENTIFIC INQUIRY

- Different kinds of questions suggest different kinds of scientific investigations. Some investigations involve observing and describing objects, organisms, or events; some involve collecting specimens; some involve experiments; some involve seeking more information; some involve discovery of new objects and phenomena; and some involve making models.

- Current scientific knowledge and understanding guide scientific investigations. Different scientific domains employ different methods, core theories, and standards to advance scientific knowledge and understanding.

- Mathematics is important in all aspects of scientific inquiry.

- Technology used to gather data enhances accuracy and allows scientists to analyze and quantify results of investigations.

- Scientific explanations emphasize evidence, have logically consistent arguments, and use scientific principles, models, and theories. The scientific community accepts and uses such explanations until displaced by better scientific ones. When such displacement occurs, science advances.

- Science advances through legitimate skepticism. Asking questions and querying other scientists' explanations is part of scientific inquiry. Scientists evaluate the explanations proposed by other scientists by examining evidence, comparing evidence, identifying faulty reasoning, pointing out statements that go beyond the evidence, and suggesting alternative explanations for the same observations.

- Scientific investigations sometimes result in new ideas and phenomena for study, generate new methods or procedures for an investigation, or develop new technologies to improve the collection of data. All of these results can lead to new investigations.

Physical Science

CONTENT STANDARD B:

As a result of their activities in grades 5-8, all students should develop an understanding of

- Properties and changes of properties in matter
- Motions and forces
- Transfer of energy

DEVELOPING STUDENT UNDERSTANDING

In grades 5-8, the focus on student understanding shifts from properties of objects and materials to the characteristic properties of the substances from which the materials are made. In the K-4 years, students learned that objects and materials can be sorted and ordered in terms of their properties. During that process, they learned that some properties, such as size, weight, and shape, can be assigned only to the object while other properties, such as color, texture, and hardness, describe the materials from which objects are made. In grades 5-8, students observe and measure characteristic properties, such as boiling points, melting points, solubility, and simple chemical changes of pure substances and use those properties to distinguish and separate one substance from another.

Students usually bring some vocabulary and primitive notions of atomicity to the science class but often lack understanding of the evidence and the logical arguments that support the particulate model of matter. Their early ideas are that the particles have

the same properties as the parent material; that is, they are a tiny piece of the substance. It can be tempting to introduce atoms and molecules or improve students' understanding of them so that particles can be used as an explanation for the properties of elements and compounds. However, use of such terminology is premature for these stu-

In grades 5-8, students observe and measure characteristic properties, such as boiling and melting points, solubility, and simple chemical changes of pure substances, and use those properties to distinguish and separate one substance from another.

dents and can distract from the understanding that can be gained from focusing on the observation and description of macroscopic features of substances and of physical and chemical reactions. At this level, elements and compounds can be defined operationally from their chemical characteristics, but few students can comprehend the idea of atomic and molecular particles.

The study of motions and the forces causing motion provide concrete experiences on which a more comprehensive understanding of force can be based in grades 9-12. By using simple objects, such as rolling balls and mechanical toys, students can move from qualitative to quantitative descriptions of moving objects and begin to describe the forces acting on the objects. Students' everyday experience is that friction causes all moving objects to slow down and stop. Through experiences in which friction is

Funny Water

In this example, Mr. B makes his plans using his knowledge and understanding of science, students, teaching, and the district science program. His understanding and ability are the results of years of studying and reflection on his own teaching. He usually introduces new topics with a demonstration to catch the students' attention. He asks questions that encourage students to develop understanding and designs activities that require students to confirm their ideas and extend them to situations within and beyond the science classroom. Mr. B encourages students to observe, test, discuss, and write by promoting individual effort as well as by forming different-sized groups of students for various activities. Immense understanding, skill, creativity, and energy are required to organize and orchestrate ideas, students, materials, and events the way Mr. B. does with apparent ease. And Mr. B. might repeat an activity five times a day, adapting it to the needs of different classes of students, or he might teach four other school subjects.

[This example highlights some components of Teaching Standards A, B, D, and E; Professional Development Standard C; 5-8 Content Standard A and B; Program Standards A, B, and D; and System Standards D.]

Mr. B. was beginning a unit that would include the development of students' understanding of the characteristic properties of substances such as boiling points, melting points, solubility, and density. He wanted students to consolidate their experiences and think about the properties of substances as a foundation for the atomic theories they would gradually come to understand in high school. He knew that the students had some vocabulary and some notions of atomicity but were likely not to have any understanding of the evidence of the particulate nature of matter or arguments that support that understanding. Mr. B. started the unit with a study of density because the concept is important and because this study allowed him to gather data on the students' current understandings about matter.

As he had done the year before, he began the study with the density of liquids. He knew that the students who had been in the district elementary schools had already done some work with liquids and that all students brought experience and knowledge from their daily lives. To clarify the knowledge, understanding, and confusion students might have, Mr. B. prepared a set of short exercises for the opening week of the unit of study.

For the first day, he prepared two density columns: using two 1-foot-high, clear plastic cylinders, he poured in layers of corn syrup, liquid detergent, colored water, vegetable oil, baby oil, and methanol. As the students arrived, they were directed into two groups to examine the columns and discuss what they saw. After 10 minutes of conversation, Mr. B. asked the students to take out their notebooks and jot down observations and thoughts about why the different liquids separated.

When the writing ceased, Mr. B. asked, "What did you observe? Do you have any explanations for what you see? What do you think is happening?" He took care to explain, "There are no right answers, and silence is OK. You need to think." Silence was followed by a few comments, and finally, a lively discussion ensued.

It's pretty

How do you get the colors to stay apart?

Like the ones on top are lighter or something like that.

The top looks like water.

I think the bottom liquids are heavier; they sink to the bottom .

It separated into different layers because each has different densities and they sit on top of each other.

"What do you mean by density?" asked Mr. B.

It's how packed the particles are.

This one is thick so it's on the bottom. This one is thinnest.

Doesn't oil have lighter density than water?

If we put a thicker liquid in, it would go to the bottom.

There's more of this one that's on the bottom.

The atoms in some are heavier than the ones in others.

Mr. B. realized how many different ways the students explained what they saw, for example, thickness and thinness, heaviness and lightness, more and less, different densities and atoms. The discussion gave him a sense for what the students were thinking. It was clear to him that the investigations he had planned for the following weeks to focus more closely on density would be worthwhile.

Mr. B. divided the class into seven groups of four the next day. On each of the group's tables were small cylinders. Mr. B warned the students not to drink the liquid. Each group was to choose one person to be the materials manager and one to be the recorder as they proceeded to find out what they could about the same liquids used the day before (all of which were available on the supply table). Only the materials manager was to come to the supply table for the liquids, and the recorders kept track of what they did. Forty minutes later, Mr. B. asked

students to clean up and gather to share their observations.

Every group identified some of the liquids. The water was easy, as was the vegetable oil. Some students knew corn syrup, others recognized the detergent. Several groups combined two and three liquids and found that some of them mixed together, and others stayed separate. Some disagreements arose about which liquid floated on which. Mr. B. suggested that interested students come back during their lunch time to try to resolve these disagreements. One group replicated the large cylinder, shook it vigorously, and was waiting to see whether the liquids would separate. Mr. B. asked that group to draw what the cylinder contents looked like now, put it on the windowsill, and check it the next day.

Mr. B. began the third day with a large density column again. This time he gave a small object to each of four students—a piece of wood, aluminum, plastic, or iron. He asked the class to predict what would happen when each of the four objects was released into the column. The students predicted and watched as some objects sank to the bottom, and others stopped somewhere in the columns.

"What do you think is going on?" asked Mr. B. "How can you explain the way these objects behaved? I don't want answers now," he went on, "I want you to try out some more things yourselves and then we'll talk." He then divided the class into four groups and gave each a large density column with the liquid layers. The students worked in their groups for 30 minutes. The discussion was animated as different objects were tried: rubber bands, a penny, a nickel, a pencil, and paper clips. Mr. B. circulated from group to group taking note of many interesting comments. With 10 minutes left in the class, he gathered the groups together and asked for some of their observations.

When we dropped something lighter in, it stopped near the top.

The rubber band is lighter than the paper clip. The paper clip is heavy so it drops down.

The rubber band has buoyancy, if you know what that means.

The nickel went all the way to the bottom because it's heavier, but the pencil wouldn't go into the last layer because it was too thick. The pencil is wood and it's lighter; the nickel is silver and it's heavier.

The nickel is denser than the pencil.

Mr. B. listened to these observations and encouraged the students to respond to one another. Occasionally he asked for a clarification—"What do you mean by that?" "How did you do that?" His primary purpose was to hear the students' ideas and encourage them to explain them to one another.

The next day he began the last of the introductory experiences. When the students came in, Mr. B. asked them to divide into their four groups and go to the tables with the density columns. Beside each column were several pieces of wood of different sizes. Students were to think and talk about what the pieces might do in the column, try them out, have more discussion, and write down some of their ideas in their science notebooks.

When enough time had passed, Mr. B. called the groups together and asked for some volunteers to read from their notebooks. Some students were struggling with what they had seen:

They stuck in the middle of the column.

The pieces are not the same weight. The bigger ones are heavier. I don't know why they all stopped in the middle.

Others seemed to understand. One student read,

If you have a block of wood and cut it into millions of pieces, each piece would have the density of the original block. If that block of wood weighed one gram and you cut it into a million pieces the weight would change. But no matter how many times you cut something, the density will not change.

When this statement was read Mr. B. asked how many people agreed with it. Most students quickly asserted "yes." But how sure were they? Mr. B. pulled out a piece of wood larger than any of those that the students had tried. "What would happen if this piece of wood were dropped into the column?" Some students said immediately that it would stop where the smaller pieces had. Others were not quite so sure. This piece was quite a bit bigger. One student asked for a show of hands. Twelve students thought this big piece of wood would sink farther and 16 thought it would sink to the same level as the others. Mr. B. dropped it in. It stopped sinking where the others had. There were a few "yeahs," a few "what's," and some puzzled looks.

As a final teaser and check on students' understanding, Mr. B. brought out two transparent containers of colorless liquids. He asked the class to gather around, took a candle and cut two quite different-sized pieces from it. The students were asked to predict what would happen when the candle pieces were put in the liquids. Mr. B. dropped the pieces into the columns: In one container the big piece sank to the bottom; in the other, the small one floated on the top. Some students had predicted this result, saying that the bigger one was heavier and therefore would sink. Others were perplexed. The two pieces were made of the same wax so they shouldn't be different. Something was wrong. Were the two liquids really the same? Mr. B. removed the pieces of wax from the containers and reversed them. This time the little one sank and the big one floated. "Unfair," came a chorus of voices. "The liquids aren't the same."

Mr. B. had used water and isopropyl alcohol. But he noticed several students were willing to explain the sinking of the larger piece of candle and not the smaller by the difference in the size of the piece.

Mr. B. closed the lesson by summing up. They had seen the density column and worked with the liquids themselves; they had tried floating objects in liquids; they had seen the pieces of wax in the liquids. What was the explanation for all these phenomena? For homework that night he asked them to do two things. They were to think about and write down any ideas they had about what was happening in all these experiences. He also asked them to think about and write about examples of these phenomena in their daily lives. After the students shared some of their observations from outside the classroom, Mr. B. would have the students observe as he boiled water to initiate discussion of boiling points.

reduced, students can begin to see that a moving object with no friction would continue to move indefinitely, but most students believe that the force is still acting if the object is moving or that it is "used up" if the motion stops. Students also think that friction, not inertia, is the principle reason objects remain at rest or require a force to move. Students in grades 5-8 associate force with motion and have difficulty understanding balanced forces in equilibrium, especially if the force is associated with static, inanimate objects, such as a book resting on the desk.

The understanding of energy in grades 5-8 will build on the K-4 experiences with light, heat, sound, electricity, magnetism, and the motion of objects. In 5-8, students begin to see the connections among those phenomena and to become familiar with the idea that energy is an important property of substances and that most change involves energy transfer. Students might have some of the same views of energy as they do of force—that it is associated with animate objects and is linked to motion. In addition, students view energy as a fuel or something that is stored, ready to use, and gets used up. The intent at this level is for students to improve their understanding of energy by experiencing many kinds of energy transfer.

GUIDE TO THE CONTENT STANDARD
Fundamental concepts and principles that underlie this standard include

PROPERTIES AND CHANGES OF PROPERTIES IN MATTER
- A substance has characteristic properties, such as density, a boiling point, and solubility, all of which are independent of the amount of the sample. A mixture of substances often can be separated into the original substances using one or more of the characteristic properties.
- Substances react chemically in characteristic ways with other substances to form new substances (compounds) with different characteristic properties. In chemical reactions, the total mass is conserved. Substances often are placed in categories or groups if they react in similar ways; metals is an example of such a group.
- Chemical elements do not break down during normal laboratory reactions involving such treatments as heating, exposure to electric current, or reaction with acids. There are more than 100 known elements that combine in a multitude of ways to produce compounds, which account for the living and nonliving substances that we encounter.

MOTIONS AND FORCES
- The motion of an object can be described by its position, direction of motion, and speed. That motion can be measured and represented on a graph.
- An object that is not being subjected to a force will continue to move at a constant speed and in a straight line.
- If more than one force acts on an object along a straight line, then the forces will reinforce or cancel one another, depending on their direction and magnitude. Unbalanced forces will cause changes in the speed or direction of an object's motion.

See Content Standard D (grades 5-8)

- Energy is a property of many substances and is associated with heat, light, electricity, mechanical motion, sound, nuclei, and the nature of a chemical. Energy is transferred in many ways.

- Heat moves in predictable ways, flowing from warmer objects to cooler ones, until both reach the same temperature.

- Light interacts with matter by transmission (including refraction), absorption, or scattering (including reflection). To see an object, light from that object—emitted by or scattered from it—must enter the eye.

- Electrical circuits provide a means of transferring electrical energy when heat, light, sound, and chemical changes are produced.

See Unifying Concepts and Processes

- In most chemical and nuclear reactions, energy is transferred into or out of a system. Heat, light, mechanical motion, or electricity might all be involved in such transfers.

- The sun is a major source of energy for changes on the earth's surface. The sun loses energy by emitting light. A tiny fraction of that light reaches the earth, transferring energy from the sun to the earth. The sun's energy arrives as light with a range of wavelengths, consisting of visible light, infrared, and ultraviolet radiation.

Life Science

CONTENT STANDARD C:
As a result of their activities in grades 5-8, all students should develop understanding of

- Structure and function in living systems
- Reproduction and heredity
- Regulation and behavior
- Populations and ecosystems
- Diversity and adaptations of organisms

DEVELOPING STUDENT UNDERSTANDING

In the middle-school years, students should progress from studying life science from the point of view of individual organisms to recognizing patterns in ecosystems and developing understandings about the cellular dimensions of living systems. For example, students should broaden their understanding from the way one species lives in its environment to populations and communities of species and the ways they interact with each other and with their environment. Students also should expand their investigations of living systems to include the study of cells. Observations and investigations should become increasingly quantitative, incorporating the use of computers and conceptual and mathematical models. Students in grades 5-8 also have the fine-motor skills to work with a light microscope and can interpret accurately what they see, enhancing their introduction to cells and microorganisms and establishing a foundation for developing understanding of molecular biology at the high school level.

Some aspects of middle-school student understanding should be noted. This period of development in youth lends itself to human biology. Middle-school students can develop the understanding that the body has organs that function together to maintain life. Teachers should introduce the general idea of structure-function in the context of human organ systems working together. Other, more specific and concrete examples, such as the hand, can be used to develop a specific understanding of structure-function in living systems. By middle-school, most students know about the basic process of sexual reproduction in humans. However, the student might have misconceptions about the role of sperm and eggs and about the sexual reproduction of flowering plants. Concerning heredity, younger middle-school students tend to focus on observable traits, and older students have some understanding that genetic material carries information.

Students understand ecosystems and the interactions between organisms and environments well enough by this stage to introduce ideas about nutrition and energy flow, although some students might be confused by charts and flow diagrams. If asked about common ecological concepts, such as community and competition between organisms, teachers are likely to hear responses based on everyday experiences rather than scientific explanations. Teachers should use the students' understanding as a basis to develop the scientific understanding.

Understanding adaptation can be particularly troublesome at this level. Many students think adaptation means that individuals change in major ways in response to environmental changes (that is, if the environment changes, individual organisms deliberately adapt).

GUIDE TO THE CONTENT STANDARD
Fundamental concepts and principles that underlie this standard include

STRUCTURE AND FUNCTION IN LIVING SYSTEMS

- Living systems at all levels of organization demonstrate the complementary nature of structure and function. Important levels of organization for structure and function include cells, organs, tissues, organ systems, whole organisms, and ecosystems.

- All organisms are composed of cells—the fundamental unit of life. Most organisms are single cells; other organisms, including humans, are multicellular.

- Cells carry on the many functions needed to sustain life. They grow and divide, thereby producing more cells. This requires that they take in nutrients, which they use to provide energy for the work that cells do and to make the materials that a cell or an organism needs.

- Specialized cells perform specialized functions in multicellular organisms. Groups of specialized cells cooperate to form a tissue, such as a muscle. Different tissues are in turn grouped together to form larger functional units, called organs. Each type of cell, tissue, and organ has a distinct structure and set of functions that serve the organism as a whole.

- The human organism has systems for digestion, respiration, reproduction, circulation, excretion, movement, control, and coordination, and for protection

See Unifying Concepts and Processes

from disease. These systems interact with one another.

- Disease is a breakdown in structures or functions of an organism. Some diseases are the result of intrinsic failures of the system. Others are the result of damage by infection by other organisms.

REPRODUCTION AND HEREDITY

- Reproduction is a characteristic of all living systems; because no individual organism lives forever, reproduction is essential to the continuation of every species. Some organisms reproduce asexually. Other organisms reproduce sexually.

- In many species, including humans, females produce eggs and males produce sperm. Plants also reproduce sexually—the egg and sperm are produced in the flowers of flowering plants. An egg and sperm unite to begin development of a new individual. That new individual receives genetic information from its mother (via the egg) and its father (via the sperm). Sexually produced offspring never are identical to either of their parents.

- Every organism requires a set of instructions for specifying its traits. Heredity is the passage of these instructions from one generation to another.

- Hereditary information is contained in genes, located in the chromosomes of each cell. Each gene carries a single unit of information. An inherited trait of an individual can be determined by one or by many genes, and a single gene can influence more than one trait. A human cell contains many thousands of different genes.

- The characteristics of an organism can be described in terms of a combination of traits. Some traits are inherited and others result from interactions with the environment.

REGULATION AND BEHAVIOR

- All organisms must be able to obtain and use resources, grow, reproduce, and maintain stable internal conditions while living in a constantly changing external environment.

- Regulation of an organism's internal environment involves sensing the internal environment and changing physiological activities to keep conditions within the range required to survive.

- Behavior is one kind of response an organism can make to an internal or environmental stimulus. A behavioral response requires coordination and communication at many levels, including cells, organ systems, and whole organisms. Behavioral response is a set of actions determined in part by heredity and in part from experience.

- An organism's behavior evolves through adaptation to its environment. How a species moves, obtains food, reproduces, and responds to danger are based in the species' evolutionary history.

POPULATIONS AND ECOSYSTEMS

- A population consists of all individuals of a species that occur together at a given place and time. All populations living together and the physical factors with which they interact compose an ecosystem.

- Populations of organisms can be categorized by the function they serve in an ecosystem. Plants and some microorganisms are producers—they make their own food. All animals, including humans, are consumers, which obtain food by eating other organisms. Decomposers, primarily bacteria and fungi, are consumers that use waste materials and dead organisms for food. Food webs identify the relationships among producers, consumers, and decomposers in an ecosystem.

- For ecosystems, the major source of energy is sunlight. Energy entering ecosystems as sunlight is transferred by producers into chemical energy through photosynthesis. That energy then passes from organism to organism in food webs.

- The number of organisms an ecosystem can support depends on the resources available and abiotic factors, such as quantity of light and water, range of temperatures, and soil composition. Given adequate biotic and abiotic resources and no disease or predators, populations (including humans) increase at rapid rates. Lack of resources and other factors, such as predation and climate, limit the growth of populations in specific niches in the ecosystem.

DIVERSITY AND ADAPTATIONS OF ORGANISMS

- Millions of species of animals, plants, and microorganisms are alive today. Although different species might look dissimilar, the unity among organisms becomes apparent from an analysis of internal structures, the similarity of their chemical processes, and the evidence of common ancestry.

- Biological evolution accounts for the diversity of species developed through gradual processes over many generations.

Species acquire many of their unique characteristics through biological adaptation, which involves the selection of naturally occurring variations in populations. Biological adaptations include changes in structures, behaviors, or physiology that enhance survival and reproductive success in a particular environment.

- Extinction of a species occurs when the environment changes and the adaptive characteristics of a species are insufficient to allow its survival. Fossils indicate that many organisms that lived long ago are extinct. Extinction of species is common; most of the species that have lived on the earth no longer exist.

Earth and Space Science

CONTENT STANDARD D:
As a result of their activities in grades 5-8, all students should develop an understanding of
- Structure of the earth system
- Earth's history
- Earth in the solar system

DEVELOPING STUDENT UNDERSTANDING

A major goal of science in the middle grades is for students to develop an understanding of earth and the solar system as a set of closely coupled systems. The idea of systems provides a framework in which students can investigate the four major interacting components of the earth system—

geosphere (crust, mantle, and core), hydrosphere (water), atmosphere (air), and the biosphere (the realm of all living things). In this holistic approach to studying the planet, physical, chemical, and biological processes act within and among the four components on a wide range of time scales to change continuously earth's crust, oceans, atmosphere, and living organisms. Students can investigate the water and rock cycles as introductory examples of geophysical and geochemical cycles. Their study of earth's history provides some evidence about co-evolution of the planet's main features—the distribution of land and sea, features of the crust, the composition of the atmosphere, global climate, and populations of living organisms in the biosphere.

By plotting the locations of volcanoes and earthquakes, students can see a pattern of geological activity. Earth has an outermost rigid shell called the lithosphere. It is made up of the crust and part of the upper mantle. It is broken into about a dozen rigid plates that move without deforming, except at boundaries where they collide. Those plates range in thickness from a few to more than 100 kilometers. Ocean floors are the tops of thin oceanic plates that spread outward from midocean rift zones; land surfaces are the tops of thicker, less-dense continental plates.

Because students do not have direct contact with most of these phenomena and the long-term nature of the processes, some explanations of moving plates and the evolution of life must be reserved for late in grades 5-8. As students mature, the concept of evaporation can be reasonably well understood as the conservation of matter combined with a primitive idea of particles

and the idea that air is real. Condensation is less well understood and requires extensive observation and instruction to complete an understanding of the water cycle.

The understanding that students gain from their observations in grades K-4 provides the motivation and the basis from which they can begin to construct a model that explains the visual and physical relationships among earth, sun, moon, and the solar system. Direct observation and satellite data allow students to conclude that earth is a moving, spherical planet, having unique features that distinguish it from other planets in the solar system. From activities with trajectories and orbits and using the earth-sun-moon system as an example, students can develop the understanding that gravity is a ubiquitous force that holds all parts of the solar system together. Energy from the sun transferred by light and other radiation is the primary energy source for processes on earth's surface and in its hydrosphere, atmosphere, and biosphere.

By grades 5-8, students have a clear notion about gravity, the shape of the earth, and the relative positions of the earth, sun, and moon. Nevertheless, more than half of the students will not be able to use these models to explain the phases of the moon, and correct explanations for the seasons will be even more difficult to achieve.

GUIDE TO THE CONTENT STANDARD
Fundamental concepts and principles that underlie this standard include

STRUCTURE OF THE EARTH SYSTEM

- The solid earth is layered with a lithosphere; hot, convecting mantle; and dense, metallic core.

See Content Standard F (grades 5-8)

- Lithospheric plates on the scales of continents and oceans constantly move at rates of centimeters per year in response to movements in the mantle. Major geological events, such as earthquakes, volcanic eruptions, and mountain building, result from these plate motions.

- Land forms are the result of a combination of constructive and destructive forces. Constructive forces include crustal deformation, volcanic eruption, and deposition of sediment, while destructive forces include weathering and erosion.

- Some changes in the solid earth can be described as the "rock cycle." Old rocks at the earth's surface weather, forming sediments that are buried, then compacted, heated, and often recrystallized into new rock. Eventually, those new rocks may be brought to the surface by the forces that drive plate motions, and the rock cycle continues.

- Soil consists of weathered rocks and decomposed organic material from dead plants, animals, and bacteria. Soils are often found in layers, with each having a different chemical composition and texture.

- Water, which covers the majority of the earth's surface, circulates through the crust, oceans, and atmosphere in what is known as the "water cycle." Water evaporates from the earth's surface, rises and cools as it moves to higher elevations, condenses as rain or snow, and falls to the surface where it collects in lakes, oceans, soil, and in rocks underground.

- Water is a solvent. As it passes through the water cycle it dissolves minerals and gases and carries them to the oceans.

- The atmosphere is a mixture of nitrogen, oxygen, and trace gases that include water vapor. The atmosphere has different properties at different elevations.

- Clouds, formed by the condensation of water vapor, affect weather and climate.

- Global patterns of atmospheric movement influence local weather. Oceans have a major effect on climate, because water in the oceans holds a large amount of heat.

- Living organisms have played many roles in the earth system, including affecting the composition of the atmosphere, producing some types of rocks, and contributing to the weathering of rocks.

EARTH'S HISTORY

- The earth processes we see today, including erosion, movement of lithospheric plates, and changes in atmospheric composition, are similar to those that occurred in the past. earth history is also influenced by occasional catastrophes, such as the impact of an asteroid or comet.

- Fossils provide important evidence of how life and environmental conditions have changed.

See Content Standard C (grades 5-8)

EARTH IN THE SOLAR SYSTEM

- The earth is the third planet from the sun in a system that includes the moon, the sun, eight other planets and their moons, and smaller objects, such as asteroids and comets. The sun, an average star, is the central and largest body in the solar system.

- Most objects in the solar system are in regular and predictable motion. Those motions explain such phenomena as the day, the year, phases of the moon, and eclipses.

See Unifying Concepts and Processes

- Gravity is the force that keeps planets in orbit around the sun and governs the rest of the motion in the solar system. Gravity alone holds us to the earth's surface and explains the phenomena of the tides.
- The sun is the major source of energy for phenomena on the earth's surface, such as growth of plants, winds, ocean currents, and the water cycle. Seasons result from variations in the amount of the sun's energy hitting the surface, due to the tilt of the earth's rotation on its axis and the length of the day.

Science and Technology

CONTENT STANDARD E:
As a result of activities in grades 5-8, all students should develop
- **Abilities of technological design**
- **Understandings about science and technology**

DEVELOPING STUDENT ABILITIES AND UNDERSTANDING

Students in grades 5-8 can begin to differentiate between science and technology, although the distinction is not easy to make early in this level. One basis for understanding the similarities, differences, and relationships between science and technology should be experiences with design and problem solving in which students can further develop some of the abilities introduced in grades K-4. The understanding of technology can be developed by tasks in which students have to design something

and also by studying technological products and systems.

In the middle-school years, students' work with scientific investigations can be complemented by activities in which the purpose is to meet a human need, solve a

In the middle-school years, students' work with scientific investigations can be complemented by activities that are meant to meet a human need, solve a human problem, or develop a product…

human problem, or develop a product rather than to explore ideas about the natural world. The tasks chosen should involve the use of science concepts already familiar to students or should motivate them to learn new concepts needed to use or understand the technology. Students should also, through the experience of trying to meet a need in the best possible way, begin to appreciate that technological design and problem solving involve many other factors besides the scientific issues.

Suitable design tasks for students at these grades should be well-defined, so that the purposes of the tasks are not confusing. Tasks should be based on contexts that are immediately familiar in the homes, school, and immediate community of the students. The activities should be straightforward with only a few well-defined ways to solve the problems involved. The criteria for success and the constraints for design should be limited. Only one or two science ideas should be involved in any particular task. Any construction involved should be readily

The Egg Drop

This rich example includes both a description of teaching and an assessment task. Mr. S. has students engage in a full design activity, designing and testing a container that can prevent an egg from breaking when dropped. The technology activity was preceded by a science unit on force and motion so that students were able to use their understanding of science in the design process. He has carefully considered commercially prepared versions of this activity but modified them to create one based on his experiences and the needs of the students. He has considered the safety of the students. The use of the videotape of former students not only provides a local context for the activity, but provides students with ideas about the designs that work and do not work. After the enjoyable day, Mr. S. requires students to reflect on what they have learned and apply it to a new, but similar problem.

[This example highlights some elements of all of the Teaching Standards; Assessment Standard A; 5-8 Content Standards B and E; Program Standard D; and System Standard D.]

As Mr. S. reviewed his syllabus for the year, he saw the next unit and smiled. On Monday they would begin the "Egg Drop"—the students, working in teams, would design a container for an uncooked egg. The time was right. During the period between the winter break and the new semester, the students had focused on the similarities and differences between science and technology. At the beginning of the second semester the students had completed activities and engaged in discussions until they demonstrated an adequate understanding of force, motion, gravity and acceleration. Now it was time to bring the knowledge of science principles to a design problem. The problem was to design a con-

tainer that could be dropped from the second floor balcony without breaking the egg.

Some variation of the egg drop activity was found in just about every middle school science book that Mr. S. had ever seen. But over the years he had come to know what worked and what didn't, where to anticipate the students would have difficulties, and just how to phrase questions and challenges the students could respond to without being overwhelmed. He had developed some aspects of the unit that were special to him and to the students in Belle Vue Middle School. He knew when he introduced the idea that at least one student would have a tale to tell about dropping a carton of eggs when carrying groceries home from the store or when removing the carton from the refrigerator. While dropping eggs from the balcony was not part of the every day experience of the students, dropping things and having them break was.

On Monday, he would set the challenge, the constraints, and the schedule. They would begin with a whole class review of what the students knew about force, acceleration, and gravity and the design principles. He would have someone write these on a chart that they could hang on the wall during the unit. Next they would identify things they had seen fall gently without breaking and about the size, shape, material, and construction of these items. Finally he would tell the students the constraints: teams would be made up of three students each; materials would be limited to the 'stuff' available on the work table; teams would have to show him a sketch before they began building their container; they would have to conduct at least two trials with their container—one with a plastic egg and one with a hard-cooked egg. For years, he had collected odds and ends—string and plastic, paper towel rolls end egg cartons, Styrofoam peanuts, cotton and other packing material. In the world outside of school, limited availability of materials was a real constraint. He was grateful that he taught in Florida where he could open the door and watch the students outside as they climbed to the second floor balcony to conduct their trial runs. He knew that if he taught up North, where they would have to do this activity from the gym balcony, he would have to plan differently as the class would have to move to and from the gym.

On Tuesday, he would have a few raw eggs for each class. He would have several students try to crush them by exerting force with their hands. He would need lab aprons, goggles, and plastic gloves for that. Then he would show the egg drop video. After the first few years, he learned to videotape the class on the day of the egg drop. He had edited a short video of some of the more spectacular egg drops—both successful and unsuccessful. The students enjoyed watching older brothers and sisters, and famous and infamous students. The students would then get into their groups and discuss the features of the containers in which the eggs broke and those in which the eggs did not break. He would challenge them to consider how they might improve the successful egg drop containers. Toward the end of the period, each group would have someone report to the class one thing the group had learned from the video and discussion.

Wednesday would be an intense day as students argued and sketched, sketched and argued, had plans approved, collected materials,

bartered with other teams for materials, and tried to build a prototype of their container.

Thursday they would begin class with a discussion of why they needed to build a prototype and why they needed to do some trial runs with plastic and hard cooked eggs. He would ask them the advantages and disadvantages of using the plastic and hard cooked eggs in the trial runs. This would give them an opportunity to consider cost and the characteristics of models. There would be time in class to work and some groups would be ready to begin the field trials. He would need a supply of trash bags to use as drop cloths.

Friday's class would begin by reminding the students that the assessment for the egg drop would not be whether the egg broke, but rather how they would be able to share what they considered as they tried to solve the problem of designing a container for an egg so that the egg would drop 15 feet and not break. He would also remind them that the egg drop was scheduled for Wednesday, ready or not.

Monday would be an uninterrupted work day. On Tuesday they would by work in their groups to determine what would be needed to make their egg drop event a success. In his plans Mr. S. noted that he would need a set-up team that would cover the ground below the balcony with trash bags. A clean up crew, again wearing plastic gloves, would gather the bags and get them into the disposal. He anticipated that they would want two class mates to have stopwatches to measure the time it took for the egg to drop. The students would want to determine where the egg should be held for the start of the egg drop. There were always heated arguments about whether the starting line was from the arm of the dropper or from some point on the container. They would need someone to call "Drop!"

Wednesday would be the day of the egg drop. Thursday, the class would begin by meeting in their small groups to discuss what worked, what didn't, why, and what they would do differently if they were to do the egg drop design experiment again. Then they would discuss these same ideas as a whole class.

Friday, the students would fill the board with characteristics of good design procedures. Then they would write and sketch in their notebooks these characteristics and what each had learned from the egg drop activity. He knew from experience that the egg drop would be an engaging activity.

The "header titles" emphasize some important components of the assessment process.

SCIENCE CONTENT: The Content Standards for Science and Technology for students in Grades 5-8 call for them to understand and be able to solve a problem by using design principles. These include the ability to design a product; evaluate technological products; and communicate the process of technological design.

ASSESSMENT ACTIVITY: Following the egg drop activity, students each prepare a report on one thing they propose in order to improve their team's container and how they would test the effectiveness of their improvement.

ASSESSMENT TYPE: Individual. embedded in teaching.

ASSESSMENT PURPOSE: The teacher will use the information to assess student understanding of the process of design and for assigning a grade.

DATA: A report, written, sketched, or both, in which students describe an improvement to the container, the anticipated gains and losses from the improvement, and how they would propose to test the new container.

CONTEXT: The egg drop activity allows students the opportunity to bring scientific principles and creativity to a problem, while developing the skills of technology and having a good time. However, the excitement of the activity can overshadow the intended outcome of developing understanding and abilities of technological design. This assessment activity provides the opportunity for students to reflect on what they have experienced and articulate what they have come to understand. The activity comes after the design of an original container, the testing of that container, a class discussion on what worked and why, what didn't work and why, what they would do differently next time, and an opportunity to make notes in a personal journal for science class.

EVALUATING STUDENT PERFORMANCE: Student progress in understanding and doing design can be evaluated by comparing the student responses in the reports with the list generated by previous classes. The astute teacher will have made sure that the list included constraints such as cost, time, materials, and trade-offs. Criteria for a quality report might also include how well the student has differentiated between the design and its evaluation. The teacher might also consider the clarity of expression, as well as alternate ways used to present the information, such as drawings.

accomplished by the students and should not involve lengthy learning of new physical skills or time-consuming preparation and assembly operations.

During the middle-school years, the design tasks should cover a range of needs, materials, and aspects of science. Suitable experiences could include making electrical circuits for a warning device, designing a meal to meet nutritional criteria, choosing a material to combine strength with insulation, selecting plants for an area of a school, or designing a system to move dishes in a restaurant or in a production line.

Such work should be complemented by the study of technology in the students' everyday world. This could be achieved by investigating simple, familiar objects through which students can develop powers of observation and analysis—for example, by comparing the various characteristics of competing consumer products, including cost, convenience, durability, and suitability for different modes of use. Regardless of the product used, students need to understand the science behind it. There should be a balance over the years, with the products studied coming from the areas of clothing, food, structures, and simple mechanical and electrical devices. The inclusion of some non-product-oriented problems is important to help students understand that technological solutions include the design of systems and can involve communication, ideas, and rules.

The principles of design for grades 5-8 do not change from grades K-4. But the complexity of the problems addressed and the extended ways the principles are applied do change.

GUIDE TO THE CONTENT STANDARD
Fundamental abilities and concepts that underlie this standard include

ABILITIES OF TECHNOLOGICAL DESIGN

IDENTIFY APPROPRIATE PROBLEMS FOR TECHNOLOGICAL DESIGN. Students should develop their abilities by identifying a specified need, considering its various aspects, and talking to different potential users or beneficiaries. They should appreciate that for some needs, the cultural backgrounds and beliefs of different groups can affect the criteria for a suitable product.

See Content Standard A (grades 5-8)

DESIGN A SOLUTION OR PRODUCT. Students should make and compare different proposals in the light of the criteria they have selected. They must consider constraints—such as cost, time, trade-offs, and materials needed—and communicate ideas with drawings and simple models.

IMPLEMENT A PROPOSED DESIGN. Students should organize materials and other resources, plan their work, make good use of group collaboration where appropriate, choose suitable tools and techniques, and work with appropriate measurement methods to ensure adequate accuracy.

EVALUATE COMPLETED TECHNOLOGICAL DESIGNS OR PRODUCTS. Students should use criteria relevant to the original purpose or need, consider a variety of factors that might affect acceptability and suitability for intended users or beneficiaries, and develop measures of quality with respect to such criteria and factors; they should also suggest improvements and, for their own products, try proposed modifications.

See Teaching
Standard B

COMMUNICATE THE PROCESS OF TECHNOLOGICAL DESIGN. Students should review and describe any completed piece of work and identify the stages of problem identification, solution design, implementation, and evaluation.

UNDERSTANDINGS ABOUT SCIENCE AND TECHNOLOGY

See Content
Standards A, F, & G
(grades 5-8)

- Scientific inquiry and technological design have similarities and differences. Scientists propose explanations for questions about the natural world, and engineers propose solutions relating to human problems, needs, and aspirations. Technological solutions are temporary; technologies exist within nature and so they cannot contravene physical or biological principles; technological solutions have side effects; and technologies cost, carry risks, and provide benefits.
- Many different people in different cultures have made and continue to make contributions to science and technology.
- Science and technology are reciprocal. Science helps drive technology, as it addresses questions that demand more sophisticated instruments and provides principles for better instrumentation and technique. Technology is essential to science, because it provides instruments and techniques that enable observations of objects and phenomena that are otherwise unobservable due to factors such as quantity, distance, location, size, and speed. Technology also provides tools for investigations, inquiry, and analysis.

- Perfectly designed solutions do not exist. All technological solutions have trade-offs, such as safety, cost, efficiency, and appearance. Engineers often build in back-up systems to provide safety. Risk is part of living in a highly technological world. Reducing risk often results in new technology.
- Technological designs have constraints. Some constraints are unavoidable, for example, properties of materials, or effects of weather and friction; other constraints limit choices in the design, for example, environmental protection, human safety, and aesthetics.
- Technological solutions have intended benefits and unintended consequences. Some consequences can be predicted, others cannot.

Science in Personal and Social Perspectives

CONTENT STANDARD F:
As a result of activities in grades 5-8, all students should develop understanding of
- Personal health
- Populations, resources, and environments
- Natural hazards
- Risks and benefits
- Science and technology in society

DEVELOPING STUDENT UNDERSTANDING

Due to their developmental levels and expanded understanding, students in grades 5-8 can undertake sophisticated study of personal and societal challenges. Building on the foundation established in grades K-4, students can expand their study of health and establish linkages among populations, resources, and environments; they can develop an understanding of natural hazards, the role of technology in relation to personal and societal issues, and learn about risks and personal decisions. Challenges emerge from the knowledge that the products, processes, technologies and inventions of a society can result in pollution and environmental degradation and can involve some level of risk to human health or to the survival of other species.

The study of science-related personal and societal challenges is an important endeavor for science education at the middle level. By middle school, students begin to realize that illness can be caused by various factors, such as microorganisms, genetic predispositions, malfunctioning of organs and organ-systems, health habits, and environmental conditions. Students in grades 5-8 tend to focus on physical more than mental health. They associate health with food and fitness more than with other factors such as safety and substance use. One very important issue for teachers in grades 5-8 is overcoming students' perceptions that most factors related to health are beyond their control.

Students often have the vocabulary for many aspects of health, but they often do not understand the science related to the terminology. Developing a scientific understanding of health is a focus of this standard.

Healthy behaviors and other aspects of health education are introduced in other parts of school programs.

By grades 5-8, students begin to develop a more conceptual understanding of ecological crises. For example, they begin to realize the cumulative ecological effects of pollution. By this age, students can study environmental issues of a large and abstract

Although students in grades 5-8 have some awareness of global issues, teachers should challenge misconceptions, such as anything natural is not a pollutant, oceans are limitless resources, and humans are indestructible as a species.

nature, for example, acid rain or global ozone depletion. However, teachers should challenge several important misconceptions, such as anything natural is not a pollutant, oceans are limitless resources, and humans are indestructible as a species.

Little research is available on students' perceptions of risk and benefit in the context of science and technology. Students sometimes view social harm from technological failure as unacceptable. On the other hand, some believe if the risk is personal and voluntary, then it is part of life and should not be the concern of others (or society). Helping students develop an understanding of risks and benefits in the areas of health, natural hazards—and science and technology in general—presents a challenge to middle-school teachers.

Middle-school students are generally aware of science-technology-society issues from the media, but their awareness is fraught with misunderstandings. Teachers should begin developing student understanding with concrete and personal examples that avoid an exclusive focus on problems.

GUIDE TO THE CONTENT STANDARD
Fundamental concepts and principles that underlie this standard include

PERSONAL HEALTH

- Regular exercise is important to the maintenance and improvement of health. The benefits of physical fitness include maintaining healthy weight, having energy and strength for routine activities, good muscle tone, bone strength, strong heart/lung systems, and improved mental health. Personal exercise, especially developing cardiovascular endurance, is the foundation of physical fitness.

- The potential for accidents and the existence of hazards imposes the need for injury prevention. Safe living involves the development and use of safety precautions and the recognition of risk in personal decisions. Injury prevention has personal and social dimensions.

- The use of tobacco increases the risk of illness. Students should understand the influence of short-term social and psychological factors that lead to tobacco use, and the possible long-term detrimental effects of smoking and chewing tobacco.

- Alcohol and other drugs are often abused substances. Such drugs change how the body functions and can lead to addiction.

- Food provides energy and nutrients for growth and development. Nutrition requirements vary with body weight, age, sex, activity, and body functioning.

- Sex drive is a natural human function that requires understanding. Sex is also a prominent means of transmitting diseases. The diseases can be prevented through a variety of precautions.

- Natural environments may contain substances (for example, radon and lead) that are harmful to human beings. Maintaining environmental health involves establishing or monitoring quality standards related to use of soil, water, and air.

POPULATIONS, RESOURCES, AND ENVIRONMENTS

- When an area becomes overpopulated, the environment will become degraded due to the increased use of resources.

- Causes of environmental degradation and resource depletion vary from region to region and from country to country.

NATURAL HAZARDS

- Internal and external processes of the earth system cause natural hazards, events that change or destroy human and wildlife habitats, damage property, and harm or kill humans. Natural hazards include earthquakes, landslides, wildfires, volcanic eruptions, floods, storms, and even possible impacts of asteroids.

- Human activities also can induce hazards through resource acquisition, urban growth, land-use decisions, and waste disposal. Such activities can accelerate many natural changes.

- Natural hazards can present personal and societal challenges because misidentifying the change or incorrectly estimating the rate and scale of change may result in either too little attention and significant

See Content Standard D (grades 5-8)

human costs or too much cost for unneeded preventive measures.

RISKS AND BENEFITS

- Risk analysis considers the type of hazard and estimates the number of people that might be exposed and the number likely to suffer consequences. The results are used to determine the options for reducing or eliminating risks.

- Students should understand the risks associated with natural hazards (fires, floods, tornadoes, hurricanes, earthquakes, and volcanic eruptions), with chemical hazards (pollutants in air, water, soil, and food), with biological hazards (pollen, viruses, bacterial, and parasites), social hazards (occupational safety and transportation), and with personal hazards (smoking, dieting, and drinking).

- Individuals can use a systematic approach to thinking critically about risks and benefits. Examples include applying probability estimates to risks and comparing them to estimated personal and social benefits.

- Important personal and social decisions are made based on perceptions of benefits and risks.

See Content
Standard E
(grades 5-8)

SCIENCE AND TECHNOLOGY IN SOCIETY

- Science influences society through its knowledge and world view. Scientific knowledge and the procedures used by scientists influence the way many individuals in society think about themselves, others, and the environment. The effect of science on society is neither entirely beneficial nor entirely detrimental.

- Societal challenges often inspire questions for scientific research, and social priorities often influence research priorities through the availability of funding for research.

- Technology influences society through its products and processes. Technology influences the quality of life and the ways people act and interact. Technological changes are often accompanied by social, political, and economic changes that can be beneficial or detrimental to individuals and to society. Social needs, attitudes, and values influence the direction of technological development.

- Science and technology have advanced through contributions of many different people, in different cultures, at different times in history. Science and technology have contributed enormously to economic growth and productivity among societies and groups within societies.

- Scientists and engineers work in many different settings, including colleges and universities, businesses and industries, specific research institutes, and government agencies.

- Scientists and engineers have ethical codes requiring that human subjects involved with research be fully informed about risks and benefits associated with the research before the individuals choose to participate. This ethic extends to potential risks to communities and property. In short, prior knowledge and consent are required for research involving human subjects or potential damage to property.

- Science cannot answer all questions and technology cannot solve all human problems or meet all human needs. Students should understand the difference between scientific and other questions. They should appreciate what science and

Science and technology have advanced through the contributions of many different people in different cultures at different times in history.

technology can reasonably contribute to society and what they cannot do. For example, new technologies often will decrease some risks and increase others.

History and Nature of Science

CONTENT STANDARD G:

As a result of activities in grades 5-8, all students should develop understanding of

- **Science as a human endeavor**
- **Nature of science**
- **History of science**

DEVELOPING STUDENT UNDERSTANDING

Experiences in which students actually engage in scientific investigations provide the background for developing an understanding of the nature of scientific inquiry, and will also provide a foundation for appreciating the history of science described in this standard.

The introduction of historical examples will help students see the scientific enterprise as more philosophical, social, and human.

Middle-school students can thereby develop a better understanding of scientific inquiry and the interactions between science and society. In general, teachers of science should not assume that students have an accurate conception of the nature of science in either contemporary or historical contexts.

To develop understanding of the history and nature of science, teachers of science can use the actual experiences of student investigations, case studies, and historical vignettes. The intention of this standard is not to develop an overview of the complete history of science. Rather, historical examples are used to help students understand scientific inquiry, the nature of scientific knowledge, and the interactions between science and society.

GUIDE TO THE CONTENT STANDARD
Fundamental concepts and principles that underlie this standard include

SCIENCE AS A HUMAN ENDEAVOR

- Women and men of various social and ethnic backgrounds—and with diverse interests, talents, qualities, and motivations—engage in the activities of science, engineering, and related fields such as the health professions. Some scientists work in teams, and some work alone, but all communicate extensively with others.

- Science requires different abilities, depending on such factors as the field of study and type of inquiry. Science is very much a human endeavor, and the work of science relies on basic human qualities, such as reasoning, insight, energy, skill, and creativity—as well as on scientific habits of mind, such as intellectual honesty, tolerance of ambiguity, skepticism, and openness to new ideas.

NATURE OF SCIENCE

- Scientists formulate and test their explanations of nature using observation, experiments, and theoretical and mathematical models. Although all scientific ideas are tentative and subject to change and improvement in principle, for most major ideas in science, there is much experimental and observational confirmation. Those ideas are not likely to change greatly in the future. Scientists do and have changed their ideas about nature when they encounter new experimental evidence that does not match their existing explanations.

- In areas where active research is being pursued and in which there is not a great deal of experimental or observational evidence and understanding, it is normal for scientists to differ with one another about the interpretation of the evidence or theory being considered. Different scientists might publish conflicting experimental results or might draw different conclusions from the same data. Ideally, scientists acknowledge such conflict and work towards finding evidence that will resolve their disagreement.

- It is part of scientific inquiry to evaluate the results of scientific investigations, experiments, observations, theoretical models, and the explanations proposed by other scientists. Evaluation includes reviewing the experimental procedures, examining the evidence, identifying faulty reasoning, pointing out statements that go beyond the evidence, and suggesting alternative explanations for the same observations. Although scientists may disagree about explanations of phenomena, about interpretations of data, or about the value of rival theories, they do agree that questioning, response to criticism, and open communication are integral to the process of

Students should understand the difference between scientific and other questions and what science and technology can and cannot reasonably contribute to society.

science. As scientific knowledge evolves, major disagreements are eventually resolved through such interactions between scientists.

HISTORY OF SCIENCE

- Many individuals have contributed to the traditions of science. Studying some of these individuals provides further understanding of scientific inquiry, science as a human endeavor, the nature of science, and the relationships between science and society.

- In historical perspective, science has been practiced by different individuals in different cultures. In looking at the history of many peoples, one finds that scientists and engineers of high achievement are considered to be among the most valued contributors to their culture.

- Tracing the history of science can show how difficult it was for scientific innovators to break through the accepted ideas of their time to reach the conclusions that we currently take for granted.

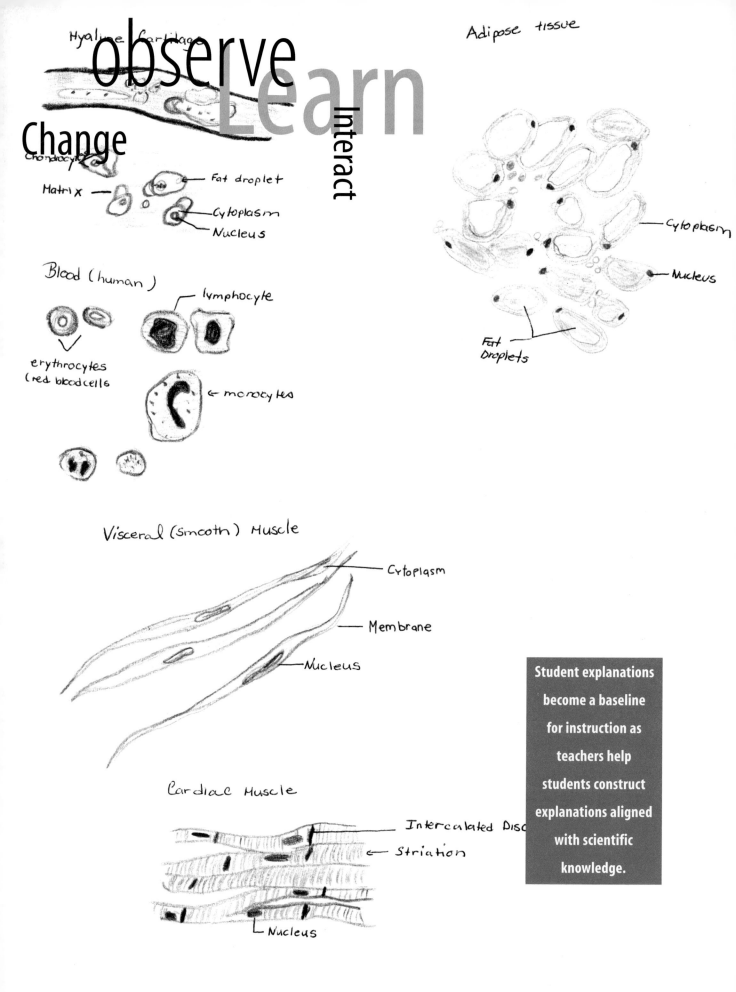

Hyaline Cartilage

observe

Learn

Change

Interact

Chondrocyte

Matrix —

Fat droplet

Cytoplasm

Nucleus

Adipose tissue

Cytoplasm

Nucleus

Fat Droplets

Blood (human)

lymphocyte

erythrocytes
(red blood cells)

← monocytes

Visceral (smooth) Muscle

Cytoplasm

Membrane

Nucleus

Cardiac Muscle

Intercalated Disc

← Striation

Nucleus

Student explanations become a baseline for instruction as teachers help students construct explanations aligned with scientific knowledge.

Content Standards: 9-12

Science as Inquiry

CONTENT STANDARD A:
As a result of activities in grades 9-12, all students should develop
- Abilities necessary to do scientific inquiry
- Understandings about scientific inquiry

DEVELOPING STUDENT ABILITIES AND UNDERSTANDING

For students to develop the abilities that characterize science as inquiry, they must actively participate in scientific investigations, and they must actually use the cognitive and manipulative skills associated with the formulation of scientific explanations. This standard describes the fundamental abilities and understandings of inquiry, as well as a larger framework for conducting scientific investigations of natural phenomena.

In grades 9-12, students should develop sophistication in their abilities and understanding of scientific inquiry. Students can understand that experiments are guided by concepts and are performed to test ideas. Some students still have trouble with variables and controlled experiments. Further, students often have trouble dealing with data that seem anomalous and in proposing explanations based on evidence and logic rather than on their prior beliefs about the natural world.

One challenge to teachers of science and to curriculum developers is making science investigations meaningful. Investigations should derive from questions and issues that have meaning for students. Scientific topics that have been highlighted by current events provide one source, whereas actual science- and technology-related problems provide another source of meaningful investigations. Finally, teachers of science should remember that some experiences begin with little meaning for students but develop meaning through active involvement, continued exposure, and growing skill and understanding.

A critical component of successful scientific inquiry in grades 9-12 includes having students reflect on the concepts that guide the inquiry. Also important is the prior establishment of an adequate knowledge base to support the investigation and help develop scientific explanations. The concepts of the world that students bring to school will shape the way they engage in science investigations, and serve as filters for their explanations of scientific phenomena. Left unexamined, the limited nature of students' beliefs will interfere with their ability to develop a deep understanding of science. Thus, in a full inquiry, instructional strategies such as small-group discussions, labeled drawings, writings, and concept mapping should be used by the teacher of science to gain information about students' current explanations. Those student explanations then become a baseline for instruction as teachers help students construct explanations aligned with scientific knowledge; teachers also help students evaluate their own explanations and those made by scientists.

Students also need to learn how to analyze evidence and data. The evidence they analyze may be from their investigations, other students' investigations, or databases. Data manipulation and analysis strategies need to be modeled by teachers of science and practiced by students. Determining the range of the data, the mean and mode values of the data, plotting the data, developing mathematical functions from the data, and looking for anomalous data are all examples of analyses students can perform. Teachers

of science can ask questions, such as "What explanation did you expect to develop from the data?" "Were there any surprises in the data?" "How confident do you feel about the accuracy of the data?" Students should answer questions such as these during full and partial inquiries.

Public discussions of the explanations proposed by students is a form of peer review of investigations, and peer review is an important aspect of science. Talking with peers about science experiences helps students develop meaning and understanding. Their conversations clarify the concepts and processes of science, helping students make sense of the content of science. Teachers of science should engage students in conversations that focus on questions, such as "How do we know?" "How certain are you of those results?" "Is there a better way to do the investigation?" "If you had to explain this to someone who knew nothing about the project, how would you do it?" "Is there an alternative scientific explanation for the one we proposed?" "Should we do the investigation over?" "Do we need more evidence?" "What are our sources of experimental error?" "How do you account for an explanation that is different from ours?"

Questions like these make it possible for students to analyze data, develop a richer knowledge base, reason using science concepts, make connections between evidence and explanations, and recognize alternative explanations. Ideas should be examined and discussed in class so that other students can benefit from the feedback. Teachers of science can use the ideas of students in their class, ideas from other classes, and ideas from texts, databases, or other sources—but scientific ideas and methods should be discussed in the fashion just described.

GUIDE TO THE CONTENT STANDARD
Fundamental abilities and concepts that underlie this standard include

ABILITIES NECESSARY TO DO SCIENTIFIC INQUIRY

IDENTIFY QUESTIONS AND CONCEPTS THAT GUIDE SCIENTIFIC INVESTIGATIONS. Students should formulate a testable hypothesis and demonstrate the logical connections between the scientific concepts guiding a hypothesis and the design of an experiment. They should demonstrate appropriate procedures, a knowledge base, and conceptual understanding of scientific investigations.

DESIGN AND CONDUCT SCIENTIFIC INVESTIGATIONS. Designing and conducting a scientific investigation requires introduction to the major concepts in the area being investigated, proper equipment, safety precautions, assistance with methodological problems, recommendations for use of technologies, clarification of ideas that guide the inquiry, and scientific knowledge obtained from sources other than the actual investigation. The investigation may also require student clarification of the question, method, controls, and variables; student organization and display of data; student revision of methods and explanations; and a public presentation of the results with a critical response from peers. Regardless of the scientific investigation performed, students must use evidence, apply logic, and construct an argument for their proposed explanations.

USE TECHNOLOGY AND MATHEMATICS TO IMPROVE INVESTIGATIONS AND COMMUNICATIONS. A variety of technologies, such as hand tools, measuring instruments, and calculators, should be an integral component of scientific investigations. The use of computers for the collection, analysis, and display of data is also a part of this standard. Mathematics plays an essential role in all aspects of an inquiry. For example, measurement is used for posing questions, formulas are used for developing explanations, and charts and graphs are used for communicating results.

FORMULATE AND REVISE SCIENTIFIC EXPLANATIONS AND MODELS USING LOGIC AND EVIDENCE. Student inquiries should culminate in formulating an explanation or model. Models should be physical, conceptual, and mathematical. In the process of answering the questions, the students should engage in discussions and arguments that result in the revision of their explanations. These discussions should be based on scientific knowledge, the use of logic, and evidence from their investigation.

RECOGNIZE AND ANALYZE ALTERNATIVE EXPLANATIONS AND MODELS. This aspect of the standard emphasizes the critical abilities of analyzing an argument by reviewing current scientific understanding, weighing the evidence, and examining the logic so as to decide which explanations and models are best. In other words, although there may be several plausible explanations, they do not all have equal weight. Students should be able to use scientific criteria to find the preferred explanations.

See Teaching
Standard B in
Chapter 3

COMMUNICATE AND DEFEND A SCIENTIFIC ARGUMENT. Students in school science programs should develop the abilities associated with accurate and effective communication. These include writing and following procedures, expressing concepts, reviewing information, summarizing data, using language appropriately, developing diagrams and charts, explaining statistical analysis, speaking clearly and logically, constructing a reasoned argument, and responding appropriately to critical comments.

UNDERSTANDINGS ABOUT SCIENTIFIC INQUIRY

See Unifying
Concepts and
Processes

- Scientists usually inquire about how physical, living, or designed systems function. Conceptual principles and knowledge guide scientific inquiries. Historical and current scientific knowledge influence the design and interpretation of investigations and the evaluation of proposed explanations made by other scientists.

- Scientists conduct investigations for a wide variety of reasons. For example, they may wish to discover new aspects of the natural world, explain recently observed phenomena, or test the conclusions of prior investigations or the predictions of current theories.

See Content
Standard E
(grades 9-12)

- Scientists rely on technology to enhance the gathering and manipulation of data. New techniques and tools provide new evidence to guide inquiry and new methods to gather data, thereby contributing to the advance of science. The accuracy and precision of the data, and therefore the quality of the exploration, depends on the technology used.

See Program
Standard C

- Mathematics is essential in scientific inquiry. Mathematical tools and models guide and improve the posing of questions, gathering data, constructing explanations and communicating results.

- Scientific explanations must adhere to criteria such as: a proposed explanation must be logically consistent; it must abide by the rules of evidence; it must be open to questions and possible modification; and it must be based on historical and current scientific knowledge.

- Results of scientific inquiry—new knowledge and methods—emerge from different types of investigations and public communication among scientists. In communicating and defending the results of scientific inquiry, arguments must be logical and demonstrate connections between natural phenomena, investigations, and the historical body of scientific knowledge. In addition, the methods and procedures that scientists used to obtain evidence must be clearly reported to enhance opportunities for further investigation.

Physical Science

CONTENT STANDARD B:
As a result of their activities in grades 9-12, all students should develop an understanding of

- **Structure of atoms**
- **Structure and properties of matter**
- **Chemical reactions**
- **Motions and forces**
- **Conservation of energy and increase in disorder**
- **Interactions of energy and matter**

DEVELOPING STUDENT UNDERSTANDING

High-school students develop the ability to relate the macroscopic properties of substances that they study in grades K-8 to the microscopic structure of substances. This development in understanding requires students to move among three domains of thought—the macroscopic world of observable phenomena, the microscopic world of molecules, atoms, and subatomic particles, and the symbolic and mathematical world of chemical formulas, equations, and symbols.

The relationship between properties of matter and its structure continues as a major component of study in 9-12 physical science. In the elementary grades, students studied the properties of matter and the classification of substances using easily observable properties. In the middle grades, they examined change of state, solutions, and simple chemical reactions, and developed enough knowledge and experience to define the properties of elements and compounds. When students observe and integrate a wide variety of evidence, such as seeing copper "dissolved" by an acid into a solution and then retrieved as pure copper when it is displaced by zinc, the idea that copper atoms are the same for any copper object begins to make sense. In each of these reactions, the knowledge that the mass of the substance does not change can be interpreted by assuming that the number of particles does not change during their rearrangement in the reaction. Studies of student understanding of molecules indicate that it will be difficult for them to comprehend the very small size and large number of particles involved. The connection between the particles and the chemical formulas that represent them is also often not clear.

It is logical for students to begin asking about the internal structure of atoms, and it will be difficult, but important, for them to know "how we know." Quality learning and the spirit and practice of scientific inquiry are lost when the evidence and argument for atomic structure are replaced by direct assertions by the teacher and text. Although many experiments are difficult to replicate in school, students can read some of the actual reports and examine the chain of evidence that led to the development of the current concept of the atom. The nature of the atom is far from totally understood; scientists continue to investigate atoms and have discovered even smaller constituents of which neutrons and protons are made.

Laboratory investigation of the properties of substances and their changes through a range of chemical interactions provide a basis for the high school graduate to understand a variety of reaction types and their applications, such as the capability to liberate elements from ore, create new drugs, manipulate the structure of genes, and synthesize polymers.

Understanding of the microstructure of matter can be supported by laboratory experiences with the macroscopic and microscopic world of forces, motion (including vibrations and waves), light, and electricity. These experiences expand upon the ones that the students had in the middle school and provide new ways of understanding the movement of muscles, the transport of materials across cell membranes, the behavior of atoms and molecules, communication technologies, and the movement of planets and galaxies. By this age, the concept of a force is better understood, but static forces in equilibrium and students' intuitive ideas about forces on projectiles and satellites still resist change through instruction for a large percentage of the students.

On the basis of their experiences with energy transfers in the middle grades, high-school students can investigate energy transfers quantitatively by measuring variables such as temperature change and kinetic energy. Laboratory investigations and descriptions of other experiments can help students understand the evidence that leads to the conclusion that energy is conserved. Although the operational distinction between temperature and heat can be fairly well understood after careful instruction, research with high-school students indicates that the idea that heat is the energy of random motion and vibrating molecules is difficult for students to understand.

GUIDE TO THE CONTENT STANDARD
Fundamental concepts and principles that underlie this standard include

STRUCTURE OF ATOMS

- Matter is made of minute particles called atoms, and atoms are composed of even smaller components. These components have measurable properties, such as mass and electrical charge. Each atom has a positively charged nucleus surrounded by negatively charged electrons. The electric force between the nucleus and electrons holds the atom together.

- The atom's nucleus is composed of protons and neutrons, which are much more massive than electrons. When an element has atoms that differ in the number of neutrons, these atoms are called different isotopes of the element.

- The nuclear forces that hold the nucleus of an atom together, at nuclear distances, are usually stronger than the electric forces that would make it fly apart. Nuclear reactions convert a fraction of the mass of interacting particles into energy, and they can release much greater amounts of energy than atomic interactions. Fission is the splitting of a large nucleus into smaller pieces. Fusion is the joining of two nuclei at extremely high temperature and pressure, and is the process responsible for the energy of the sun and other stars.

- Radioactive isotopes are unstable and undergo spontaneous nuclear reactions, emitting particles and/or wavelike radiation. The decay of any one nucleus cannot be predicted, but a large group of identical nuclei decay at a predictable rate. This predictability can be used to estimate the age of materials that contain radioactive isotopes.

STRUCTURE AND PROPERTIES OF MATTER

- Atoms interact with one another by transferring or sharing electrons that are furthest from the nucleus. These outer electrons govern the chemical properties of the element.

- An element is composed of a single type of atom. When elements are listed in order according to the number of protons (called the atomic number), repeating patterns of physical and chemical properties identify families of elements with similar properties. This "Periodic Table" is a consequence of the repeating pattern of outermost electrons and their permitted energies.

- Bonds between atoms are created when electrons are paired up by being transferred or shared. A substance composed of a single kind of atom is called an element. The atoms may be bonded together into molecules or crystalline solids. A compound is formed when two or more kinds of atoms bind together chemically.

- The physical properties of compounds reflect the nature of the interactions among its molecules. These interactions are determined by the structure of the molecule, including the constituent atoms and the distances and angles between them.

- Solids, liquids, and gases differ in the distances and angles between molecules or atoms and therefore the energy that binds them together. In solids the structure is nearly rigid; in liquids molecules or atoms move around each other but do not move apart; and in gases molecules or atoms move almost independently of each other and are mostly far apart.

- Carbon atoms can bond to one another in chains, rings, and branching networks to form a variety of structures, including synthetic polymers, oils, and the large molecules essential to life.

CHEMICAL REACTIONS

See Content Standard C (Grades 9-12)

- Chemical reactions occur all around us, for example in health care, cooking, cosmetics, and automobiles. Complex chemical reactions involving carbon-based molecules take place constantly in every cell in our bodies.

- Chemical reactions may release or consume energy. Some reactions such as the burning of fossil fuels release large amounts of energy by losing heat and by emitting light. Light can initiate many chemical reactions such as photosynthesis and the evolution of urban smog.

- A large number of important reactions involve the transfer of either electrons (oxidation/reduction reactions) or hydrogen ions (acid/base reactions) between reacting ions, molecules, or atoms. In other reactions, chemical bonds are broken by heat or light to form very reactive radicals with electrons ready to form new bonds. Radical reactions control many processes such as the presence of ozone and greenhouse gases in the atmosphere, burning and processing of fossil fuels, the formation of polymers, and explosions.

- Chemical reactions can take place in time periods ranging from the few femtoseconds (10^{-15} seconds) required for an atom to move a fraction of a chemical bond distance to geologic time scales of billions of years. Reaction rates depend on how often the reacting atoms and molecules encounter one another, on the temperature, and on the properties—including shape—of the reacting species.

- Catalysts, such as metal surfaces, accelerate chemical reactions. Chemical reactions in living systems are catalyzed by protein molecules called enzymes.

MOTIONS AND FORCES

- Objects change their motion only when a net force is applied. Laws of motion are used to calculate precisely the effects of forces on the motion of objects. The magnitude of the change in motion can be calculated using the relationship F = ma, which is independent of the nature of the force. Whenever one object exerts force on another, a force equal in magnitude and opposite in direction is exerted on the first object.

- Gravitation is a universal force that each mass exerts on any other mass. The strength of the gravitational attractive force between two masses is proportional to the masses and inversely proportional to the square of the distance between them.

- The electric force is a universal force that exists between any two charged objects. Opposite charges attract while like charges repel. The strength of the force is proportional to the charges, and, as with gravitation, inversely proportional to the square of the distance between them.

- Between any two charged particles, electric force is vastly greater than the gravitational force. Most observable forces such as those exerted by a coiled spring or friction may be traced to electric forces acting between atoms and molecules.

- Electricity and magnetism are two aspects of a single electromagnetic force. Moving electric charges produce magnetic forces, and moving magnets produce electric forces. These effects help students to understand electric motors and generators.

CONSERVATION OF ENERGY AND THE INCREASE IN DISORDER

See Content Standard C (grades 9-12)

- The total energy of the universe is constant. Energy can be transferred by collisions in chemical and nuclear reactions, by light waves and other radiations, and in many other ways. However, it can never be destroyed. As these transfers occur, the matter involved becomes steadily less ordered.

- All energy can be considered to be either kinetic energy, which is the energy of motion; potential energy, which depends on relative position; or energy contained by a field, such as electromagnetic waves.

- Heat consists of random motion and the vibrations of atoms, molecules, and ions. The higher the temperature, the greater the atomic or molecular motion.

- Everything tends to become less organized and less orderly over time. Thus, in all energy transfers, the overall effect is that the energy is spread out uniformly. Examples are the transfer of energy from hotter to cooler objects by conduction, radiation, or convection and the warming of our surroundings when we burn fuels.

INTERACTIONS OF ENERGY AND MATTER

See Content Standard D (grades 9-12)

- Waves, including sound and seismic waves, waves on water, and light waves, have energy and can transfer energy when they interact with matter.

- Electromagnetic waves result when a charged object is accelerated or decelerated. Electromagnetic waves include radio waves (the longest wavelength), microwaves, infrared radiation (radiant heat), visible light, ultraviolet radiation, x-rays, and gamma rays. The energy of electromagnetic waves is carried in packets whose magnitude is inversely proportional to the wavelength.

- Each kind of atom or molecule can gain or lose energy only in particular discrete amounts and thus can absorb and emit light only at wavelengths corresponding to these amounts. These wavelengths can be used to identify the substance.

- In some materials, such as metals, electrons flow easily, whereas in insulating materials such as glass they can hardly flow at all. Semiconducting materials have intermediate behavior. At low temperatures some materials become superconductors and offer no resistance to the flow of electrons.

Life Science

CONTENT STANDARD C:
As a result of their activities in grades 9-12, all students should develop understanding of
- The cell
- Molecular basis of heredity
- Biological evolution
- Interdependence of organisms
- Matter, energy, and organization in living systems
- Behavior of organisms

DEVELOPING STUDENT UNDERSTANDING

Students in grades K-8 should have developed a foundational understanding of life sciences. In grades 9-12, students' understanding of biology will expand by incorporating more abstract knowledge, such as the structure and function of DNA, and more comprehensive theories, such as evolution. Students' understandings should encompass scales that are both smaller, for example, molecules, and larger, for example, the biosphere.

Teachers of science will have to make choices about what to teach that will most productively develop student understanding of the life sciences. All too often, the criteria for selection are not clear, resulting in an overemphasis on information and an underemphasis on conceptual understanding. In describing the content for life sciences, the national standards focus on a small number of general principles that can serve as the basis for teachers and students to develop further understanding of biology.

Because molecular biology will continue into the twenty-first century as a major frontier of science, students should understand the chemical basis of life not only for its own sake, but because of the need to take informed positions on some of the practical and ethical implications of humankind's capacity to manipulate living organisms.

In general, students recognize the idea of species as a basis for classifying organisms, but few students will refer to the genetic basis of species. Students may exhibit a general understanding of classification. However, when presented with unique organisms, students sometimes appeal to "everyday" classifications, such as viewing jellyfish as fish because of the term "fish," and penguins as amphibians because they live on land and in water.

Although students may indicate that they know about cells, they may say that living systems are made of cells but not molecules, because students often associate molecules only with physical science.

Students have difficulty with the fundamental concepts of evolution. For example, students often do not understand natural

Fossils

The investigation in this example centers on the use of fossils to develop concepts about variation of characteristics in a population, evolution—including indicators of past environments and changes in those environments, the role of climate in biological adaptation, and use of geological data. High-school students generally exhibit interest in fossils and what the fossils indicate about organisms and their habitats. Fossils can be purchased from scientific supply houses, as well as collected locally in some places. In the investigation described here, the students conduct an inquiry to answer an apparently simple question: Do two slightly different fossils represent an evolutionary trend? In doing the activity, students rely on prior knowledge from life science. They use mathematical knowledge and skill. The focus of the discussion is to explain organized data.

[This example highlights some elements of Teaching Standards A, B, D, and E; 9-12 Content Standards A, C, D and the Unifying Concepts and Processes; and Program Standards A and C.]

The investigation begins with a task that students originally perceive as easy—describing the characteristics of two brachiopods to see if change has occurred. The student inquiries begin when the teacher, Mr. D., gives each student two similar but slightly different fossils and asks the students if they think an evolutionary trend can be discerned. The openness and ambiguity of the question results in mixed responses. Mr. D. asks for a justification of each answer and gently challenges the students' responses by posing questions such as: "How do you know? How could you support your answer? What evidence would you

need? What if these fossils were from the same rock formation? How do you know that the differences are not normal variations in this species? What if the two fossils were from rock formations deposited 10 millions years apart? Can you tell if evolution has or has not occurred by examining only two samples?"

Mr. D. shows students two trays, each with about 100 carefully selected fossil brachiopods. He asks the students to describe the fossils. After they have had time to examine the fossils, he hears descriptions such as "They look like butterflies," and "They are kind of triangular with a big middle section and ribs." Then he asks if there are any differences between the fossils in the two trays. The students quickly conclude that they cannot really tell any differences based on the general description, so Mr. D. asks how they could tell if the fossil populations were different. From the ensuing discussion, students determine that quantitative description of specific characteristics, such as length, width, and number of ribs are most helpful.

Mr. D. places the students in groups of four and presents them with two trays of brachiopods. They are told to measure, record, and graph some characteristics of the brachiopod populations. The students decide what they want to measure and how to do it. They work for a class period measuring and entering their data on length and width of the brachiopods in the populations in a computer database. When all data are entered, summarized, and graphed, the class results resemble those displayed in the figure.

The students begin examining the graphs showing frequency distribution of the length and width of fossils. As the figure

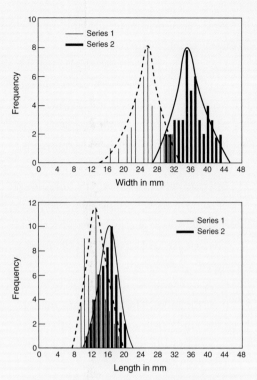

Figure 1. Graph showing characteristics of branchiopod populations.

indicates, the results for either dimension show a continuous variation for the two populations. Students observe that regardless of the dimension measured, the mean for the two populations differs.

After the graphs are drawn, Mr. D. asks the students to explain the differences in the populations. The students suggest several general explanations: evolution has not occurred—these are simply different kinds of brachiopods; evolution has occurred—the differences in the means for length and width demonstrate evolutionary change in the populations; evolution has not occurred—the differences are a result of normal variations in the populations.

Mr. D. takes time to provide some background information that the students should consider. He notes that evolution occurs in populations, and changes in a population's

environment result in selection for those organisms best fit for the new environment. He continues with a few questions that again challenge the students' thinking: Did the geological evidence indicate the environment changed? How can you be sure that the fossils were not from different environments and deposited within a scale of time that would not explain the degree of evolutionary change? Why would natural selection for differences in length and width of brachiopods occur? What differences in structure and function are represented in the length and width of brachiopods?

The students must use the evidence from their investigations and other reviews of scientific literature to develop scientific explanations for the aforementioned general explanations. They take the next class period to complete this assignment.

After a day's work by the students on background research and preparation, Mr. D. holds a small conference at which the students' papers are presented and discussed. He focuses students on their ability to ask skeptical questions, evaluate the use of evidence, assess the understanding of geological and biological concepts, and review aspects of scientific inquiries. During the discussions, students are directed to address the following questions: What evidence would you look for that might indicate these brachiopods were the same or different species? What constitutes the same or different species? Were the rocks in which the fossils were deposited formed at the same or different times? How similar or different were the environments of deposition of the rocks? What is the effect of sample size on reliability of conclusions?

selection because they fail to make a conceptual connection between the occurrence of new variations in a population and the potential effect of those variations on the long-term survival of the species. One misconception that teachers may encounter involves students attributing new variations

Many misconceptions about the process of natural selection can be changed through instruction.

to an organism's need, environmental conditions, or use. With some help, students can understand that, in general, mutations occur randomly and are selected because they help some organisms survive and produce more offspring. Other misconceptions center on a lack of understanding of how a population changes as a result of differential reproduction (some individuals producing more offspring), as opposed to all individuals in a population changing. Many misconceptions about the process of natural selection can be changed through instruction.

GUIDE TO THE CONTENT STANDARD
Fundamental concepts and principles that underlie this standard include

THE CELL

See Unifying Concepts and Processes

- Cells have particular structures that underlie their functions. Every cell is surrounded by a membrane that separates it from the outside world. Inside the cell is a concentrated mixture of thousands of different molecules which form a variety of specialized structures that carry out such cell functions as energy production, transport of molecules, waste disposal, synthesis of new molecules, and the storage of genetic material.

- Most cell functions involve chemical reactions. Food molecules taken into cells react to provide the chemical constituents needed to synthesize other molecules. Both breakdown and synthesis are made possible by a large set of protein catalysts, called enzymes. The breakdown of some of the food molecules enables the cell to store energy in specific chemicals that are used to carry out the many functions of the cell.

- Cells store and use information to guide their functions. The genetic information stored in DNA is used to direct the synthesis of the thousands of proteins that each cell requires.

- Cell functions are regulated. Regulation occurs both through changes in the activity of the functions performed by proteins and through the selective expression of individual genes. This regulation allows cells to respond to their environment and to control and coordinate cell growth and division.

- Plant cells contain chloroplasts, the site of photosynthesis. Plants and many microorganisms use solar energy to combine molecules of carbon dioxide and water into complex, energy rich organic compounds and release oxygen to the environment. This process of photosynthesis provides a vital connection between the sun and the energy needs of living systems.

- Cells can differentiate, and complex multicellular organisms are formed as a highly organized arrangement of differentiated cells. In the development of these multicellular organisms, the progeny from a single cell form an embryo in which the cells multiply and differentiate to form the many specialized cells, tissues and organs that comprise the final organism. This differentiation is regulated through the expression of different genes.

THE MOLECULAR BASIS OF HEREDITY

See Content Standard B (grades 9-12)

- In all organisms, the instructions for specifying the characteristics of the organism are carried in DNA, a large polymer formed from subunits of four kinds (A, G, C, and T). The chemical and structural properties of DNA explain how the genetic information that underlies heredity is both encoded in genes (as a string of molecular "letters") and replicated (by a templating mechanism). Each DNA molecule in a cell forms a single chromosome.

- Most of the cells in a human contain two copies of each of 22 different chromosomes. In addition, there is a pair of chromosomes that determines sex: a female contains two X chromosomes and a male contains one X and one Y chromosome. Transmission of genetic information to offspring occurs through egg and sperm cells that contain only one representative from each chromosome pair. An egg and a sperm unite to form a new individual. The fact that the human body is formed from cells that contain two copies of each chromosome—and therefore two copies of each gene—explains many features of human heredity, such as how variations that are hidden in one generation can be expressed in the next.

- Changes in DNA (mutations) occur spontaneously at low rates. Some of these changes make no difference to the organism, whereas others can change cells and organisms. Only mutations in germ cells can create the variation that changes an organism's offspring.

BIOLOGICAL EVOLUTION

See Unifying Concepts and Processes

- Species evolve over time. Evolution is the consequence of the interactions of (1) the potential for a species to increase its numbers, (2) the genetic variability of offspring due to mutation and recombination of genes, (3) a finite supply of the resources required for life, and (4) the ensuing selection by the environment of those offspring better able to survive and leave offspring.

- The great diversity of organisms is the result of more than 3.5 billion years of evolution that has filled every available niche with life forms.

- Natural selection and its evolutionary consequences provide a scientific explanation for the fossil record of ancient life forms, as well as for the striking molecular similarities observed among the diverse species of living organisms.

- The millions of different species of plants, animals, and microorganisms that live on earth today are related by descent from common ancestors.

- Biological classifications are based on how organisms are related. Organisms are classified into a hierarchy of groups and subgroups based on similarities which reflect their evolutionary relationships. Species is the most fundamental unit of classification.

THE INTERDEPENDENCE OF ORGANISMS

- The atoms and molecules on the earth cycle among the living and nonliving components of the biosphere.
- Energy flows through ecosystems in one direction, from photosynthetic organisms to herbivores to carnivores and decomposers.
- Organisms both cooperate and compete in ecosystems. The interrelationships and interdependencies of these organisms may generate ecosystems that are stable for hundreds or thousands of years.
- Living organisms have the capacity to produce populations of infinite size, but environments and resources are finite. This fundamental tension has profound effects on the interactions between organisms.
- Human beings live within the world's ecosystems. Increasingly, humans modify ecosystems as a result of population growth, technology, and consumption. Human destruction of habitats through direct harvesting, pollution, atmospheric changes, and other factors is threatening current global stability, and if not addressed, ecosystems will be irreversibly affected.

MATTER, ENERGY, AND ORGANIZATION IN LIVING SYSTEMS

See Unifying Concepts and Processes

- All matter tends toward more disorganized states. Living systems require a continuous input of energy to maintain their chemical and physical organizations. With death, and the cessation of energy input, living systems rapidly disintegrate.

- The energy for life primarily derives from the sun. Plants capture energy by absorbing light and using it to form strong (covalent) chemical bonds between the atoms of carbon-containing (organic) molecules. These molecules can be used to assemble larger molecules with biological activity (including proteins, DNA, sugars, and fats). In addition, the energy stored in bonds between the atoms (chemical energy) can be used as sources of energy for life processes.
- The chemical bonds of food molecules contain energy. Energy is released when the bonds of food molecules are broken and new compounds with lower energy bonds are formed. Cells usually store this energy temporarily in phosphate bonds of a small high-energy compound called ATP.
- The complexity and organization of organisms accommodates the need for obtaining, transforming, transporting, releasing, and eliminating the matter and energy used to sustain the organism.
- The distribution and abundance of organisms and populations in ecosystems are limited by the availability of matter and energy and the ability of the ecosystem to recycle materials.
- As matter and energy flows through different levels of organization of living systems—cells, organs, organisms, communities—and between living systems and the physical environment, chemical elements are recombined in different ways. Each recombination results in storage and dissipation of energy into

the environment as heat. Matter and energy are conserved in each change.

THE BEHAVIOR OF ORGANISMS

- Multicellular animals have nervous systems that generate behavior. Nervous systems are formed from specialized cells that conduct signals rapidly through the long cell extensions that make up nerves. The nerve cells communicate with each other by secreting specific excitatory and inhibitory molecules. In sense organs, specialized cells detect light, sound, and specific chemicals and enable animals to monitor what is going on in the world around them.

- Organisms have behavioral responses to internal changes and to external stimuli. Responses to external stimuli can result from interactions with the organism's own species and others, as well as environmental changes; these responses either can be innate or learned. The broad patterns of behavior exhibited by animals have evolved to ensure reproductive success. Animals often live in unpredictable environments, and so their behavior must be flexible enough to deal with uncertainty and change. Plants also respond to stimuli.

- Like other aspects of an organism's biology, behaviors have evolved through natural selection. Behaviors often have an adaptive logic when viewed in terms of evolutionary principles.

- Behavioral biology has implications for humans, as it provides links to psychology, sociology, and anthropology.

Earth and Space Science

CONTENT STANDARD D:

As a result of their activities in grades 9-12, all students should develop an understanding of

- Energy in the earth system
- Geochemical cycles
- Origin and evolution of the earth system
- Origin and evolution of the universe

DEVELOPING STUDENT UNDERSTANDING

During the high school years, students continue studying the earth system introduced in grades 5-8. At grades 9-12, students focus on matter, energy, crustal dynamics, cycles, geochemical processes, and the expanded time scales necessary to understand events in the earth system. Driven by sunlight and earth's internal heat, a variety of cycles connect and continually circulate energy and material through the components of the earth system. Together, these cycles establish the structure of the earth system and regulate earth's climate. In grades 9-12, students review the water cycle as a carrier of material, and deepen their understanding of this key cycle to see that it is also an important agent for energy transfer. Because it plays a central role in establishing and maintaining earth's climate and the production of many mineral and fossil fuel resources, the students' explorations are also directed toward the carbon cycle. Students use and extend their understanding of how the processes of radiation, convection, and conduction transfer energy through the earth system.

In studying the evolution of the earth system over geologic time, students develop a deeper understanding of the evidence, first introduced in grades 5-8, of earth's past and unravel the interconnected story of earth's dynamic crust, fluctuating climate, and evolving life forms. The students' studies develop the concept of the earth system existing in a state of dynamic equilibrium. They will discover that while certain properties of the earth system may fluctuate on short or long time scales, the earth system will generally stay within a certain narrow range for millions of years. This long-term stability can be understood through the working of planetary geochemical cycles and the feedback processes that help to maintain or modify those cycles.

As an example of this long-term stability, students find that the geologic record suggests that the global temperature has fluctuated within a relatively narrow range, one that has been narrow enough to enable life to survive and evolve for over three billion years. They come to understand that some of the small temperature fluctuations have produced what we perceive as dramatic effects in the earth system, such as the ice ages and the extinction of entire species. They explore the regulation of earth's global temperature by the water and carbon cycles. Using this background, students can examine environmental changes occurring today and make predictions about future temperature fluctuations in the earth system.

Looking outward into deep space and deep time, astronomers have shown that we live in a vast and ancient universe. Scientists assume that the laws of matter are the same in all parts of the universe and over billions

. . . as many as half of the students in this age group will need many concrete examples and considerable help in following the multistep logic necessary to develop the understandings described here.

of years. It is thus possible to understand the structure and evolution of the universe through laboratory experiments and current observations of events and phenomena in the universe.

Until this grade level, astronomy has been largely restricted to the behavior of objects in the solar system. In grades 9-12, the study of the universe becomes more abstract as students expand their ability to comprehend large distances, long time scales, and the nature of nuclear reactions. The age of the universe and its evolution into galaxies, stars, and planets—and eventually life on earth—fascinates and challenges students.

The challenge of helping students learn the content of this standard will be to present understandable evidence from sources that range over immense timescales—and from studies of the earth's interior to observations from outer space. Many students are capable of doing this kind of thinking, but as many as half will need concrete examples and considerable help in following the multistep logic necessary to develop the understandings described in this standard. Because direct experimentation is usually not possible for many concepts associated with earth and space science, it is important to maintain the spirit of inquiry by focusing the teaching on questions that can be answered by using observational data, the knowledge base of science, and processes of reasoning.

GUIDE TO THE CONTENT STANDARD
Fundamental concepts and principles that underlie this standard include

ENERGY IN THE EARTH SYSTEM
- Earth systems have internal and external sources of energy, both of which create heat. The sun is the major external source of energy. Two primary sources of internal energy are the decay of radioactive isotopes and the gravitational energy from the earth's original formation.

See content Standard B (grades 9-12)

- The outward transfer of earth's internal heat drives convection circulation in the mantle that propels the plates comprising earth's surface across the face of the globe.
- Heating of earth's surface and atmosphere by the sun drives convection within the atmosphere and oceans, producing winds and ocean currents.
- Global climate is determined by energy transfer from the sun at and near the earth's surface. This energy transfer is influenced by dynamic processes such as cloud cover and the earth's rotation, and static conditions such as the position of mountain ranges and oceans.

GEOCHEMICAL CYCLES
- The earth is a system containing essentially a fixed amount of each stable chemical atom or element. Each element can exist in several different chemical reservoirs. Each element on earth moves among reservoirs in the solid earth,

oceans, atmosphere, and organisms as part of geochemical cycles.
- Movement of matter between reservoirs is driven by the earth's internal and external sources of energy. These movements are often accompanied by a change in the physical and chemical properties of the matter. Carbon, for

It is important to maintain the spirit of inquiry by focusing the teaching on questions that can be answered by using observational data, the knowledge base of science, and processes of reasoning.

example, occurs in carbonate rocks such as limestone, in the atmosphere as carbon dioxide gas, in water as dissolved carbon dioxide, and in all organisms as complex molecules that control the chemistry of life.

THE ORIGIN AND EVOLUTION OF THE EARTH SYSTEM
- The sun, the earth, and the rest of the solar system formed from a nebular cloud of dust and gas 4.6 billion years ago. The early earth was very different from the planet we live on today.
- Geologic time can be estimated by observing rock sequences and using fossils to correlate the sequences at various locations. Current methods include using the known decay rates of radioactive isotopes present in rocks to measure the time since the rock was formed.
- Interactions among the solid earth, the oceans, the atmosphere, and organisms have resulted in the ongoing evolution of

the earth system. We can observe some changes such as earthquakes and volcanic eruptions on a human time scale, but many processes such as mountain building and plate movements take place over hundreds of millions of years.

- Evidence for one-celled forms of life—the bacteria—extends back more than 3.5 billion years. The evolution of life caused dramatic changes in the composition of the earth's atmosphere, which did not originally contain oxygen.

THE ORIGIN AND EVOLUTION OF THE UNIVERSE

See Content
Standard A
(grades 9-12)

- The origin of the universe remains one of the greatest questions in science. The "big bang" theory places the origin between 10 and 20 billion years ago, when the universe began in a hot dense state; according to this theory, the universe has been expanding ever since.

- Early in the history of the universe, matter, primarily the light atoms hydrogen and helium, clumped together by gravitational attraction to form countless trillions of stars. Billions of galaxies, each of which is a gravitationally bound cluster of billions of stars, now form most of the visible mass in the universe.

- Stars produce energy from nuclear reactions, primarily the fusion of hydrogen to form helium. These and other processes in stars have led to the formation of all the other elements.

Science and Technology

CONTENT STANDARD E:
As a result of activities in grades 9-12, all students should develop
- Abilities of technological design
- Understandings about science and technology

DEVELOPING STUDENT ABILITIES AND UNDERSTANDING

This standard has two equally important parts—developing students' abilities of technological design and developing students' understanding about science and technology. Although these are science education standards, the relationship between science and technology is so close that any presentation of science without developing an understanding of technology would portray an inaccurate picture of science.

In the course of solving any problem where students try to meet certain criteria within constraints, they will find that the ideas and methods of science that they know, or can learn, can be powerful aids. Students also find that they need to call on other sources of knowledge and skill, such as cost, risk, and benefit analysis, and aspects of critical thinking and creativity. Learning experiences associated with this standard should include examples of technological achievement in which science has played a part and examples where technological advances contributed directly to scientific progress.

Students can understand and use the design model outlined in this standard. Students respond positively to the concrete, practical, outcome orientation of design problems before they are able to engage in the abstract, theoretical nature of many scientific inquiries. In general, high school students do not distinguish between the roles of science and technology. Helping them do so is implied by this standard. This lack of distinction between science and technology is further confused by students' positive perceptions of science, as when they associate it with medical research and use the common phrase "scientific progress." However, their association of technology is often with environmental problems and another common phrase, "technological problems." With regard to the connection between science and technology, students as well as many adults and teachers of science indicate a belief that science influences technology. This belief is captured by the common and only partially accurate definition "technology is applied science." Few students understand that technology influences science. Unraveling these misconceptions of science and technology and developing accurate concepts of the role, place, limits, possibilities and relationships of science and technology is the challenge of this standard.

The choice of design tasks and related learning activities is an important and difficult part of addressing this standard. In choosing technological learning activities, teachers of science will have to bear in mind some important issues. For example, whether to involve students in a full or partial design problem; or whether to engage them in meeting a need through technology or in studying the technological work of others. Another issue is how to select a task that brings out the various ways in which science

and technology interact, providing a basis for reflection on the nature of technology while learning the science concepts involved.

In grades 9-12, design tasks should explore a range of contexts including both those immediately familiar in the homes, school, and community of the students and those from wider regional, national, or global contexts. The tasks should promote different ways to tackle the problems so that different design solutions can be implemented by different students. Successful completion of design problems requires that the students meet criteria while addressing conflicting constraints. Where constructions are involved, these might draw on technical skills and understandings developed within the science program, technical and craft skills developed in other school work, or require developing new skills.

Over the high school years, the tasks should cover a range of needs, of materials, and of different aspects of science. For example, a suitable design problem could include assembling electronic components to control a sequence of operations or analyzing the features of different athletic shoes to see the criteria and constraints imposed by the sport, human anatomy, and materials. Some tasks should involve science ideas drawn from more than one field of science. These can be complex, for example, a machine that incorporates both mechanical and electrical control systems.

Although some experiences in science and technology will emphasize solving problems and meeting needs by focusing on products, experience also should include problems about system design, cost, risk, benefit, and very importantly, tradeoffs.

Because this study of technology occurs within science courses, the number of these activities must be limited. Details specified in this standard are criteria to ensure quality and balance in a small number of tasks and are not meant to require a large number of such activities. Many abilities and understandings of this standard can be developed as part of activities designed for other content standards.

GUIDE TO THE CONTENT STANDARD
Fundamental abilities and concepts that underlie this standard include

ABILITIES OF TECHNOLOGICAL DESIGN

See Content
Standard A
(grades 9-12)

IDENTIFY A PROBLEM OR DESIGN AN OPPORTUNITY. Students should be able to identify new problems or needs and to change and improve current technological designs.

PROPOSE DESIGNS AND CHOOSE BETWEEN ALTERNATIVE SOLUTIONS. Students should demonstrate thoughtful planning for a piece of technology or technique. Students should be introduced to the roles of models and simulations in these processes.

IMPLEMENT A PROPOSED SOLUTION. A variety of skills can be needed in proposing a solution depending on the type of technology that is involved. The construction of artifacts can require the skills of cutting, shaping, treating, and joining common materials—such as wood, metal, plastics, and textiles. Solutions can also be implemented using computer software.

EVALUATE THE SOLUTION AND ITS CONSEQUENCES. Students should test any solution against the needs and criteria it was

designed to meet. At this stage, new criteria not originally considered may be reviewed.

COMMUNICATE THE PROBLEM, PROCESS, AND SOLUTION. Students should present their results to students, teachers, and others in a variety of ways, such as orally, in writing, and in other forms—including models, diagrams, and demonstrations.

See Teaching
Standard B

UNDERSTANDINGS ABOUT SCIENCE AND TECHNOLOGY

- Scientists in different disciplines ask different questions, use different methods of investigation, and accept different types of evidence to support their explanations. Many scientific investigations require the contributions of individuals from different disciplines, including engineering. New disciplines of science, such as geophysics and biochemistry often emerge at the interface of two older disciplines.

- Science often advances with the introduction of new technologies. Solving technological problems often results in new scientific knowledge. New technologies often extend the current levels of scientific understanding and introduce new areas of research.

- Creativity, imagination, and a good knowledge base are all required in the work of science and engineering.

- Science and technology are pursued for different purposes. Scientific inquiry is driven by the desire to understand the natural world, and technological design is driven by the need to meet human needs and solve human problems. Technology, by its nature, has a more direct effect on society than science because its purpose is to solve human problems, help humans adapt, and fulfill human aspirations. Technological solutions may create new problems. Science, by its nature, answers questions that may or may not directly influence humans. Sometimes scientific advances challenge people's beliefs and practical explanations concerning various aspects of the world.

- Technological knowledge is often not made public because of patents and the financial potential of the idea or invention. Scientific knowledge is made public through presentations at professional meetings and publications in scientific journals.

Science in Personal and Social Perspectives

CONTENT STANDARD F:
As a result of activities in grades 9-12, all students should develop understanding of
- **Personal and community health**
- **Population growth**
- **Natural resources**
- **Environmental quality**
- **Natural and human-induced hazards**
- **Science and technology in local, national, and global challenges**

DEVELOPING STUDENT UNDERSTANDING

The organizing principles for this standard do not identify specific personal and societal challenges, rather they form a set of conceptual organizers, fundamental under-

standings, and implied actions for most contemporary issues. The organizing principles apply to local as well as global phenomena and represent challenges that occur on scales that vary from quite short—for example, natural hazards—to very long—for example, the potential result of global changes.

By grades 9-12, many students have a fairly sound understanding of the overall functioning of some human systems, such

The organizing principles apply to local as well as global phenomena.

as the digestive, respiratory, and circulatory systems. They might not have a clear understanding of others, such as the human nervous, endocrine, and immune systems. Therefore, students may have difficulty with specific mechanisms and processes related to health issues.

Most high school students have a concept of populations of organisms, but they have a poorly developed understanding of the relationships among populations within a community and connections between populations and other ideas such as competition for resources. Few students understand and apply the idea of interdependence when considering interactions among populations, environments, and resources. If, for example, students are asked about the size of populations and why some populations would be larger, they often simply describe rather than reason about interdependence or energy flow.

Students may exhibit a general idea of cycling matter in ecosystems, but they may center on short chains of the cyclical process

Photosynthesis

In this example, Ms. M. believes that her understanding of the history of scientific ideas enriches her understanding of the nature of scientific inquiry. She also wants the students to understand how ideas in science develop, change, and are influenced by values, ideas, and resources prevalent in society at any given time. She uses an historical approach to introduce an important concept in life science. She provokes an interest in the topic by purposely showing an overhead beyond what is developmentally appropriate for high-school students. Her lecture is interrupted with questions that encourage discussion among students. The research activity, primarily using print material which she has been collecting for a long time, includes discussion. The questions about factors that might influence contemporary research return the students to issues that are of immediate concern to them.

[This example highlights some elements of Teaching Standards A and B; 9-12 Content Standards A, C, F and G; and Program Standard B.]

Ms. M. was beginning the second round of planning for the high-school biology class. She had set aside three weeks for a unit on green plants. Now it was time to decide what would happen during those three weeks. Students came to the class with some knowledge and understanding about green plants, but they still had many questions. As a way to get students to focus some of their questions, and to highlight the interdependence of science and civilization, she was going to begin the unit with a lecture on photosynthesis. Lecturing was something she seldom did. However, the purpose here was not to lay out the details of the photosynthetic process, but to illustrate how the scientific community's knowledge of photosynthesis had changed over time.

She would begin the lecture by putting a transparency on the overhead projector of that detailed diagram of photosynthesis which had been sent to her free from one of the pharmaceutical companies. One of the high-school textbooks that she kept as a reference said that scientists now had described 80 separate but interdependent reactions that made up photosynthesis. The high-school students would not study these reactions. Rather, she wanted the students to observe the complexity of the current knowledge about photosynthesis, and this diagram was a useful introduction to her lecture. She would ask the students how long the scientific community had known about these many complex reactions; why this knowledge was important; how they had come to know so much; was there still more detail to be described?

Next she would ask the students to tell her what they already knew about photosynthesis. She expected most would recall that carbon dioxide, water, sugar, oxygen and sunlight were important and many would recall growing plants in dark cupboards and under boxes in middle school. The next two questions would have to be worded carefully: Why is photosynthesis so important or, put another way, what is the fundamental question that photosynthesis answers? And how long have scientists known about photosynthesis?

With this introduction, she would lecture about the seventeenth century experiment of van Helmont and his tree and his conclusion that the weight of the plants came from water. Ms. M. would pause. "Was van Helmont wrong?", she would ask the students. She expected them to have difficulty conceiving that van Helmont had conducted an experiment, which they knew was essential to science, but that he had not obtained the answer they knew was correct. Ms. M. would help them analyze the experiment and the conclusions that could legitimately be drawn from it. She would then introduce more of the context of van Helmont's investigation: the prevailing belief about plants as a combination of fire and earth and how van Helmont's study was designed to refute this belief. She would comment that many researchers chose to repeat the tree study, and then she would allow students to discuss how (or whether) van Helmont's study had contributed to the science of photosynthesis.

She would then continue her historical lecture using similar details from several other episodes. She would describe how chemists had learned to collect gases from chemical reactions, how Priestley used these new techniques, and how he then observed the effect that gases from plants produced on burning candles. She would note that Priestley did not know about oxygen, but viewed it as a purer form of air. She would mention how Ingenhousz expanded Priestley's finding by showing that the air was changed only when the plants were kept in sunlight, and how de Saussure confirmed that carbon dioxide was a gas needed for the same effect. She would detail how James Hutton had been involved in industrial debates about the quality of coal and was interested in why coal burned. He had interpreted plant imprints in coal as a clue that something from the sun was being stored in

plants and then fossilized as coal. The "something" would later be released again as light and heat as the coal burned. But Hutton had no concept of chemical or light energy—concepts introduced only decades later by Julius Mayer. Ms. M. would stop her history here. Students would review how various factors had shaped the development of early knowledge about photosynthesis. She would record and organize their views on the chalkboard. From this they would develop a set of questions for continuing the history on their own.

Ms. M. had collected a number of textbooks from different periods in the century. She would introduce them as a resource for sketching the changing status of knowledge about photosynthesis. She would have the students work in groups of five. Each group would prepare a brief presentation on ideas of photosynthesis during a particular historical period. After two days to gather information, each group would share the result of their research and together they would identify or infer what discoveries had been made in each period. Then, using the questions they had formulated earlier, the students would return to their groups to determine how each discovery had occurred. They would identify factors such as new technologies that were relevant to conducting investigations, the sources of funding for various research projects, the personal interests of researchers, occasions of luck or chance, and the theories that had guided research. Finally, each group would share two patterns that they had uncovered and how they had reached their conclusion.

Through this activity, students would come to realize that scientific understanding does not emerge all at once or fully formed. Further, the students recognized that each new concept reflected the personal backgrounds, time, and place of its discoverers. At the very end of the period Ms. M would ask the students to speculate on what scientists might ask about photosynthesis today or in the future, and what factors might shape their research.

and express the misconception that matter is created and destroyed at each step of the cycle rather than undergoing continuous transformation. Instruction using charts of the flow of matter through an ecosystem and emphasizing the reasoning involved with the entire process may enable students to develop more accurate conceptions.

Many high-school students hold the view that science should inform society about various issues and society should set policy about what research is important. In general, students have rather simple and naive ideas about the interactions between science and society. There is some research supporting the idea that S-T-S (science, technology, and society) curriculum helps improve student understanding of various aspects of science- and technology-related societal challenges.

GUIDE TO THE CONTENT STANDARD
Fundamental concepts and principles that underlie this standard include

PERSONAL AND COMMUNITY HEALTH

See Content Standard C (grades 9-12)

- Hazards and the potential for accidents exist. Regardless of the environment, the possibility of injury, illness, disability, or death may be present. Humans have a variety of mechanisms—sensory, motor, emotional, social, and technological— that can reduce and modify hazards.

- The severity of disease symptoms is dependent on many factors, such as human resistance and the virulence of the disease-producing organism. Many diseases can be prevented, controlled, or cured. Some diseases, such as cancer, result from specific body dysfunctions and cannot be transmitted.

- Personal choice concerning fitness and health involves multiple factors. Personal goals, peer and social pressures, ethnic and religious beliefs, and understanding of biological consequences can all influence decisions about health practices.

- An individual's mood and behavior may be modified by substances. The modification may be beneficial or detrimental depending on the motives, type of substance, duration of use, pattern of use, level of influence, and short- and long-term effects. Students should understand that drugs can result in physical dependence and can increase the risk of injury, accidents, and death.

- Selection of foods and eating patterns determine nutritional balance. Nutritional balance has a direct effect on growth and development and personal well-being. Personal and social factors— such as habits, family income, ethnic heritage, body size, advertising, and peer pressure—influence nutritional choices.

- Families serve basic health needs, especially for young children. Regardless of the family structure, individuals have families that involve a variety of physical, mental, and social relationships that influence the maintenance and improvement of health.

- Sexuality is basic to the physical, mental, and social development of humans. Students should understand that human sexuality involves biological functions, psychological motives, and cultural, ethnic, religious, and technological influences. Sex is a basic and powerful force that has consequences to individuals' health and to society. Students should understand various methods of controlling the reproduction process and that each method has a different type of effectiveness and different health and social consequences.

POPULATION GROWTH

- Populations grow or decline through the combined effects of births and deaths, and through emigration and immigration. Populations can increase through linear or exponential growth, with effects on resource use and environmental pollution.

- Various factors influence birth rates and fertility rates, such as average levels of affluence and education, importance of children in the labor force, education and employment of women, infant mortality rates, costs of raising children, availability and reliability of birth control methods, and religious beliefs and cultural norms that influence personal decisions about family size.

- Populations can reach limits to growth. Carrying capacity is the maximum number of individuals that can be supported in a given environment. The limitation is not the availability of space, but the number of people in relation to resources and the capacity of earth systems to support human beings. Changes in technology can cause significant changes, either positive or negative, in carrying capacity.

NATURAL RESOURCES

- Human populations use resources in the environment in order to maintain and improve their existence. Natural

resources have been and will continue to be used to maintain human populations.

- The earth does not have infinite resources; increasing human consumption places severe stress on the natural processes that renew some resources, and it depletes those resources that cannot be renewed.

- Humans use many natural systems as resources. Natural systems have the capacity to reuse waste, but that capacity is limited. Natural systems can change to an extent that exceeds the limits of organisms to adapt naturally or humans to adapt technologically.

ENVIRONMENTAL QUALITY

- Natural ecosystems provide an array of basic processes that affect humans. Those processes include maintenance of the quality of the atmosphere, generation of soils, control of the hydrologic cycle, disposal of wastes, and recycling of nutrients. Humans are changing many of these basic processes, and the changes may be detrimental to humans.

See Content Standard C (grades 9-12)

- Materials from human societies affect both physical and chemical cycles of the earth.

- Many factors influence environmental quality. Factors that students might investigate include population growth, resource use, population distribution, overconsumption, the capacity of technology to solve problems, poverty, the role of economic, political, and religious views, and different ways humans view the earth.

NATURAL AND HUMAN-INDUCED HAZARDS

- Normal adjustments of earth may be hazardous for humans. Humans live at the interface between the atmosphere driven

See Content Standard D (grades 9-12)

by solar energy and the upper mantle where convection creates changes in the earth's solid crust. As societies have grown, become stable, and come to value aspects of the environment, vulnerability to natural processes of change has increased.

- Human activities can enhance potential for hazards. Acquisition of resources, urban growth, and waste disposal can accelerate rates of natural change.

- Some hazards, such as earthquakes, volcanic eruptions, and severe weather, are rapid and spectacular. But there are slow and progressive changes that also result in problems for individuals and societies. For example, change in stream channel position, erosion of bridge foundations, sedimentation in lakes and harbors, coastal erosions, and continuing erosion and wasting of soil and landscapes can all negatively affect society.

- Natural and human-induced hazards present the need for humans to assess potential danger and risk. Many changes in the environment designed by humans bring benefits to society, as well as cause risks. Students should understand the costs and trade-offs of various hazards—ranging from those with minor risk to a few people to major catastrophes with major risk to many people. The scale of events and the accuracy with which scientists and engineers can (and cannot) predict events are important considerations.

SCIENCE AND TECHNOLOGY IN LOCAL, NATIONAL, AND GLOBAL CHALLENGES

See Content Standard E (grades 9-12)

- Science and technology are essential social enterprises, but alone they can only indicate what can happen, not what should happen. The latter involves human decisions about the use of knowledge.

- Understanding basic concepts and principles of science and technology should precede active debate about the economics, policies, politics, and ethics of various science- and technology-related challenges. However, understanding science alone will not resolve local, national, or global challenges.

- Progress in science and technology can be affected by social issues and challenges. Funding priorities for specific health problems serve as examples of ways that social issues influence science and technology.

- Individuals and society must decide on proposals involving new research and the introduction of new technologies into society. Decisions involve assessment of alternatives, risks, costs, and benefits and consideration of who benefits and who suffers, who pays and gains, and what the risks are and who bears them. Students should understand the appropriateness and value of basic questions—"What can happen?"— "What are the odds?"—and "How do scientists and engineers know what will happen?"

- Humans have a major effect on other species. For example, the influence of humans on other organisms occurs through land use—which decreases space available to other species—and pollution—which changes the chemical composition of air, soil, and water.

History and Nature of Science

DEVELOPING STUDENT UNDERSTANDING

The *National Science Education Standards* use history to elaborate various aspects of scientific inquiry, the nature of science, and science in different historical and cultural perspectives. The standards on the history and nature of science are closely aligned with the nature of science and historical episodes described in the American Association for the Advancement of Science *Benchmarks for Science Literacy*. Teachers

Scientists have ethical traditions. Scientists value peer review, truthful reporting about the methods and outcomes of investigations, and making public the results of work.

of science can incorporate other historical examples that may accommodate different interests, topics, disciplines, and cultures—as the intention of the standard is to develop an understanding of the human dimensions of science, the nature of scientific knowledge, and the enterprise of science in society—and not to develop a comprehensive understanding of history.

Little research has been reported on the use of history in teaching about the nature of science. But learning about the history of science might help students to improve their general understanding of science. Teachers should be sensitive to the students' lack of knowledge and perspective on time, duration, and succession when it comes to historical study. High school students may have difficulties understanding the views of historical figures. For example, students may think of historical figures as inferior because they did not understand what we do today. This "Whiggish perspective" seems to hold for some students with regard to scientists whose theories have been displaced.

GUIDE TO THE CONTENT STANDARD
Fundamental concepts and principles that underlie this standard include

SCIENCE AS A HUMAN ENDEAVOR
- Individuals and teams have contributed and will continue to contribute to the scientific enterprise. Doing science or engineering can be as simple as an individual conducting field studies or as complex as hundreds of people working on a major scientific question or technological problem. Pursuing science as a career or as a hobby can be both fascinating and intellectually rewarding.
- Scientists have ethical traditions. Scientists value peer review, truthful reporting about the methods and outcomes of investigations, and making

public the results of work. Violations of such norms do occur, but scientists responsible for such violations are censured by their peers.

- Scientists are influenced by societal, cultural, and personal beliefs and ways of viewing the world. Science is not separate from society but rather science is a part of society.

NATURE OF SCIENTIFIC KNOWLEDGE

- Science distinguishes itself from other ways of knowing and from other bodies of knowledge through the use of empirical standards, logical arguments, and skepticism, as scientists strive for the best possible explanations about the natural world.

- Scientific explanations must meet certain criteria. First and foremost, they must be consistent with experimental and observational evidence about nature, and must make accurate predictions, when appropriate, about systems being studied. They should also be logical, respect the rules of evidence, be open to criticism, report methods and procedures, and make knowledge public. Explanations on how the natural world changes based on myths, personal beliefs, religious values, mystical inspiration, superstition, or authority may be personally useful and socially relevant, but they are not scientific.

- Because all scientific ideas depend on experimental and observational confirmation, all scientific knowledge is, in principle, subject to change as new evidence becomes available. The core ideas of science such as the conservation of energy or the laws of motion have been

subjected to a wide variety of confirmations and are therefore unlikely to change in the areas in which they have been tested. In areas where data or understanding

Science distinguishes itself from other ways of knowing and from other bodies of knowledge through the use of empirical standards, logical arguments, and skepticism.

are incomplete, such as the details of human evolution or questions surrounding global warming, new data may well lead to changes in current ideas or resolve current conflicts. In situations where information is still fragmentary, it is normal for scientific ideas to be incomplete, but this is also where the opportunity for making advances may be greatest.

HISTORICAL PERSPECTIVES

- In history, diverse cultures have contributed scientific knowledge and technologic inventions. Modern science began to evolve rapidly in Europe several hundred years ago. During the past two centuries, it has contributed significantly to the industrialization of Western and non-Western cultures. However, other, non-European cultures have developed scientific ideas and solved human problems through technology.

- Usually, changes in science occur as small modifications in extant knowledge. The daily work of science and engineering results in incremental advances in our understanding of the world and our

An Analysis of a Scientific Inquiry

By the "header titles" this example emphasizes some important components of the assessment process. Any boundary between assessment and teaching is lost in this example. Students engage in an analytic activity that requires them to use their understanding of all the science content standards. The activity assumes that they have maintained journals throughout their high school career and have had much previous experience with analyzing scientific inquiry. It would be unreasonable to expect them to successfully complete such an analysis without prior experience. The assessment task requires the use of criteria developed by the class and the teacher together for self assessment and peer assessment. Students may elect to improve the analysis or do another. The teacher uses the data to decide what further inquiries, analyses, or evaluations students might do.

[This example highlights Teaching Standards A, C, and E; Assessments Standards A, B, and E; and 9-12 Content Standard G.]

SCIENCE CONTENT: This activity focuses on all aspects of the Content Standard on the History and Nature of Science: Science as a human endeavor, nature of scientific knowledge, and historical perspectives on science.

ASSESSMENT ACTIVITY: Students read an account of an historical or contemporary scientific study and report on it.

ASSESSMENT TYPE: Performance, individual, group, public.

ASSESSMENT PURPOSE: The teacher uses the information gathered in this activity for assigning grades and for planning further activities involving analysis or inquiry.

DATA: Students' individual reports; student reviews of their peers' work; and teacher's observations.

CONTEXT: This assessment activity is appropriate at the end of 12th grade. Throughout the high school science program, students have read accounts of scientific studies and the social context in which the studies were conducted. Students sometimes read the scientist's own account of the investigation and sometimes an account of the investigation written by another person. The earlier the investigation, the more likely that the high school students are able to read and understand the scientist's original account. Reports by scientists on contemporary studies are likely to be too technical for students to understand, but accounts in popular science books or magazines should be accessible to high school students. Examples of contemporary and historical accounts appropriate to this activity include

Goodfield's *An Imagined World*

Weiner's *The Beak of the Finch*

Watson's *The Double Helix*

Darwin's *Voyage of the Beagle*

Project Physics Readers

In each student's science journal are notes on his or her own inquiries and the inquiries read about throughout the school science career, including an analysis of historical context in which the study was conducted. After completing each analysis, the science teacher had reviewed and commented on the analysis as well as on the student's developing sophistication in doing analysis. Questions that guided each student's analysis include

What factors—personal, technological, cultural, and/or scientific—led this person to the investigation?

How was the investigation designed and why was it designed as it was?

What data did the investigator collect?

How did the investigator interpret the data?

How were the investigator's conclusions related to the design of the investigation and to major theoretical or cultural assumptions, if any?

How did the investigator try to persuade others? Were the ideas accepted by contemporaries? Are they accepted today? Why or why not?

How did the results of this investigation influence the investigator, fellow investigators, and society more broadly?

Were there ethical dimensions to this investigation? If so, how were they resolved?

What element of this episode seems to you most characteristic or most revealing about the process of science? Why?

ASSESSMENT EXERCISE

Each student in the class selects an account of one scientific investigation and analyzes it using the questions above. When the analyses are completed, they are handed in to the teacher who passes them out to other members of the class for peer review. Prior to the peer reviews, the teacher and the class have reviewed the framework for analysis and established criteria for evaluating the quality of the analyses. The teacher reviews the peer reviews and, if appropriate, returns them to the author. The author will have the opportunity to revise the analysis on the basis of the peer review before submitting it to the teacher for a grade.

EVALUATION OF STUDENT RESPONSES

The teacher's grade will be based both on the student's progress in conducting such analyses and on how well the analysis meets the criteria set by the teacher in consultation with the class.

ability to meet human needs and aspirations. Much can be learned about the internal workings of science and the nature of science from study of individual scientists, their daily work, and their efforts to advance scientific knowledge in their area of study.

■ Occasionally, there are advances in science and technology that have important and long-lasting effects on science and society. Examples of such advances include the following

Copernican revolution

Newtonian mechanics

Relativity

Geologic time scale

Plate tectonics

Atomic theory

Nuclear physics

Biological evolution

Germ theory

Industrial revolution

Molecular biology

Information and communication

Quantum theory

Galactic universe

Medical and health technology

■ The historical perspective of scientific explanations demonstrates how scientific knowledge changes by evolving over time, almost always building on earlier knowledge.

References for Further Reading

SCIENCE AS INQUIRY

AAAS (American Association for the Advancement of Science). 1993. Benchmarks for Science Literacy. New York: Oxford University Press.

AAAS (American Association for the Advancement of Science). 1989. Science for All Americans: A Project 2061 Report on Literacy Goals in Science, Mathematics, and Technology. Washington DC.: AAAS.

Bechtel, W. 1988. Philosophy of Science: An Overview for Cognitive Science. Hillsdale, NJ: Lawrence Earlbaum.

Bingman, R. 1969. Inquiry Objectives in the Teaching of Biology. Boulder, CO and Kansas City, MO: Biological Sciences Curriculum Study and Mid-Continent Regional Educational Laboratory.

Carey, S., R. Evans, M. Honda, E. Jay, and C. Unger. 1989. An experiment is when you try it and see if it works: A study of grade 7 students' understanding of the construction of scientific knowledge. International Journal of Science Education, 11(5): 514-529.

Chinn, C.A., and W.F. Brewer. 1993. The role of anomalous data in knowledge acquisition: A theoretical framework and implications for science instruction. Review of Educational Research, 63(1): 1-49.

Connelly, F.M., M.W. Wahlstrom, M. Finegold, and F. Elbaz. 1977. Enquiry Teaching in Science: A Handbook for Secondary School Teachers. Toronto, Ontario: Ontario Institute for Studies in Education.

Driver, R. 1989. Students' conceptions and the learning of science: Introduction. International Journal of Science Education, 11(5): 481-490.

Duschl, R.A. 1990. Restructuring Science Education: The Importance of Theories and Their Development. New York: Teachers College Press.

Duschl, R.A., and R.J. Hamilton, eds. 1992. Philosophy of Science, Cognitive Psychology, and Educational Theory and Practice. Albany, NY: State University of New York Press.

Glaser, R. 1984. Education and thinking: The role of knowledge. American Psychologist, 39(2): 93-104.

Grosslight, L., C. Unger, E. Jay, and C.L. Smith. 1991. Understanding models and their use in science: Conceptions of middle and high school students and experts. [Special issue] Journal of Research in Science Teaching, 28(9): 799-822.

Hewson, P.W., and N.R. Thorley. 1989. The conditions of conceptual change in the classroom. International Journal of Science Education, 11(5): 541-553.

Hodson, D. 1992. Assessment of practical work: Some considerations in philosophy of science. Science & Education, 1(2): 115-134.

Hodson, D. 1985. Philosophy of science, science and science education. Studies in Science Education, 12: 25-57.

Kyle, W. C. Jr. 1980. The distinction between inquiry and scientific inquiry and why high school students should be cognizant of the distinction. Journal of Research in Science Teaching, 17(2): 123-130.

Longino, H.E. 1990. Science as Social Knowledge: Values and Objectivity in Scientific Inquiry. Princeton, NJ: Princeton University Press.

Mayer, W.V., ed. 1978. BSCS Biology Teachers' Handbook, third edition. New York: John Wiley and Sons.

Metz, K.E. 1991. Development of explanation: Incremental and fundamental change in children's physics knowledge. [Special issue] Journal of Research in Science Teaching, 28(9): 785-797.

NRC (National Research Council). 1988. Improving Indicators of the Quality of Science and Mathematics Education in Grades K-12. R.J. Murnane, and S.A. Raizen, eds. Washington, DC: National Academy Press.

NSRC (National Science Resources Center). 1996. Resources for Teaching Elementary School Science. Washington, DC: National Academy Press.

Ohlsson, S. 1992. The cognitive skill of theory articulation: A neglected aspect of science education. Science & Education, 1(2): 181-192.

Roth, K.J. 1989. Science education: It's not enough to 'do' or 'relate.' The American Educator, 13(4): 16-22; 46-48.

Rutherford, F.J. 1964. The role of inquiry in science teaching. Journal of Research in Science Teaching, 2: 80-84.

Schauble, L., L.E. Klopfer, and K. Raghavan. 1991. Students' transition from an engineering model to a science model of experimentation. [Special issue] Journal of Research in Science Teaching, 28(9): 859-882.

Schwab, J.J. 1958. The teaching of science as inquiry. Bulletin of the Atomic Scientists, 14: 374-379.

Schwab, J.J. 1964. The teaching of science as enquiry. In The Teaching of Science, J.J. Schwab and P.F. Brandwein, eds.: 3-103. Cambridge, MA: Harvard University Press.

Welch, W.W., L.E. Klopfer, G.S. Aikenhead, and J.T. Robinson. 1981. The role of inquiry in science education: Analysis and recommendations. Science Education, 65(1): 33-50.

PHYSICAL SCIENCE, LIFE SCIENCE, AND EARTH AND SPACE SCIENCE

AAAS (American Association for the Advancement of Science). 1993. Benchmarks for Science Literacy. New York: Oxford University Press.

AAAS (American Association for the Advancement of Science). 1989. Science for All Americans: A Project 2061 Report on Literacy Goals in Science, Mathematics, and Technology. Washington, DC: AAAS.

Driver, R., A. Squires, P. Rushworth, and V. Wood-Robinson. 1994. *Making Sense of Secondary Science: Research into Children's Ideas.* London: Routledge.

Driver, R., E. Guesne, and A. Tiberghien, eds. 1985. *Children's Ideas in Science.* Philadelphia, PA.: Open University Press.

Fensham, P. J., R. F. Gunstone, and R. T. White, eds. 1994. *The Content of Science: A Constructivist Approach to Its Teaching and Learning.* Bristol, PA: Falmer Press.

Harlen, W. 1988. *The Teaching of Science.* London: Fulton.

NSTA (National Science Teachers Association). 1992. *Scope, Sequence, Coordination. The Content Core: A Guide for Curriculum Designers.* Washington, DC: NSTA.

Osborne, R.J., and P. Freyberg. 1985. *Learning in Science: The Implications of 'Children's Science.'* New Zealand: Heinemann.

PHYSICAL SCIENCE

AAPT (American Association of Physics Teachers). 1988. Course Content in High School Physics. *High School Physics: Views from AAPT.* College Park, MD: AAPT.

AAPT (American Association of Physics Teachers). 1986. *Guidelines for High School Physics Programs.* Washington, DC: AAPT.

ACS (American Chemical Society). 1996. *FACETS Foundations and Challenges to Encourage Technology-based Science.* Dubuque, Iowa: Kendall/Hunt.

ACS (American Chemical Society). 1993. *ChemCom: Chemistry in the Community,* second ed. Dubuque, Iowa: Kendall/Hunt.

LIFE SCIENCE

BSCS (Biological Sciences Curriculum Study). 1993. *Developing Biological Literacy: A Guide to Developing Secondary and Post-Secondary Biology Curricula.* Colorado Springs, CO: BSCS.

Jacob, F. 1982. *The Possible and the Actual.* Seattle: University of Washington Press.

Medawar, P.B., and J.S. Medawar. 1977. *The Life Science: Current Ideas of Biology.* New York: Harper and Row.

Moore, J.A. 1993. *Science as a Way of Knowing: The Foundations of Modern Biology.* Cambridge, MA: Harvard University Press.

Morowitz, H.J. 1979. Biological Generalizations and Equilibrium Organic Chemistry. In *Energy Flow in Biology: Biological Organization as a Problem in Thermal Physics.* Woodbridge, CT: Oxbow Press.

NRC (National Research Council). 1990. *Fulfilling the Promise: Biology Education in Our Nation's Schools.* Washington, DC: National Academy Press.

NRC (National Research Council). 1989. *High-School Biology Today and Tomorrow.* Washington, DC: National Academy Press.

EARTH AND SPACE SCIENCE

AGI (American Geological Institute). 1991. *Earth Science Content Guidelines Grades K-12.* Alexandria, VA: AGI.

AGI (American Geological Institute). 1991. *Earth Science Education for the 21st Century: A Planning Guide.* Alexandria, VA: AGI.

NRC (National Research Council). 1993. *Solid-Earth Sciences and Society: A Critical Assessment.* Washington, DC: National Academy Press.

SCIENCE AND TECHNOLOGY

AAAS (American Association for the Advancement of Science). 1993. *Benchmarks for Science Literacy.* New York: Oxford University Press.

AAAS (American Association for the Advancement of Science). 1989. *Science for All Americans: A Project 2061 Report on Literacy Goals in Science, Mathematics, and Technology.* New York: Oxford University Press.

Johnson, J. 1989. Technology: A Report of the Project 2061 Phase I Technology Panel. Washington, DC: American Association for the Advancement of Science.

Selby, C.C. 1993. Technology: From myths to realities. Phi Delta Kappan, 74(9): 684-689.

SCIENCE IN PERSONAL AND SOCIAL PERSPECTIVES

AAAS (American Association for the Advancement of Science). 1993. Benchmarks for Science Literacy. New York: Oxford University Press.

Gore, A. 1992. Earth in the Balance: Ecology and the Human Spirit. Boston: Houghton Mifflin.

Meadows, D.H., D.L. Meadows, and J. Randers. 1992. Beyond the Limits: Confronting Global Collapse, Envisioning a Sustainable Future. Post Mills, VT: Chelsea Green.

Miller, G.T. 1992. Living in the Environment: An Introduction to Environmental Science, 7th ed. Belmont, CA: Wadsworth.

Moore, J. 1985. Science as a Way of Knowing II: Human Ecology. Baltimore, MD: American Society of Zoologists.

NRC (National Research Council). 1993. Solid-Earth Sciences and Society. Washington, DC: National Academy Press.

Silver, C.S., and R.S. DeFries. 1990. One Earth, One Future: Our Changing Global Enviroment. Washington, DC: National Academy Press.

HISTORY AND NATURE OF SCIENCE

In addition to references for Science as Inquiry, the following references are suggested.

AAAS (American Association for the Advancement of Science). 1993. Benchmarks for Science Literacy. New York: Oxford University Press.

Bakker, G., and L. Clark. 1988. Explanation: An Introduction to the Philosophy of Science. Mountain View, CA: Mayfield.

Cohen, I.B. 1985. Revolution in Science. Cambridge, MA: The Belknap Press of Harvard University Press.

Hacking, I. 1983. Representing and Intervening: Introductory Topics in the Philosophy of Natural Science. New York: Cambridge University Press.

Hoyingen-Huene, P. 1987. Context of discovery and context of justification. Studies in History and Philosophy of Science, 18(4): 501-515.

Klopfer, L. 1992. A historical perspective on the history and nature of science on school science programs. In Teaching About the History and Nature of Science and Technology: Background Papers, Biological Sciences Curriculum Study and Social Science Education Consortium: 105-129. Colorado Springs, CO: Biological Sciences Curriculum Study.

Machamer, P. 1992. Philosophy of science: An overview for educators. In Teaching About the History and Nature of Science and Technology: Background Papers, Biological Sciences Curriculum Study and Social Science Education Consortium: 9-17. Colorado Springs, CO: Biological Sciences Curriculum Study.

Malley, M. 1992. The Nature and History of Science. In Teaching About the History and Nature of Science and Technology: Background Papers, Biological Sciences Curriculum Study and Social Science Education Consortium: 67-79. Colorado Springs, CO: Biological Sciences Curriculum Study.

Moore, J.A. 1993. Science as a Way of Knowing: The Foundations of Modern Biology. Cambridge, MA.: Harvard University Press.

NRC (National Research Council). 1995. On Being a Scientist: Responsible Conduct in Research. 2nd ed. Washington, DC: National Academy Press.

Russell, T.L. 1981. What history of science, how much, and why? Science Education 65 (1): 51-64.

observe

Learn

Interact

Change

The alignment of assessment with curriculum and teaching is one of the most critical pieces of science education reform.

CHAPTER 7

SEVEN

Science Education Program Standards

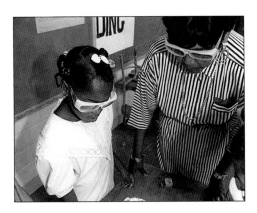

The program standards are criteria for the quality of and conditions for school science programs. They focus on issues at the school and district levels that relate to opportunities for students to learn and opportunities for teachers to teach science. ▌ The first three standards provide criteria to be used in making judgments about the quality of the K-12 science program. Those standards are directed at individuals and groups responsible for the design, development, selection, and adaptation of science programs. People involved include teachers, department chairs, curriculum directors, administrators, publishers, and school committees. Each school and district must translate the standards into programs that are consistent with the content, teaching, and assessment standards, as well as reflect the context and policies of the local district. Because the content standards outline what students should know, understand, and be able to do without describing the organization of the program of study, program standards A, B, and C focus on criteria for the design of the program, course of study, and curriculum. In contrast, standards D, E, and F describe the conditions necessary to implement a comprehensive program that provides appropriate opportunities for all students to learn science.

The Standards

The program standards are rooted in the assumptions that thoughtful design and implementation of science programs at the school and district levels are necessary to provide comprehensive and coordinated experiences for all students across grade levels, and that coordinated experiences result in more effective learning. But a balance must be maintained. To the extent that district and school policies and consequent decisions provide guidance, support, and coordination among teachers, they can enhance the science program. However, if policies become restrictive and prescriptive, they make it difficult for teachers to use their professional ability in the service of their students.

PROGRAM STANDARD A:
All elements of the K-12 science program must be consistent with the other *National Science Education Standards* and with one another and developed within and across grade levels to meet a clearly stated set of goals.

- In an effective science program, a set of clear goals and expectations for students must be used to guide the design, implementation, and assessment of all elements of the science program.
- Curriculum frameworks should be used to guide the selection and development of units and courses of study.
- Teaching practices need to be consistent with the goals and curriculum frameworks.
- Assessment policies and practices should be aligned with the goals, student expectations, and curriculum frameworks.
- Support systems and formal and informal expectations of teachers must be aligned with the goals, student expectations and curriculum frameworks.
- Responsibility needs to be clearly defined for determining, supporting, maintaining, and upgrading all elements of the science program.

IN AN EFFECTIVE SCIENCE PROGRAM, A SET OF CLEAR GOALS AND EXPECTATIONS FOR STUDENTS MUST BE USED TO GUIDE THE DESIGN, IMPLEMENTATION, AND ASSESSMENT OF ALL ELEMENTS OF THE SCIENCE PROGRAM.
A science program begins with the goals and expectations for student achievement; it also includes the selection and organization of science content into curriculum frameworks, ways of teaching, and assessment strategies. The goals for a science program provide the statements of philosophy and the vision that drive the program and the statements of purpose that the program is designed to achieve.

See Teaching
Standard A

See Program
Standard B

**CURRICULUM FRAMEWORKS SHOULD
BE USED TO GUIDE THE SELECTION
AND DEVELOPMENT OF UNITS AND
COURSES OF STUDY.** The curriculum
framework provides a guide for moving the
vision presented in the goals closer to reality. Teachers use the guide as they select and
design specific school and classroom work.
By specifying the sequence of topics in the
curriculum, the guide ensures articulation
and coherence across the curriculum. Using
the framework, teachers design instruction
that is based on the prior experiences of students but avoids unnecessary repetition. The
framework guides the students as they move
through their schooling.

**TEACHING PRACTICES NEED TO BE
CONSISTENT WITH THE GOALS AND
CURRICULUM FRAMEWORKS.** The program standards do not prescribe specific
teaching behaviors, nor should district or
school policies. There are many ways to teach
science effectively while adhering to the basic
tenets of the *National Science Education
Standards*, but they must be consistent with
the goals and framework of the district.

See Teaching
Standard C

**ASSESSMENT POLICIES AND PRACTICES
SHOULD BE ALIGNED WITH THE GOALS,
STUDENT EXPECTATIONS, AND CURRICU-
LUM FRAMEWORKS.** Within the science
program, the alignment of assessment with
curriculum and teaching is one of the most
critical pieces of science education reform. If
the assessment system at the school and district levels does not reflect the *Standards* and
measure what is valued, the likelihood of
reform is greatly diminished. Assessing only

factual information inevitably leads to
emphasis on factual teaching—a situation all
too prevalent in schools today. Decision
makers at the school and district levels, as
well as community leaders and parents, must
realize the nature of the science that is being
taught and the strategies by which student
understanding can be assessed. This will
require letting go of some traditional methods of accountability and developing new
assessment policies and practices at the
classroom and district levels that are consistent with the program goals of the district
and the assessment standards.

**SUPPORT SYSTEMS AND FORMAL AND
INFORMAL EXPECTATIONS OF TEACHERS
MUST BE ALIGNED WITH THE GOALS,
STUDENT EXPECTATIONS, AND CURRICU-
LUM FRAMEWORKS.** An effective science
program requires an adequate support system, including resources of people, time,
materials and finance, opportunities for staff
development, and leadership that works
toward the goals of the program. It is encoded formally in policy documents such as a
teacher's handbook and informally in the
unwritten norms that determine routines.
The support system must support classroom
teachers in teaching science as described in
the *Standards*.

**RESPONSIBILITY NEEDS TO BE CLEARLY
DEFINED FOR DETERMINING, SUPPORT-
ING, MAINTAINING, AND UPGRADING
ALL ELEMENTS OF THE SCIENCE
PROGRAM.** Although all school personnel
have responsibilities, clearly defined leadership at the school and district levels is

See Teaching
Standard F

required for an effective science program. Leadership can be vested in a variety of people, including teachers, school administrators, and science coordinators. Who provides such leadership is not as critical as ensuring that the responsibilities for support, maintenance, assessment, review, revision, and improvement of the program are effectively carried out so that students have opportunities to learn and teachers have the opportunity to teach.

The alignment needed in a science program can be illustrated by considering scientific inquiry. The ability to understand and conduct scientific inquiry is an important goal for students in any science program. To accomplish this goal, teachers must provide students with many opportunities to engage in and reflect on inquiry about natural phenomena. The district and school must provide curriculum frameworks that highlight inquiry and the support of materials and time to make this type of teaching possible. And assessment tasks should require students to demonstrate an understanding of inquiry and an ability to inquire.

PROGRAM STANDARD B:
The program of study in science for all students should be developmentally appropriate, interesting, and relevant to students' lives; emphasize student understanding through inquiry; and be connected with other school subjects.

- The program of study should include all of the content standards.
- Science content must be embedded in a variety of curriculum patterns that are developmentally appropriate, interesting, and relevant to students' lives.

- The program of study must emphasize student understanding through inquiry.
- The program of study in science should connect to other school subjects.

This standard sets criteria for the work of curriculum designers and developers, whether in school districts, research and development institutions, or commercial publishing houses. It also sets criteria for those who select curricula.

THE PROGRAM OF STUDY SHOULD INCLUDE ALL OF THE CONTENT STANDARDS.
Science content, as defined by the *Standards*, includes eight categories—unifying concepts and processes in science, science as inquiry, physical science, life science, earth and space science, science and technology, science in personal and social perspectives, and history and nature of science. An effective science program includes activities for students to achieve understanding and ability in all categories.

SCIENCE CONTENT MUST BE EMBEDDED IN A VARIETY OF CURRICULUM PATTERNS THAT ARE DEVELOPMENTALLY APPROPRIATE, INTERESTING, AND RELEVANT TO STUDENTS' LIVES.
Curriculum includes not only the content, but also the structure, organization, balance, and means of presentation of the content in the classroom. Designing curricula considers the teaching and assessment standards, as well as the program standards and the content standards.

The translation of content into curricula can and should take many forms. The *Standards* do not prescribe a single curriculum for students to achieve the content standards. On the contrary, for students to experience science fully and to meet the goals of science education, a variety of curriculum patterns, structures, and emphases should be included in the activities, units, and courses that make up a total science program.

Regardless of organization, the science program should emphasize understanding natural phenomena and science-related social issues that students encounter in everyday life. Because inquiries into most natural phenomena and the process of resolving social issues that are science related involve understanding and ability from more than one content standard, science programs will contain activities, units, and courses that are designed to require knowledge and skill from more than one content standard. As an example, a unit on the quality of a river might emphasize the outcomes specified in the content standard on science as inquiry. At the same time, the unit might increase students' understanding of science in personal and social perspectives, life science, physical science, and earth and space science.

If teachers are to teach for understanding as described in the content standards, then coverage of great amounts of trivial, unconnected information must be eliminated from the curriculum. Integrated and thematic approaches to curriculum can be powerful; however they require skill and understanding in their design and implementation.

See Teaching Standard A

Effective science curriculum materials are developed by teams of experienced teachers, scientists, and science curriculum specialists using a systematic research and development process that involves repeated cycles of design, trial teaching with children,

evaluation, and revision. Because this research and development process is labor intensive and requires considerable scientific, technical, and pedagogical expertise, teachers and school district personnel usually begin the design and development of a curriculum that meets local goals and frameworks with a careful examination of externally produced science materials. These materials are modified and adapted to meet the goals of the district and of teachers in that district, and to use the resources of the local community. However, care should be taken that in the adaptation of externally produced materials to local needs, the original intended purpose and design are not undermined.

Districtwide goals and expectations for student achievement, as well as the curriculum frameworks, serve to ensure coherence and articulation across grades, but they must not constrain the creativity and responsiveness of teachers in schools. While high-quality curriculum materials provide a critical base for teaching science, especially for new teachers and others new to teaching science as described in the *Standards*, teachers must have the flexibility to meet the science program goals in a variety of ways by adjusting and adapting curriculum materials to match their own and their students' strengths and interests.

The content standards are designed to be developmentally appropriate and to build understanding of basic ideas across the grade levels. In designing curricula, care should be taken to return to concepts in successive years so that students have the opportunity to increase and deepen their understanding and ability as they mature.

This gradual development of understanding and ability will be realized only if the concepts and capabilities designated for each grade level are congruent with the students' mental, affective, and physical abilities. Providing a range of student activities promotes learning, and some activities can be slightly beyond the students' developmental level. However, it is inappropriate to require students to learn terms and perform activities that are far beyond their cognitive and physical developmental level.

See Content Standard A (all grade levels)

THE PROGRAM OF STUDY MUST EMPHASIZE STUDENT UNDERSTAND-ING THROUGH INQUIRY. Inquiry is a set of interrelated processes by which scientists and students pose questions about the natural world and investigate phenomena; in doing so, students acquire knowledge and develop a rich understanding of concepts, principles, models, and theories. Inquiry is a critical component of a science program at all grade levels and in every domain of science, and designers of curricula and programs must be sure that the approach to content, as well as the teaching and assessment strategies, reflect the acquisition of scientific understanding through inquiry. Students then will learn science in a way that reflects how science actually works.

THE PROGRAM OF STUDY IN SCIENCE SHOULD CONNECT TO OTHER SCHOOL SUBJECTS. Student achievement in science and in other school subjects such as social studies, language arts, and technology is enhanced by coordination between and among the science program and other programs. Furthermore, such coordination can make maximal use of time in a crowded

school schedule. As an example, the National Standards for Geography include knowledge about land forms, as does the earth and space science standard. A combined geography and science unit is natural. Oral and written communication skills are developed in science when students record, summarize, and communicate the results of inquiry to their class, school, or community. Coordination suggests that these skills receive attention in the language arts program as well as in the science program.

PROGRAM STANDARD C: The science program should be coordinated with the mathematics program to enhance student use and understanding of mathematics in the study of science and to improve student understanding of mathematics.

Science requires the use of mathematics in the collection and treatment of data and in the reasoning used to develop concepts, laws, and theories. School science and mathematics programs should be coordinated so that students learn the necessary mathematical skills and concepts before and during their use in the science program.

Coordination of science and mathematics programs provides an opportunity to advance instruction in science beyond the purely descriptive. Students gathering data in a science investigation should use tools of data analysis to organize these data and to formulate hypotheses for further testing. Using data from actual investigations from science in mathematics courses, students encounter all the anomalies of authentic problems—inconsistencies, outliers, and

The Solar System

In this example, students engage in an inquiry activity that includes both science and mathematics providing prerequisite knowledge for constructing physical models. Ms. B. begins by asking students what they already know about the solar system and maintains their interest by pointing out that some science and technology that they accept as ordinary have not always existed. In a careful sequence, each lesson in the inquiry builds on previous lessons. Students observe stars for a period of time, discuss patterns they observe, and seek confirmation of the patterns through additional observations. Students use manipulatives such as globes, rulers, and protractors to develop understanding. Mathematics is integral to this inquiry, so Ms. B has worked with the mathematics instructor to ensure coordination.

[This example highlights some elements of Teaching Standards A, B, D and E; 5-8 Content Standards A, B, F, and G, as well as Unifying Concepts and Processes; and Program Standards A, B, C, and D.]

Ms. B. was beginning the study of the solar system with the eighth grade class. In preparation for building models of the solar system, she wanted the students to estimate the circumference of the earth. The activity was designed to allow students to think and act like astronomers 500 years ago. She had spent some time with the mathematics teacher in order to coordinate part of the study with him. In fact, some of the science work would actually take place in the math class.

Ms. B. set the stage by reviewing what the students already knew about the solar system, especially about the earth, sun, and moon. Then they talked briefly about building models and determined that to make a scale model they would have to know how big each object in the solar system was and also the distances between them. Ms. B. asked whether they knew these facts about the sun, moon and earth. Someone said they could look it up. But Ms. B. said that although they could get the answer this way, instead they were going to try to find out for themselves, similar to the way astronomers learned new things.

She asked the students how they thought the circumference of the earth was measured. Someone said by measuring on a map. Someone else said by flying around it keeping track of the distance. Ms. B. told them, however, that Columbus had an approximate, but limited, idea of how big the earth was before anyone had gone around it. She said they were going to determine the circumference of the earth using the North Star. Ms. B. gave each student a diagram of the North Star and the stars of the Big and Little Dipper, drawn to scale. The stars were oriented the way they would be looking due north at about 8:00 p.m. in their town. She directed the students to observe and make sketches of the positions of the Big Dipper, the Little Dipper, and the North Star at dark and at least two hours later.

Several days later students compared notes on the stars. Almost everyone had found them, many for the first time. When they compared their observations, everyone had seen the stars move, but most students noticed that the North Star seemed to stay in the same place. They agreed that everyone should observe one more time that night to confirm their observations. But for the moment it was agreed to assume—with the majority—that the North Star didn't seem to move at all.

With these observations, Ms. B. said, they were ready to try to find the circumference of the earth. She challenged each group of four to use their globes to answer the question: "Since the North Star didn't appear to move, what direction would it be if you were standing at the North Pole?" After some time for thinking, discussing and moving the globe around, the class shared their answers. Several groups said it would be right overhead. Asked to explain why, they used their globes to illustrate that if it were not, it wouldn't stay due north as the earth turned.

Ms. B. then drew a sketch of the earth, with the familiar Western Hemisphere facing her, on the blackboard. She drew an arrow straight up from the North Pole, pointing to the North Star, and she also made a dot on the equator at the edge of her sketch on the Gilbert and Ellis Islands in the Pacific. She asked: "Which way is the North Star for someone in the Gilbert and Ellis Islands?"

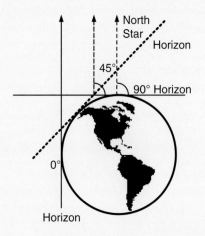

Figure 1. Ms. B.'s Sketch of the earth

Each group was directed to reach a consensus of where to draw the arrow from the Gilbert and Ellis Islands on the sketch, but some could not. Each group, and the holdouts, put an arrow on the board to illustrate their answer. One arrow pointed straight up, and the rest pointed at a range of angles, most toward a point near the top of the blackboard. How could they find out who was accurate? Ms. B. suggested that they use what they knew to try to decide who among the groups might be right. To help the students get started on this task, she asked each group how high up they thought the North Star was. According to where their arrows pointed, most had assumed that the North Star was only a few earth diameters above the North Pole. Ms. B. then asked what the students thought the distance to the North Star really was compared with the size of the earth. Now many students said that it must be very far away because it's a star and stars are very far away. In the end consensus was reached that if the North Star were very far away—a great many earth diameters—the straight up arrow in the sketch would point to this star, no matter where one was on the drawing of the earth.

Then Ms. B. drew a line straight across the top of the earth in her sketch to indicate the horizon at the North Pole, pointing out that on the blackboard the angle from the horizon to the North Star was 90 degrees. If you were standing on the North Pole you would look straight up to see the North Star. She asked the students where the inhabitants of the Gilbert and Ellis Islands on the equator, 1/4 of the way around the earth away, would look. She also made a mark on her diagram

1/8 of the earth's circumference south from the North Pole and asked at what angle above the horizon the inhabitants there would have to look to find the North Star. Discussion followed, with a variety of different quick answers. Ms. B. challenged the groups to use their compasses and protractors to make a drawing that would give them the answers. When the groups had come up with some ideas, she led them in a discussion on how the angle changed as the distance around the earth from the pole changed. They agreed that it got smaller and smaller, going from 90 degrees at the pole to 45 degrees 1/8 of the way around, and 0 degrees at the equator.

The next day, Ms. B. put a graph with the three points the students had found so far on the board. She asked how they could predict the angle of the North Star for two points, A and B, which she added to the graph, one halfway between the 45 degree point and the pole and the other halfway between the 45 degree point and the equator? The students suggested a straight line on the graph which fitted their three points would represent the relationship between the angle and distance around the earth. The students also agreed that this was just a guess. Ms. B. asked how they could be more certain and they decided they could go back to their drawing, use their protractors to put A and B on it, and measure what the angle of the North Star would be.

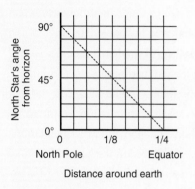

Figure 2. Ms. B.'s Graph

The result of their graphic investigation confirmed that a straight line seemed to be a good graph for the relationship between the angle formed by the North Star and the horizon and distance around the earth.

Ms. B. then told them that in Columbus' day it was known from ground travel that the distance between a town in Scandinavia where the North Star angle was 67 degrees and another in Italy where the North Star angle was 43 degrees was about 3,000 miles. People who knew what the students now knew could figure out the circumference of the earth. The groups were to take their data to math class where they would have time to figure out the earth's circumference and then proceed to look in the library for the best modern value.

The next day, the class discussed how well they had done in getting a value for the earth's size. In succeeding days they calculated the distance to the moon and its circumference and looked up the same information for the sun. They also learned how modern astronomers calculate distances and size. Finally, using the data, each group designed a scale model of the sun, moon, and earth.

errors—which they might not encounter with contrived textbook data.

If teachers of mathematics use scientific examples and methods, understanding in both disciplines will be enhanced. For mathematics, coordination reinforces the perspective of investigation and experimentation that is emphasized in the National Council of Teachers of Mathematics (NCTM) standards. The mathematics that students should understand and use in the study of science as articulated in the NCTM mathematics standards are listed in Table 7.1.

Connecting the science and mathematics programs requires coordination at the school and district levels. Those who develop guiding frameworks must work together to ensure that the potential for connection is in place at the district level. At the school level, teachers of mathematics and science must develop and implement a coordinated program.

PROGRAM STANDARD D:
The K-12 science program must give students access to appropriate and sufficient resources, including quality teachers, time, materials and equipment, adequate and safe space, and the community.

- **The most important resource is professional teachers.**
- **Time is a major resource in a science program.**
- **Conducting scientific inquiry requires that students have easy, equitable, and frequent opportunities to use a wide range of equipment, materials, supplies, and other resources for experimentation and direct investigation of phenomena.**
- **Collaborative inquiry requires adequate and safe space.**
- **Good science programs require access to the world beyond the classroom.**

Learning science requires active inquiry into the phenomena of the natural world. Such inquiry requires rich and varied resources in an adequate and safe environment. The specific criteria for a science learning environment will depend on many factors such as the needs of the students and the characteristics of the science program. A student with rich experience in a topic might need access to additional resources within or outside the school; a student with a different language background might need supporting materials in that language; a student with a physical disability might need specially designed equipment; and a student with little experience using computer technology might need a tutor or a tutorial program. District policy makers and those in charge of budget allocations must provide the resources, and then school-level administrators and teachers must make sure that, once allocated, the resources are well used.

THE MOST IMPORTANT RESOURCE IS PROFESSIONAL TEACHERS. Needless to say, students must have access to skilled, professional teachers. Teachers must be prepared to teach science to students with diverse strengths, needs, experiences, and approaches to learning. Teachers must know the content they will teach, understand the nature of learning, and use a range of teaching strategies for science. Hiring practices must ensure that teachers are prepared to teach science and should include successful teachers of science in the selection of their new colleagues.

See System Standard D

TABLE 7.1. EXAMPLES OF MATHEMATICS THAT STUDENTS SHOULD USE AND UNDERSTAND

GRADES K-4

Measure, collect, and organize data

Explore chance

Recognize and describe patterns

Use variables to express relationships

Develop skills of estimation and judgment

GRADES 5-8

Represent situations verbally, numerically, graphically, geometrically, or symbolically

Use estimations

Identify and use functional relationships

Develop and use tables, graphs, and rules to describe situations

Use statistical methods to describe, analyze, evaluate, and make decisions

Use geometry in solving problems

Create experimental and theoretical models of situations involving probabilities

GRADES 9-12

Develop ability to use realistic applications and modeling in trigonometry

Understand connections within a problem situation, its model as a function in symbolic form, and the graph of that function

Use functions that are constructed as models of real-world problems

Know how to use statistics and probability

Source: NCTM, 1989

Districts should use the professional development standards to provide teachers with opportunities to develop and enhance the needed capabilities for effective science teaching. Funding and professional time for such development is an essential part of district budgets.

The emphasis on the need for professional teachers of science does not diminish the need for other school personnel who enhance the science program. In addition to an administrative team and teaching colleagues, other support personnel might include the resource librarian, a laboratory technician, or maintenance staff.

TIME IS A MAJOR RESOURCE IN A SCIENCE PROGRAM. Science must be allocated sufficient time in the school program every day, every week, and every year. The content standards define scientific literacy; the amount of time required to achieve scientific literacy for all students depends on the particular program. The time devoted to science education must be allocated to meet the needs of an inquiry-based science program. No matter what the scheduling model, a school schedule needs to provide sufficient and flexible use of time to accommodate the needs of the students and what is being learned. In addition to time with students and with colleagues, teachers of science also spend considerable time preparing materials, setting up activities, creating the learning environment, and organizing student experiences. This time must be built into the daily teaching schedule.

CONDUCTING SCIENTIFIC INQUIRY REQUIRES THAT STUDENTS HAVE EASY, EQUITABLE, AND FREQUENT OPPORTUNITIES TO USE A WIDE RANGE OF EQUIPMENT, MATERIALS, SUPPLIES, AND OTHER RESOURCES FOR EXPERIMENTATION AND DIRECT INVESTIGATION OF PHENOMENA. Some equipment is general purpose and should be part of every school's science inventory, such as magnifiers or microscopes of appropriate sophistication, measurement tools, tools for data analysis, and computers with software for supporting investigations. Other materials are topic specific, such as a water table for first graders or a reduced-resistance air table for physics investigations; such specialized materials also need to be made available. Many materials are consumable and need to be replenished regularly. Furthermore, policy makers need to bear in mind that equipment needs to be upgraded frequently and requires preventive maintenance.

Given that materials appropriate for inquiry-based science teaching are central to achieving the educational goals set forth in the *Standards*, it is critical that an effective infrastructure for material support be a part of any science program. School systems need to develop mechanisms to identify exemplary materials, store and maintain them, and make them accessible to teachers in a timely fashion. Providing an appropriate infrastructure frees teachers' time for more appropriate tasks and ensures that the necessary materials are available when needed. Because science inquiry is broader than first-hand investigation, print, video, and technology sources of information and simulation are also required. These are included in the materials-support infrastructure.

The teaching standards consistently make reference to the responsiveness and flexibility to student interests that must be evidenced in classrooms that reflect effective science teaching. The content standard on inquiry sets the expectation that students will develop the ability to perform a full inquiry. For such inquiry-based teaching to become a reality, in addition to what is regularly maintained in the school and district, every teacher of science needs an easily accessible budget for materials and equipment as well as for unanticipated expenses that arise as students and teachers pursue their work.

COLLABORATIVE INQUIRY REQUIRES ADEQUATE AND SAFE SPACE. There must be space for students to work together in groups, to engage safely in investigation with materials, and to display both work in progress and finished work. There also must be space for the safe and convenient storage of the materials needed for science. At the lower grade levels, schools do not need separate rooms for laboratories. In fact, it is an advantage in terms of long-term studies and making connections between school subject areas to have science as an integral part of the classroom environment. At the upper grade levels, laboratories become critical to provide the space, facilities, and equipment needed for inquiry and to ensure that the teacher and students can conduct investigations without risk. All spaces where students do inquiry must meet appropriate safety regulations.

GOOD SCIENCE PROGRAMS REQUIRE ACCESS TO THE WORLD BEYOND THE CLASSROOM. District and school leaders must allocate financial support to provide opportunities for students to investigate the world outside the classroom. This may mean budgeting for trips to nearby points of interest, such as a river, archaeological site, or nature preserve; it could include contracting with local science centers, museums, zoos, and horticultural centers for visits and programs. Relationships should be developed with local businesses and industry to allow students and teachers access to people and the institutions, and students must be given access to scientists and other professionals in higher education and the medical establishment to gain access to their expertise and the laboratory settings in which they work. Communication technology has made it possible for anyone to access readily people throughout the world. This communication technology should be easily accessible to students.

Much of this standard is acknowledged as critical, even if unavailable, for students in secondary schools. It must be emphasized, however, that this standard applies to the entire science program and all students in all grades. In addition, this standard demands quality resources that often are lacking and seem unattainable in some schools or districts. Missing resources must not be an excuse for not teaching science. Many teachers and schools "make do" or improvise under difficult circumstances (e.g., crowded classrooms, time borrowed from other subjects, and materials purchased with personal funds). A science program based on the *National Science Education Standards* is a program constantly moving toward replacing such improvisation with necessary resources.

PROGRAM STANDARD E:
All students in the K-12 science program must have equitable access to opportunities to achieve the *National Science Education Standards*.

See System Standard E

All students, regardless of sex, cultural or ethnic background, physical or learning disabilities, future aspirations, or interest in science, should have the opportunity to attain high levels of scientific literacy. By adopting this principle of equity and excellence, the *Standards* prescribe the inclusion of all students in challenging science learning opportunities and define a high level of understanding that all students should achieve. In particular, the commitment to science for all implies inclusion of those who traditionally have not received encouragement and opportunity to pursue science—women and girls, students of color, students with disabilities, and students with limited English proficiency. It implies attention to various styles of learning, adaptations to meet the needs of special students and differing sources of motivation. And it also implies providing opportunities for those students interested in and capable of moving beyond the basic program. Given this diversity of student needs, experiences, and backgrounds, and the goal that all students will achieve a common set of standards, schools must support high-quality, diverse, and varied opportunities to learn science.

The understandings and abilities described in the content standards are outcomes for all students; they do not represent different expectations for different groups of students. Curriculum developers, local policy makers, and teachers of science must make decisions about and provide the resources required to accommodate the different rates of learning.

The principles of equity and excellence have implications for the grouping of students. There are science activities for which grouping is appropriate and activities for which grouping is not appropriate. Decisions about grouping are made by considering the purpose and demands of the activity and the needs, abilities, and interests of students. A *Standards*-based science program ensures that all students participate in challenging activities adapted to diverse needs.

The principles of equity and excellence also bear on Program Standard A—coherence and consistency—and Program Standard B—curriculum. All dimensions of a science program adhere to the principle of science for all. Themes and topics chosen for curricula should support the premise that men and women of diverse backgrounds engage in and participate in science and have done so throughout history. Teaching practice is responsive to diverse learners, and the community of the classroom is one in which respect for diversity is practiced. Assessment practices adhere to the standard of fairness and do not unfairly assume the perspective or experience of a particular group. Assessment practices also are modified appropriately to accommodate the needs of students with disabilities or other special conditions.

PROGRAM STANDARD F:
Schools must work as communities that encourage, support, and sustain teachers as they implement an effective science program.

- Schools must explicitly support reform efforts in an atmosphere of openness and trust that encourages collegiality.
- Regular time needs to be provided and teachers encouraged to discuss, reflect, and conduct research around science education reform.
- Teachers must be supported in creating and being members of networks of reform.
- An effective leadership structure that includes teachers must be in place.

Many previous reform efforts have failed because little attention was paid to the connection between teacher enhancement, curriculum development, and the school as a social and intellectual community. Teachers with new ideas, skills, and exemplary materials often worked in an environment where reform was not valued or supported.

See Teaching Standard F

SCHOOLS MUST EXPLICITLY SUPPORT REFORM EFFORTS IN AN ATMOSPHERE OF OPENNESS AND TRUST THAT ENCOURAGES COLLEGIALITY. All too frequently today the norms of relationships in schools promote isolation, conformity, competition, and distrust—and teachers are treated as technicians. Significant change is called for in the vision of science education reform described by the *Standards*. Collegiality, openness, and trust must be valued; teachers must be acknowledged and treated as professionals whose work requires understanding and ability. This change cannot happen within the science program alone; it demands the transformation of entire schools into communities of adult learners focused on the study and improvement of teaching and learning. Without movement toward the school as a community of learners engaged in reflective practice, the vision of science teaching and learning promoted by the *Standards* is unlikely to flourish.

See Professional Development Standard C

REGULAR TIME NEEDS TO BE PROVIDED AND TEACHERS ENCOURAGED TO DISCUSS, REFLECT, AND CONDUCT RESEARCH AROUND SCIENCE EDUCATION REFORM. The transformation of schools into centers of inquiry requires explicit action to remove destructive practical and policy constraints to reform. Schedules must be realigned, time provided, and human resources deployed such that teachers can come together regularly to discuss individual student learning needs and to reflect and conduct research on practice. In a community of learners, teachers work together to design the curriculum and assessment. They also design and take part in other professional growth activities. Time must be available for teachers to observe other classrooms, team teach, use external resources, attend conferences, and hold meetings during the school day.

TEACHERS MUST BE SUPPORTED IN CREATING AND BEING MEMBERS OF NETWORKS OF REFORM. For teachers to study their own teaching and their students' learning effectively and work constructively with their colleagues, they need tangible and moral support. Collaboration must be developed with outside institutions such as colleges and universities, professional societies, science-rich centers, museums, and business and industry to ensure that the expertise needed for growth and change is available from within and outside the school. Teachers need the opportunity to become part of the larger world of professional teachers of science through participating in networks, attending conferences, and other means.

Teachers of science also need material support. As communities of learners, schools should make available to teachers professional journals, books, and technologies that will help them advance their knowledge. These same materials support teachers as they use research and reflection to improve their teaching.

AN EFFECTIVE LEADERSHIP STRUCTURE THAT INCLUDES TEACHERS MUST BE IN PLACE. Developing a community of learners requires strong leadership, but that leadership must change dramatically from the hierarchical and authoritarian leadership often in place in schools and in school districts today. Leadership should emerge from a shared vision of science education and from an understanding of the professional, social, and cultural norms of a school that is a community of learners.

The leadership structure might take many forms, but it inevitably requires that teachers and administrators rethink traditional roles and responsibilities and take on new ones. School leaders must structure and sustain suitable support systems for the work that teachers do. They are responsible for ensuring that agreed-upon plans for time, space, and resources are carried out. They must model the behaviors they seek by becoming learners themselves with the teaching staff. They are advocates for the school program in the district and community. They monitor the work of the school and the staff and provide corrective feedback that enhances effective functioning.

There are many possible ways to structure a community of learners that reflect the norms and demands described in this standard. However, regardless of the structure, roles and responsibilities must be explicit and accountability clearly assigned.

CHANGING EMPHASES

The *National Science Education Standards* envision change throughout the system. The program standards encompass the following changes in emphases:

LESS EMPHASIS ON	MORE EMPHASIS ON
Developing science programs at different grade levels independently of one another	Coordinating the development of the K-12 science program across grade levels
Using assessments unrelated to curriculum and teaching	Aligning curriculum, teaching, and assessment
Maintaining current resource allocations for books	Allocating resources necessary for hands-on inquiry teaching aligned with the *Standards*
Textbook- and lecture-driven curriculum	Curriculum that supports the *Standards* and includes a variety of components, such as laboratories emphasizing inquiry and field trips
Broad coverage of unconnected factual information	Curriculum that includes natural phenomena and science-related social issues that students encounter in everyday life
Treating science as a subject isolated from other school subjects	Connecting science to other school subjects, such as mathematics and social studies
Science learning opportunities that favor one group of students	Providing challenging opportunities for all students to learn science
Limiting hiring decisions to the administration	Involving successful teachers of science in the hiring process
Maintaining the isolation of teachers	Treating teachers as professionals whose work requires opportunities for continual learning and networking
Supporting competition	Promoting collegiality among teachers as a team to improve the school
Teachers as followers	Teachers as decision makers

References for Further Reading

Anderson, R., and H. Pratt. 1995. Local Leadership for Science Education Reform. Dubuque, IA: Kendall/Hunt.

Clewell, B.C., B.T. Anderson, and M.E. Thorpe. 1992. Breaking the Barriers: Helping Female and Minority Students Succeed in Mathematics and Science. San Francisco: Jossey-Bass.

Cole, M., and P. Griffin, eds. 1987. Contextual Factors in Education: Improving Science and Mathematics for Minorities and Women. Madison, WI: Committee on Research on Mathematics, Science, and Technology Education, Wisconsin Center for Education Research.

Darling-Hammond, L. 1993. Reframing the school reform agenda: Developing capacity for school transformation. Phi Beta Kappan, June, 1993.

Fullan, M., and S. Stiegelbauer. 1991. The New Meaning of Educational Change, 2nd ed. New York: Teachers College Press.

Geography Education Standards Project. 1994. Geography for Life. Washington, DC: National Geographic Research and Exploration.

Lieberman, A., ed. 1988. Building a Professional Culture in Schools. New York: Teachers College Press.

NCTM (National Council of Teachers of Mathematics). 1989. Curriculum Evaluation Standards for School Mathematics. Reston, VA: NCTM.

Oakes, J. 1990. Multiplying Inequalities: The Effect of Race, Social Class, and Tracking on Opportunities to Learn Mathematics and Science. Santa Monica, CA: RAND Corporation.

Porter, A. 1993. School delivery standards. Educational Researcher 22(5): 24-30.

Stevenson, H.W., and J.W. Stigler. 1992. The Learning Gap: Why Our Schools Are Failing and What We Can Learn from Japanese and Chinese Education. New York: Summit Books.

observe

Change

Learn

Interact

Changing the
pedagogical practices
of higher education is
a necessary condition
for changing
pedagogical practices
in schools

Science Education System Standards

The science education system standards provide criteria for judging the performance of the components of the science education system responsible for providing schools with necessary financial and intellectual resources. ▌ Despite the frequent use of the term "educational system," the meaning often is unclear. Systems in nature are composed of subsystems, and are themselves subsystems of some larger system. The educational system may be viewed as a similar hierarchy. ▌ A view of a system requires understanding the whole in terms of interacting component subsystems, boundaries, inputs and outputs, feedback, and relationships. In the education system, the school is the central institution for public education. The school includes many components that interact, for example, teaching, administration, and finance. The school is a component subsystem of a local district, which is a subsystem of a state educational system.

States are part of a national education system. Schools are also components of a local community that can include colleges and universities, nature centers, parks and museums, businesses, laboratories, community organizations, and various media.

The primary function of the science education system is to supply society with scientifically literate citizens. Information and resources (typically financial) energize the system. The nature of the information, the magnitude of resources, and the paths along which they flow are directed by policies that are contained in instruments such as legislation, judicial rulings, and budgets.

Systems can be represented in a variety of ways, depending on the purpose and the information to be conveyed. For example, Figure 8.1 depicts the overlap among three systems that influence the practice of science education. This type of representation is a reminder that actions taken in one system have implications not only for science education but for other systems as well.

Coordination of action among the systems can serve as a powerful force for change. But if actions are at cross purposes, their effects can be negated and create waste and conflict. The overlap in Figure 8.1 illustrates that the

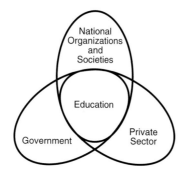

Figure 8-1. The overlap of three systems that influence science education.

day-to-day activities of science classrooms are influenced directly and indirectly by many organizations which are themselves systems. Government agencies, national organizations and societies, and private sector special-interest groups at the local, regional, state, and national levels are three among many. Each organization has an executive officer and governing body that ultimately are responsible for the organization's

State education agencies generally have more direct influence on science classroom activities than federal agencies.

activities and influence on science education.

A brief discussion of one aspect of one organization—government—contributes to the understanding of science education as a system. The power of government organizations to influence classroom science derives from two sources: (1) constitutional, legislative, or judicial authority and (2) political and economic action. Because education is not specifically mentioned as a federal power in the U.S. Constitution, authority for education resides in states or localities. Federal dollars may be targeted for specific uses, but because the dollars flow through state agencies to local districts, their use is subject to modification to meet state objectives. State education agencies generally have more direct influence on science classroom activities than federal agencies.

We can also consider the science education system as a network to facilitate thinking about the system's many interacting compo-

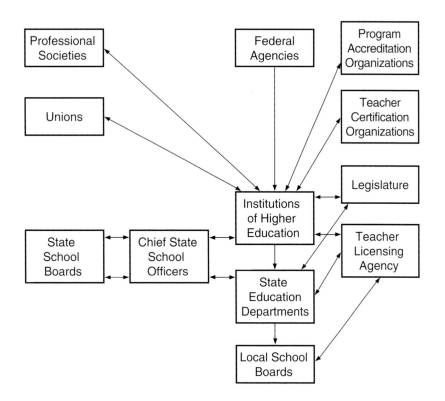

Figure 8.2. Some organizations that affect the preparation, certification, and employment of teachers.

nents. Components of the science education system serve a variety of functions that influence the classroom practice of science education. Functions generally decided at the state (but sometimes the local) level include the content of the school science curriculum, the characteristics of the science program, the nature of science teaching, and assessment practices. For any of these functions, many different organizations and responsible individuals interact. Figure 8.2 depicts how individuals and agencies from different systems interact in the preparation, certification, and employment of teachers of science.

Components of the science education system that have a major influence on teacher certification fit into four categories: (1) professional societies (such as the National

Science Teachers Association, American Association of Physics Teachers, National Association of Biology Teachers, American Geological Institute, American Chemical Society), (2) program-accrediting agencies (such as the National Board for Professional Teaching Standards, which certifies teachers, and the National Council for Accreditation of Teacher Education, which certifies teacher education programs), (3) government agencies, and (4) institutions of higher education operating within and across national, state, and local levels.

Professional societies usually are not thought of as accrediting agencies, but their membership standards describe what it means to be a professional teacher of science. Teacher accrediting agencies certify the quality of certain aspects of teaching, such as teacher education programs. The greatest authority and interaction around matters of teacher certification occur at the state level and involves state departments of education, state credentialing agencies, institutions of higher education, and state-level professional organizations. However, state policies are influenced by the federal government and national organizations, as well as by local districts. And ultimately, state policies are put into practice at the local level in the form of local school board employment policies and practices.

When thinking about the science education system, it is important to remember that organizations and agencies are composed of individuals who implement policies and practices.

The Standards

See Program
Standard A

SYSTEM STANDARD A:
Policies that influence the practice of science education must be congruent with the program, teaching, professional development, assessment, and content standards while allowing for adaptation to local circumstances.

This standard places consistency in the foreground of science education policy and practice. If the practice of science education is to undergo radical improvement, policies must support the vision contained in the *Standards*.

State and national policies are consistent with the program standards when, as a

whole, the regulations reflect the program standards. For example, state regulations for class size, for time in the school day devoted to science, and for science laboratory facilities, equipment, and safety should meet the program standards. Also, requirements of national organizations that accredit schools should be based on the program standards.

State and national policies are consistent with the teaching and professional development standards when teacher employment practices are consistent with them. State policies and practices that influence the prepara-

If the practice of science education is to undergo radical improvement, policies must support the vision contained in the Standards.

tion, certification, and continuing professional development of teachers should be congruent with the teaching and professional development standards. The pedagogical methods employed at institutions of higher education and the requirements of national organizations for the certification of teachers and accreditation of teacher education programs also must reflect the *Standards*.

State and federal assessment practices should reflect the content and assessment standards, whether to describe student achievement, to determine if a school or district is providing the opportunities for all students to learn science, to monitor the system, or to certify teachers.

State and national policies are consistent with the content standards when state curriculum frameworks reflect the content standards adapted to state and local needs. For example, students in grades K-4 are expected to understand the characteristics of organisms. The content standards do not specify which organisms should be used as examples; states and local districts should choose organisms in the children's local environment. Schools in desert environments might achieve this outcome using one type of organism, while schools in coastal regions might use another. This kind of flexibility should be a part of state policy instruments such as curriculum frameworks.

SYSTEM STANDARD B:
Policies that influence science education should be coordinated within and across agencies, institutions, and organizations.

This standard emphasizes coordination of policies and the practices defined in them. The separation of responsibilities for education and poor communication among organizations responsible for science education are barriers to achieving coordination. Individuals and organizations must understand the vision contained in the *Standards*, as well as how their practices and policies influence progress toward attaining that vision.

When individuals and organizations share a common vision, there are many ways to improve coordination. For example, intra- and inter-organizational policies should be reviewed regularly to eliminate conflicting regulations and redundancy of initiatives. Significant information needs to flow freely within and across organizations. That communication should be clear and readily understandable by individuals in other organizations, as well as by the general public.

At colleges and universities, the science and education faculties need to engage in cooperative planning of courses and programs for prospective teachers. In a broader context, scientific and teaching society policies should support the integration of science content and pedagogy called for in the *Standards*.

One example of the need for coordination is the various state-level requirements for knowing and understanding science content. Because different agencies are involved, the content of science courses in institutions of higher education for prospective teachers could be different from the subject-matter competence required for teacher licensure, and both could be different from the science content requirements of the state curriculum framework. Other examples include coordination between those who set requirements for graduation from high school and those who set admissions requirements for colleges and universities. Likewise, coordination is needed between those who determine curricula and the needs and demands of business and industry.

SYSTEM STANDARD C:
Policies need to be sustained over sufficient time to provide the continuity necessary to bring about the changes required by the *Standards*.

Achieving the vision contained in the *Standards* will take more than a few years to accomplish. Standard C has particular implications for organizations whose policies are set by elected or politically appointed leaders. New administrations often make radical changes in policy and initiatives and this practice is detrimental to education change, which takes longer than the typical 2- or 4-year term of elected office. Changes that will bring contemporary science education practices to the level of quality specified in the *Standards* will require a sustained effort.

Policies calling for changes in practice need to provide sufficient time for achieving the change, for the changes in practice to affect student learning, and for changes in student learning to affect the scientific literacy of the general public. Further, policies should include plans and resources for assessing their affects over time. If school-based educators are to work enthusiastically toward achieving the *Standards*, they need reassurance that organizations and individuals in the larger system are committed for the long term.

SYSTEM STANDARD D:
Policies must be supported with resources.

See Program Standard D

Standard D focuses on the resources necessary to fuel science education reform. Such resources include time in the school day devoted to science, exemplary teachers, thoughtfully crafted curriculum frameworks, science facilities, and apparatus and supplies. If policies are enacted without consideration for the resources needed to implement them, schools, teachers, and students are placed in the untenable position of meeting demands without the availability of the requisite resources.

For example, state resource allocations for science education must be sufficient to meet program standards for classroom practices. Policies mandating inquiry approaches to teaching science need to contain provisions for supplying the necessary print and media materials, laboratories and laboratory sup-

plies, scientific apparatus, technology, and time in the school day with reasonable class size required by this approach. Policies calling for improved science achievement should

For schools to meet the Standards, *student learning must be viewed as the primary purpose of schooling, and policies must support that purpose.*

contain provisions for students with special needs. Policies requiring new teaching skills need to contain provisions for professional development opportunities and the time for teachers to meet the demands of the policy.

Resources are in short supply, and decisions about their allocation are difficult to make. Some resource-allocation questions that are regularly faced by local and state school boards include the proportion of hours in the school day to be allocated to science; the proportion of the school budget to be allocated to science education for underachieving, special-needs, or talented science students; and the assignments of the most experienced and talented teachers. The mandates contained in policies are far too often more ambitious in vision than realistic in providing the required resources.

SYSTEM STANDARD E:
Science education policies must be equitable.

Equity principles repeated in the introduction and in the program, teaching, professional development, assessment, and content standards follow from the well-documented barriers to learning science for

See Program Standard E

students who are economically deprived, female, have disabilities, or from populations underrepresented in the sciences. These equity principles must be incorporated into science education policies if the vision of the standards is to be achieved. Policies must reflect the principle that all students are challenged and have the opportunity to achieve the high expectations of the content standards. The challenge to the larger system is to support these policies with necessary resources.

SYSTEM STANDARD F:
All policy instruments must be reviewed for possible unintended effects on the classroom practice of science education.

Even when as many implications as possible have been carefully considered, well-intentioned policies can have unintended effects. For schools to meet the *Standards*, student learning must be viewed as the primary purpose of schooling, and policies must support that purpose. The potential benefits of any policy that diverts teachers and students from their essential work must be weighed against the potential for lowered achievement.

Unless care is taken, policies intended to improve science education might actually have detrimental effects on learning. For instance, policies intended to monitor the quality of science teaching can require extensive student time to take tests. And teacher time to correct them and file reports on scores can take valuable time away from learning and teaching science. To reduce unintended effects, those who actually implement science education policies, such as teachers and other educators, should be

constantly involved in the review of those policies. Only in this way can the policies be continuously improved.

SYSTEM STANDARD G:
Responsible individuals must take the opportunity afforded by the standards-based reform movement to achieve the new vision of science education portrayed in the *Standards*.

This standard acknowledges the role that individuals play in making changes in social systems, such as the science education system. Ultimately, individuals working within and across organizations are responsible for progress. The primary responsibility for standards-based reform in science education resides with individuals in the science education and science communities.

Teachers play an active role in the formulation of science education policy, especially those policies for which they will be held accountable. They should be provided with the time to exercise this responsibility, as well as the opportunity to develop the knowledge and skill to discharge it. Teachers also work within their professional organizations to influence policy.

All members of the science education community have responsibility for communicating and moving toward the vision of school science set forth in the *Standards*. In whatever ways possible, they need to take an active role in formulating science education policy.

Scientists must understand the vision of science education in the *Standards* and their role in achieving the vision. They need to recognize the important contributions of science education to the vitality of the scientific

Implementing Standards-Based Reform:

A District Advisory Committee for Science Education

This example centers on a district-level advisory committee that has been assigned the task of implementing science education standards. The committee has completed a thorough review of the National Science Education Standards *and model standards from the state department of education and has overseen the development of science standards by the district. The committee comprises the science supervisor (chair), six outstanding science teachers (two elementary, two middle school, and two high school), a principal, a parent, two scientists (one from a local university and one from a local industry), and two science educators from a nearby university. The committee is well into the process of implementing a standards-based science education program consisting of a district curriculum, a professional development plan, and a district- and school-level assessment process. They already have completed a review of the current science education program (K-12), engaged in an exercise where they created a "desired" program based on standards, and clarified the discrepancies between the desired and actual programs. This exercise identified specific aspects of their program that needed improvement. The committee had developed a shared vision as it completed the exercise of creating a program for the district, one based on science education standards. Now the committee's task was to identify activities and resources that would enable the district to begin to enact the vision.*

The example illustrates the system standards by focusing on the coordinated performance of several components of the science education system—namely, the role of school district administration within the district, personnel from a regional education laboratory, scientists, and science educators. The committee understands that its mission is to work with school personnel to bring together the financial, intellectual, and material resources necessary to achieve the vision expressed in the science education standards. The committee is aware that several components of the system will need to change. Members of the committee have attended several leadership institutes that helped them realize the role of policies (formal and informal) and familiarized them with curriculum materials, staff development, and assessment examples that were aligned with the Standards.

In the example, the committee has divided into several subcommittees that have the tasks of working with different groups within and outside the district to coordinate resources and individual efforts to improve science education in the district. One subcommittee contacted the university concerning the alignment of courses with standards. Many district personnel received their initial undergraduate preservice preparation at the university and take courses there for continuing education units, and, in some cases, for advanced degrees. A second subcommittee talked with the new district superintendent. A third subcommittee periodically was assigned the task of determining teachers' needs for professional development and met with three separate teachers' groups representing elementary, middle, and high schools.

[This example illustrates System Standards A, B, C, D, F, and G; Professional Development Standards A and B; and Program Standards A, D, and F.]

COMMITTEE MEETING 1

The agenda for this meeting consisted of reports from the three subcommittees.

SCHOOL/UNIVERSITY SUBCOMMITTEE: The report was not encouraging. Subcommittee members reported that university scientists and science educators were "reluctant" to modify their courses for the district because they had degree programs that had been approved, they had incorporated what they thought would be the most up-to-date science, and they met teacher certification requirements. The subcommittee members pointed out the district need to stress science as inquiry, introduce authentic assessments, and otherwise support the standards-based district programs for preservice teachers and in professional development.

After the report, committee discussion focused on what the subcommittee might say at their next meeting at the university. The committee decided to suggest that it would seek help with their professional development from another college in the state if the university would not change. The subcommittee decided to present its plan to the Eisenhower Consortium at the nearby regional laboratory.

DISTRICT SUPERINTENDENT'S SUBCOMMITTEE: This subcommittee reported general support from the new superintendent until requests were reviewed that included (1) reallocation of funds to increase support for professional development, (2) support for the materials to implement an inquiry-based program, and (3) adoption of new assessments aligned with standards. The superintendent was reluctant to shift funds because some school personnel and parents would think that science was getting too much support, she had heard that some teachers preferred textbooks and not inquiry-oriented materials, and she had questions about the new assessment practices. The subcommittee was disappointed but encouraged that the superintendent had nevertheless approved its request to present the plan to the board of education.

TEACHER SUBCOMMITTEE: This subcommittee presented a positive and encouraging report. Most of the teachers understood the importance of science education standards and appreciated their proposed roles in designing their own professional development and the science program. The teachers felt involved and that their positions were understood because they had engaged in a "year of dialogue" on the *National Science Education Standards* and had participated in development of the district standards.

The meeting concluded with preparation for the presentation to the board of education. The presentation would include an overview of the *National Science Education Standards* and the district standards, a summary of the committee's work over the past year, and a discussion of specific requests.

COMMITTEE MEETING 2 AT THE BOARD OF EDUCATION

The committee began with introductions and a brief summary of its work. Much to the surprise of the superintendent, the presentation suddenly shifted to a hands-on science activity in which all participated. The activity was inquiry oriented and introduced the nature of science and technology. Two middle-school teachers conducted the workshop. After the activity, other teachers joined the discussion to point out how the activity aligned with standards, how it provided ample opportunities to learn concepts and skills, and how an assessment was incorporated in the instructional sequence.

The superintendent, scientists, science educators, and school-board members present were all impressed. The superintendent and the board said they would review the committee requests at their next study sessions.

COMMITTEE MEETING 3

By the time of this meeting, everyone had learned the outcome of the board meeting and the follow up from the school/university subcommittee.

SUPERINTENDENT SUBCOMMITTEE:

The board had been impressed with the nature of the presentation and the thoroughness of the committee's work. Although the board and the superintendent remained hesitant to provide the full professional development funds requested, they approved a pilot program in seven schools. In each of those schools, the staff had expressed strong interest in participating in the professional development program designed to support their desire to move their curriculum and instruction into alignment with the new standards.

The subcommittee decided that this was an almost ideal solution and one it should have presented to the board. The pilot will allow time to improve the professional development opportunities and align them with

the curriculum materials being reviewed, as well as to demonstrate that the plan to move toward alignment with the standards will improve district programs. The subcommittee still has a way to go to obtain the superintendent's unqualified support, but it is making progress. "It would have been so easy with the former superintendent and before the last board election. This whole process takes time, and we need continuity as we move through the implementation. Results don't come quickly," observed one of the teachers on the subcommittee.

SCHOOL/UNIVERSITY SUBCOMMITTEE:

Several events had occurred since the subcommittee's last report, and the subcommittee also had some good news. The university could not see any major changes in its undergraduate preservice program in the near future because of budget cuts and lack of familiarity with the standards by the professors in the science disciplines. But the university had been persuaded by the director of the Eisenhower Consortium at the regional educational laboratory to offer an inservice program in several of the district schools; the program would be co-led by a teacher and a university professor. The consortium director had played a part in the review of the *National Science Education Standards*, and as a result, he was empathetic to the subcommittee's concerns. He also was able to assist in identifying outstanding science curriculum materials for the teachers in the district to review.

The committee wrapped up the meeting with satisfaction that they had made some short-term gains but still had several major hurdles to clear in the years ahead.

SUMMARY

The importance of all individuals and groups having a common vision should be apparent from this example. The common vision made it possible for the committee, the director of the regional laboratory, and the receptive teachers and principals in the district to arrive at common solutions with relative ease. Contrast this with the new superintendent, who has not had the time to reach the same vision or goals as the others (or might have a very different vision). With common vision, coordination among people, institutions, and groups—such as that between the committee and the regional educational laboratory—becomes possible. When coordination occurs, the resources of both organizations are most effectively used, and time is not wasted trying to reconcile differences. The ultimate indicator of coordination is the allocation of resources in support of a common vision. Consider how the effectiveness of the professional development of teachers in the district could have been improved if the faculty at the local university had shared the vision of the outstanding teachers on the committee.

None of the events in this scenario could have occurred if the individuals involved had not taken personal responsibility for working patiently toward standards-based reform. Coordination and the allocation of resources do not happen on their own; individuals acting in a distributed leadership capacity must take responsibility to work together to fulfill the vision of the *Standards*.

enterprise and welcome teachers of science as legitimate members of the scientific community. Scientists must take the time to become informed about what is expected in science education in schools and then take active roles in support of policies to strengthen science education in their local communities.

In higher education, 2- and 4-year college professors need to model exemplary science pedagogy and science curriculum practices. Teachers need to be taught science in college in the same way they themselves will teach science in school. Changing the pedagogical practices of higher education is a necessary condition for changing pedagogical practices in schools. The culture of higher education is such that the requisite changes will occur only if individual professors take the initiative. Concerned administrators must encourage and support such change. In addition, college and university administrators must coordinate the efforts of science and education faculty in the planning of courses and programs for prospective teachers.

Helping the ordinary citizen understand the new vision of school science is a particularly challenging responsibility for the members of the science education and scientific communities. Because the new vision of school science may be a departure from their own science experience, people outside of science education might find the new vision difficult to accept. However, their understanding and support is essential. Without it, science education will not have the consistent political and long-term economic support necessary to realize the vision.

Parents should understand the goals of school science and the resources necessary to achieve them. They must work with teachers to foster their children's science education and participate in the formulation of science education policy.

Taxpayers need to understand the benefits to larger society of a scientifically literate citizenry. They need to understand the goals of school science and the need for science facilities and apparatus to support science learning. They need to be active in schools and on school boards.

Managers in the private sector should understand the benefits to their businesses of a scientifically literate work force and bring their resources to bear on improving science education. They and their employees should promote science education in schools in whatever ways possible.

Managers and employees of industrial- and university-research laboratories, museums, nature parks, and other science-rich institutions need to understand their roles and responsibilities for the realization of the vision of science education portrayed in the *Standards*.

Last, but most important, students need to understand the importance of science in their present and future lives. They need to take responsiblity for developing their understanding and ability in science.

CHANGING EMPHASES

The emphasis charts for system standards are organized around shifting the emphases at three levels of organization within the education system—district, state, and federal. The three levels of the system selected for these charts are only representative of the many components of the science education system that need to change to promote the vision of science education described in the *National Science Education Standards*.

FEDERAL SYSTEM

LESS EMPHASIS ON	MORE EMPHASIS ON
Financial support for developing new curriculum materials not aligned with the *Standards*	Financial support for developing new curriculum materials aligned with the *Standards*
Support by federal agencies for professional development activities that affect only a few teachers	Support for professional development activities that are aligned with the *Standards* and promote systemwide changes
Agencies working independently on various components of science education	Coordination among agencies responsible for science education
Support for activities and programs that are unrelated to *Standards*-based reform	Support for activities and programs that successfully implement the *Standards* at state and district levels
Federal efforts that are independent of state and local levels	Coordination of reform efforts at federal, state, and local levels
Short-term projects	Long-term commitment of resources to improving science education

STATE SYSTEM

LESS EMPHASIS ON	MORE EMPHASIS ON
Independent initiatives to reform components of science education	Partnerships and coordination of reform efforts
Funds for workshops and programs having little connection to the *Standards*	Funds to improve curriculum and instruction based on the *Standards*
Frameworks, textbooks, and materials based on activities only marginally related to the *Standards*	Frameworks, textbooks, and materials adoption criteria aligned with national and state standards
Assessments aligned with the traditional content of science education	Assessments aligned with the *Standards* and the expanded view of science content
Current approaches to teacher education	University/college reform of teacher education to include science-specific pedagogy aligned with the *Standards*
Teacher certification based on formal, historically based requirements	Teacher certification that is based on understanding and abilities in science and science teaching

DISTRICT SYSTEM

LESS EMPHASIS ON	MORE EMPHASIS ON
Technical, short-term, in-service workshops	Ongoing professional development to support teachers
Policies unrelated to *Standards*-based reform	Policies designed to support changes called for in the *Standards*
Purchase of textbooks based on traditional topics	Purchase or adoption of curriculum aligned with the *Standards* and on a conceptual approach to science teaching, including support for hands-on science materials
Standardized tests and assessments unrelated to *Standards*-based program and practices	Assessments aligned with the *Standards*
Administration determining what will be involved in improving science education	Teacher leadership in improvement of science education
Authority at upper levels of educational system	Authority for decisions at level of implementation
School board ignorance of science education program	School board support of improvements aligned with the *Standards*
Local union contracts that ignore changes in curriculum, instruction, and assessment	Local union contracts that support improvements indicated by the *Standards*

References for Further Reading

AAAS (American Association for the Advancement of Science). 1990. The Liberal Art of Science: Agenda for Action. Washington, DC: AAAS.

ASCD (Association for Supervision and Curriculum Development). 1992. Using Curriculum Frameworks for Systemic Reform. Alexandria, VA: ASCD.

Berryman, S.E., and T.R. Bailey. 1992. The Double Helix of Education & the Economy. New York: The Institute on Education and the Economy, Teachers College, Columbia University.

Blank, R.K., and M. Dalkilic. 1992. State Policies on Science and Mathematics Education 1992. Washington, DC: Council of Chief State School Officers, State Education Assessment Center.

The Business Roundtable. 1992. Essential Components of a Successful Education System: Putting Policy into Practice. New York: The Business Roundtable.

The Business Roundtable. 1989. Essential Components of a Successful Education System: The Business Roundtable Education Public Policy Agenda. New York: The Business Roundtable.

Carnegie Commission on Science, Technology, and Government. 1991. In the National Interest: The Federal Government in the Reform of K-12 Math and Science Education. New York: Carnegie Corporation.

Cohen, D.K., and D.L. Ball. 1990. Policy and practice: An overview. Educational Evaluation and Policy Analysis, 12 (3): 347-353.

Cohen, D.K., and D.L. Ball. 1990. Relations between policy and practice: A commentary. Educational Evaluation and Policy Analysis, 12 (3): 249-256.

The Commission on Chapter 1. 1992. Making Schools Work for Children in Poverty: A New Framework. Washington, DC: The Commission on Chapter 1.

Consortium for Policy Research in Education. 1991. Putting the Pieces Together: Systemic School Reform. CPRE Policy Brief R8-06-4/91. New Brunswick, NJ: Consortium for Policy Research in Education.

Darling-Hammond, L., and A. Wise. 1985. Beyond standardization: State standards and school improvement. Elementary School Journal, 85 (3): 315-336.

ECS (Education Commission of the States). 1991. Restructuring the Education System: A Consumer's Guide, Vol. 1. Denver, CO: ECS.

Fuhrman, S.H. 1993. The politics of coherence. In Designing Coherent Education Policy: Improving the System, S.H. Fuhrman, ed., 1-34. San Francisco: Jossey-Bass Publishers.

Fuhrman, S.H., and D. Massell. 1992. Issues and Strategies in Systemic Reform. New Brunswick, NJ: Consortium for Policy Research in Education.

Fullan, M. 1982. The Meaning of Educational Change. New York: Teachers College Press.

Madaus, G. 1985. Test scores as administrative mechanisms in educational policy. Phi Delta Kappan, 66 (9): 611-617.

Marshall, R., and M. Tucker. 1992. Thinking for a Living: Education and the Wealth of Nations. New York: Basic Books.

NBPTS (National Board for Professional Teaching Standards). 1991. Toward High and Rigorous Standards for the Teaching Profession: Initial Policies and Perspectives of the National Board for Professional Teaching Standards, 3rd edition. Washington, DC: NBPTS.

NGA (National Governors' Association, Task Force on School Leadership). 1986. Time for Results: The Governors' 1991 Report on Education. Washington, DC: NGA.

NRC (National Research Council). 1993. A Nationwide Education Support System for Teachers and Schools. Washington, DC: National Academy Press.

NSTA (National Science Teachers Association). 1992. NSTA Standards for Science Teacher Certification. Washington, DC: NSTA.

NSTA (National Science Teachers Association). 1983. NSTA Standards for Science Teacher Preparation. Washington, DC: NSTA.

Oakes, J. 1987. Improving Inner-City Schools: Current Directions in Urban District Reform. Santa Monica, CA: RAND Corporation.

O'Day, J.A., and M.S. Smith. 1993. Systemic reform and educational opportunities. In Designing Coherent Education Policy: Improving the System, S.H. Fuhrman, ed., 1-34. San Francisco: Jossey-Bass Publishers.

Rigden, D. 1992. Business and the Schools: A Guide to Effective Programs. 2nd edition. New York: Council for Aid to Education.

Sarason, S.B. 1990. The Predictable Failure of Educational Reform: Can We Change Course Before It's Too Late? San Francisco: Jossey-Bass Publishers.

Shavelson, R.J., L.M. McDonnell, and J. Oakes, eds. 1989. Indicators for Monitoring Mathematics and Science Education: A Sourcebook. Santa Monica, CA: RAND Corporation.

Sigma Xi. 1994. Scientists, Educators and National Standards: Action at the Local Level. Research Triangle Park, NC: Sigma Xi.

Tyson-Bernstein, H. 1988. America's Textbook Fiasco: A Conspiracy of Good Intentions. Washington, DC: Council for Basic Education.

Wilson, K.G., and B. Daviss. 1994. Redesigning Education. New York: Henry Holt.

observe

Learn

Interact

Change

OF ATOMS H TO Ar

Achieving the high
standards outlined for
science education
requires and deserves
the combined and
continued support of
all Americans.

Epilogue

The *National Science Education Standards* describe a vision and provide a first step on a journey of educational reform that might take a decade or longer. At this point, the easy portion of the journey is complete; we have a map. The scientific and education communities have labored to reach agreement on what students should understand and be able to do, how students should be taught, and means for assessing students' understandings, abilities, and dispositions in science. The *Standards* took an insightful and innovative step by suggesting that the responsibility for improving scientific literacy extends beyond those in classrooms and schools to the entire educational system. ▌ The real journey of educational reform and the consequent improvement of scientific literacy begins with the implementation of these standards. The National Research Council now passes the challenge to all those who must assume the ultimate responsibility for reform. Scientists, science teacher educators, state departments of education, local school boards, business and industry, governmental and nongovernmental agencies, school administrators, teachers, parents, and students all have a role to play.

Science teachers have been involved in the development of the science education standards, because they have a central role in implementing them. But it would be a massive injustice and complete misunderstanding of the *Standards* if science teachers were left with the full responsibility for implementation. All of the science education community—curriculum developers, superintendents, supervisors, policy makers, assessment specialists, scientists, teacher educators—must act to make the vision of these standards a reality. Anyone who has read all or part of the *Standards* has some responsibility in the reform of science education. With distributed leadership and coordinated changes in practice among all who have responsibility for science education reform, advances in science education can rapidly accumulate and produce recognizable improvement in the scientific literacy of all students and future citizens.

Recognizing the challenge these standards present, we encourage

- Students to use the *Standards* to set personal learning goals and experience the satisfaction of understanding the natural world;

- Teachers of science to use the *Standards* as the basis for improving science content, teaching, and assessment;

- Science supervisors to use the *Standards* to implement new, long-range plans for improving science education at the state and local levels;

- Science educators to change programs in colleges and universities and develop exemplary materials based on the *Standards;*

- School administrators to focus attention on the need for materials, equipment, and staff development aligned with the *Standards;*

- Those who work in museums, zoos, and science centers to use the *Standards* as an opportunity to collaborate in providing rich science learning experiences for students;

- Parents and community members to use the *Standards* to contribute to their children's science education and generate support for higher-quality school science programs;

- Scientists and engineers to use the *Standards* to work with school personnel to initiate and sustain the improvement of school science programs;

- Business and industry to use the *Standards* to help schools and science teachers with guidance and resources for developing high-quality programs; and

- Legislators and public officials to strive for policies and funding priorities aligned with the *National Science Education Standards.*

The challenge is large, significant, and achievable. It also is too much to place on the shoulders of any one group. Achieving the high standards outlined for science education requires the combined and continued support of all Americans.

Appendix

NATIONAL COMMITTEE ON SCIENCE EDUCATION STANDARDS AND ASSESSMENT

Klausner, Richard D. (Chair), Director, National Cancer Institute, NIH, Bethesda, Maryland.

Ebert*, James D. (Past Chair), Professor of Biology, The Johns Hopkins University, Baltimore, Maryland.

Alberts*, Bruce, President, National Academy of Sciences, Washington, District of Columbia.

Alexander*, Joseph K., Jr., Deputy Assistant Administrator for Science, Environmental Protection Agency, Washington, District of Columbia.

Arceneaux, Janice M. H., Specialist, Magnet Programs Department, Houston Independent School District, Houston, Texas.

Atkin, Myron J., Professor of Education, Stanford University, Palo Alto, California.

Barton*, Jacqueline K., Professor of Chemistry, Division of Chemistry and Chemical Engineering, California Institute of Technology, Pasadena, California.

Belter, Catherine A., Chair, National Parent Teacher Association Education Commission, Springfield, Virginia.

Boyce, Joseph M., Mars Scientist, Solar System Exploration Division, NASA, Washington, District of Columbia

Brown, Rexford G., Founding Executive Director, P.S. 1, Denver, Colorado.

Brunkhorst, Bonnie J., Professor of Science Education, Geology, Institute for Science Education, California State University, San Bernadino, California.

Bugliarello, George, President, Polytechnic University, Brooklyn, New York.

Chamot*, Dennis, Associate Executive Director, Commission on Engineering and Technical Systems, National Research Council, Washington, District of Columbia.

Delacote, Goery, Executive Director, The Exploratorium, San Francisco, California.

Frye, Shirley M., Mathematics Educator, Scottsdale, Arizona.

Glaser, Robert, Director, Learning Research and Development Center, University of Pittsburgh, Pittsburgh, Pennsylvania.

Goodlad, John I., Director, Center for Educational Renewal; Professor of Education, University of Washington, Seattle, Washington.

Hernandez, Sonia C., Special Assistant to the Superintendents of Public Instruction, California State Department of Education, Sacramento, California.

Keller, Thomas E., President, Council of State Science Supervisors; Science Education Specialist, Maine Department of Education, Augusta, Maine.

Lang*, Michael, Past President, Council of State Science Supervisors; Instructional Specialist for Science, Phoenix Urban Systemic Initiative, Phoenix, Arizona.

Linder-Scholer, William, Executive Director, SCIMATH(MN), St. Paul, Minnesota.

LongReed, William, Biology Teacher, Tuba City High School, Tuba City, Arizona.

McLain, Sandra Stephens, Science Teacher, Joseph Keels Elementary School, Columbia, South Carolina.

Malcom*, Shirley M., Head, Directorate for Education and Human Resources Program, American Association for the Advancement of Science, Washington, District of Columbia.

Mills, Richard P., Commissioner of Education, Vermont State Department of Education, Montpelier, Vermont.

Mohling, Wendell G., Associate Executive Director, National Science Teachers Association, Arlington, Virginia.

Oakes, Jeannie, Professor of Education, University of California, Los Angeles, California.

Oglesby, James R., Dissemination Director, Project 2061, American Association for the Advancement of Science, Washington, District of Columbia.

Ollie, C. Arthur, Assistant Minority Leader, Iowa State House of Representatives, Clinton, Iowa.

Payzant*, Thomas W., Assistant Secretary for Elementary and Secondary Education, Department of Education, Washington, District of Columbia.

Rowe, Mary Budd, Professor of Science Education, Stanford University, Palo Alto, California.

Russell, Juanester Colbert, Principal, Daniel Boone Elementary School, University City, Missouri.

Sanchez, Bobby J., Southern Regional Coordinator, New Mexico MESA, Las Cruces, New Mexico.

Scott, Lana, Client Services, Epic Systems Corporation, Madison, Wisconsin.

Stokes, Gerald M., Director, Global Studies Program, Pacific Northwest Laboratory, Richland, Washington.

Tinker, Robert F., Physicist and Chief Science Officer, Technical Education Research Center, Cambridge, Massachusetts.

Trimble, Virginia L., Professor of Physics, University of California at Irvine, Irvine, California; Astronomy Department, University of Maryland at College Park, College Park, Maryland.

Wyatt, Terry L., Teacher, Physics and Chemistry, Roy C. Start High School, Toledo, Ohio.

Zen, E-an, Professor, Department of Geology, University of Maryland, College Park, Maryland.

past members

CHAIR'S ADVISORY COMMITTEE

Klausner, Richard D. (Chair), Director, National Cancer Institute, NIH, Bethesda, Maryland.

Aldridge, Bill G., Director of Special Projects, Former Executive Director, National Science Teachers Association, Arlington, Virginia.

Carley, Wayne, Executive Director, National Association of Biology Teachers, Reston, Virginia

Gates*, James, Past Executive Director, National Council of Teachers of Mathematics, Reston, Virginia.

Groat, Charles, Executive Director, Center for Coastal Energy and Environmental Resources, Baton Rouge, Louisiana. (Earth Sciences Coalition)

Lapp, Douglas, Executive Director, National Science Resources Center, Washington, District of Columbia.

McWethy*, Patricia, Executive Director, National Science Education Leadership Association, Arlington, Virginia.

Rosen, Linda, Executive Director, National Council of Teachers of Mathematics, Reston, Virginia.

Rutherford, James, Chief Education Officer and Director, Project 2061, American Association for the Advancement of Science, Washington, District of Columbia.

Speece, Susan P., Associate Dean of Instruction, Division of Mathematics, Science, and Engineering, Fresno City College, Fresno, California. (National Association of Biology Teachers)

Spooner, William, Director, High School Education, North Carolina Department of Public Instruction, Raleigh, North Carolina. (Council of State Science Supervisors)

Stage, Elizabeth K., Co-Director, New Standards Project—Science, Oakland, California.

Stith, James H., Professor of Physics, Ohio State University, Columbus, Ohio. (American Association of Physics Teachers)

Ware, Sylvia, Director, Education Division, American Chemical Society, Washington, District of Columbia.

Wheeler, Gerald F., Executive Director, National Science Teachers Association, Arlington, Virginia.

past members

EXECUTIVE EDITORIAL COMMITTEE

Klausner, Richard D. (Chair), Director, National Cancer Institute, NIH, Bethesda, Maryland.

Alberts, Bruce, President, National Academy of Sciences, Washington, District of Columbia.

Black, Paul, Professor, Science Education, Center for Educational Studies, King's College, London, United Kingdom.

Brunkhorst, Bonnie J., Professor of Science Education, Geology, Institute for Science Education, California State University, San Bernadino, California.

Ezell, Danine L., Teacher, Biology and General Science; Computer/Math/Science Magnet Coordinator, Bell Junior High School, San Diego, California.

Kahle, Jane Butler, Condit Professor of Science Education, Miami University, Oxford, Ohio.

Pine, Jerome, Professor of Biophysics, Physics Department, California Institute of Technology, Pasadena, California.

Rutherford, James, Chief Education Officer and Director, Project 2061, American Association for the Advancement of Science, Washington, District of Columbia.

Spooner, William, Director, High School Education, North Carolina Department of Public Instruction, Raleigh, North Carolina.

Stokes, Gerald, Director, Global Studies Program, Battelle Pacific Northwest Laboratory, Richland, Washington.

WORKING GROUP ON SCIENCE CONTENT STANDARDS

Bybee, Rodger W. (Chair), Executive Director, Center for Science, Mathematics, and Engineering Education, National Research Council, Washington, District of Columbia.

Abella, Isaac D., Professor of Physics, University of Chicago, Chicago, Illinois.

Borgford, Christie L., Project Director, The Role of the Laboratory, Department of Chemistry, Portland State University, Portland, Oregon.

Eisenkraft, Arthur, Science Coordinator, Bedford Public Schools, Bedford, New York.

Elgin, Sarah C., Professor of Biology, Biochemistry and Molecular Biophysics, Washington University, St. Louis, Missouri.

Ezell, Danine L., Teacher, Biology and General Science; Computer/Math/Science Magnet Coordinator, Bell Junior High School, San Diego, California.

Gray, JoAnne S., Assistant Principal, Staff Development, Lillian R. Nicholson Specialty School for Science and Math, Chicago, Illinois; formerly Science Department Chair, George Henry Corliss High School, Chicago, Illinois.

Heikkinen, Henry W., Co-Director, Mathematics and Science Teaching Center; Professor of Chemistry and Biochemistry, University of Northern Colorado, Greeley, Colorado.

Jackson, Laura A., Elementary and Middle Level Science Specialist, Columbia Public School District, Columbia, Missouri.

Marinez, Diana I., Dean, Science and Technology College, Texas A&M University, Corpus Christi, Texas.

Moore, C. Bradley, Professor, Department of Chemistry, University of California, Berkeley, California.

Pratt, Harold A., Senior Staff Associate, Biological Sciences Curriculum Study, Colorado Springs, Colorado.

Ridky, Robert W., Associate Professor, Department of Geology, University of Maryland, College Park, Maryland.

Smith, Patricia J., Teacher and Chair (retired), Science Department, Air Academy High School, Colorado Springs, Colorado.

Sneider, Cary, Director, Astronomy and Physics Education, Lawrence Hall of Science, University of California, Berkeley, California.

Snow, John, Dean, College of Geosciences, University of Oklahoma, Norman, Oklahoma.

Sydner-Gordon, Judith, TEAMS, Science Distance Learning Instructor, Los Angeles County Office of Education, Downey, California.

Williams, David R., Earth Science Teacher, Caesar Rodney Junior High School, Camden, Delaware.

WORKING GROUP ON SCIENCE TEACHING STANDARDS

Worth, Karen (Chair), Senior Associate, Education Development Center; Faculty Member, Wheelock College, Newton, Massachusetts.

Altman, Lynn Talton., Science Coordinator, Greenville County School District, Greenville, South Carolina.

Bingman, Kenneth J., Biology Teacher, Shawnee Mission West High School, Shawnee Mission, Kansas.

Brooks, Rhonda, Physical Science Teacher, Albuquerque Academy, Albuquerque, New Mexico.

Dyasi, Hubert M., Director, The Workshop Center for Open Education, City College of New York, New York.

Gallagher, James J., Professor of Science Education, College of Education, Michigan State University, East Lansing, Michigan.

Kuerbis, Paul J., Professor, Education Department, The Colorado College, Colorado Springs, Colorado.

Lopez-Freeman, Maria Alicia, Director, Center for Teacher Leadership, California Science Project, University of California, Office of the President, Oakland, California.

Loucks-Horsley, Susan, Senior Associate, The National Center for Improving Science Education, Tucson, Arizona.

Padilla, Michael J., Department of Science Education, University of Georgia, Athens, Georgia.

Pine, Jerry, Professor of Biophysics, Physics Department, California Institute of Technology, Pasadena, California.

Sink, Judy K., Instructor, Science Laboratory, Appalachian State University; Teacher, Hardin Park Elementary School, Boone, North Carolina.

Sprague, Susan, Director, Science/Social Science Resource Center, Mesa Public Schools, Mesa, Arizona.

Van Burgh, Dana, Jr., Co-Director, Project FutureScience; Teacher (retired), Earth Science and Field Science Programs, Dean Morgan Junior High School, Casper, Wyoming.

Walton, Edward D., Coordinator, Physical Science, Center for Science and Mathematics Education, California State Polytechnic University, Pomona, California.

Ward, Debra Susan L., Science and Mathematics Teacher, Carlisle Public Schools, Carlisle, Arkansas.

Zook, Douglas P., Assistant Professor of Science Education, Boston University, Boston, Massachusetts.

WORKING GROUP ON SCIENCE ASSESSMENT STANDARDS

Champagne, Audrey B. (Chair), Professor of Chemistry, Department of Chemistry; Professor of Education, Department of Educational Theory and Practice, State University of New York at Albany, Albany, New York.

Badders, William D., Science Resource Teacher, Cleveland Public Schools, Cleveland, Ohio.

Black, Paul J., Professor of Science Education, Center for Educational Studies, King's College, London, United Kingdom.

Bond, Lloyd, Professor, Education Research Methodology, Center for Education Research and Evaluation, University of North Carolina, Greensboro, North Carolina.

Clark, Richard C., Science Specialist (retired), Minnesota Department of Education, Minneapolis, Minnesota.

Comfort, Kathleen B., Senior Research Associate, Project 2061, American Association for the Advancement of Science, Washington, District of Columbia.

Greeno, James G., Professor of Education, School of Education, Stanford University, Stanford, California.

Kimmel, Ernest W., Jr., Executive Director, Academic Services, College Board Programs, Educational Testing Service, Princeton, New Jersey.

Kjeldsen, Barbara J., School Counselor, Kokomo High School Downton Campus, Kokomo, Indiana.

Lawrenz, Frances, Professor of Science Education, Department of Curriculum and Instruction, University of Minnesota, Minneapolis, Minnesota.

Litman, Doris L., Director (retired), Division of Science Education, Pittsburgh Public Schools, Pittsburgh, Pennsylvania.

Minstrell, James, Teacher (retired), Physics and Integrated Physics and Mathematics, Mercer Island High School, Mercer Island, Washington.

Pane, Henrietta, Teacher, Westgate Elementary School; K-6 Science Facilitator, Westside Community Schools, Omaha, Nebraska.

Sisk, Jane S., Mathematics and Science Teacher, Mayfield Boys' Treatment Center, Calloway County Schools, Mayfield, Kentucky.

St. John, Mark, President, Inverness Research Associates, Inverness, California.

Weiss, Iris, President, Horizon Research, Inc., Chapel Hill, North Carolina.

White, David J., Math/Science Coordinator, Barre Town School District, Barre Town, Vermont.

ADDITIONAL INDIVIDUALS WHO LENT SUPPORT TO THE PROJECT

Alberts, Bruce, President, National Academy of Sciences, Washington, District of Columbia.

Anderson, Don L., Professor of Geophysics, Seismological Laboratory, California Institute of Technology, Pasadena, California.

Ayala, Francisco J., Donald Bren Professor of Biological Sciences, University of California, Irvine, California.

Billington, David T., Professor, Civil Engineering and Operations Research, School of Engineering and Applied Science, Princeton University, Princeton, New Jersey.

Carlyon, Earl, Manchester High School, Manchester, Connecticut.

Duschl, Richard A., Associate Professor of Science Education, University of Pittsburgh, Pittsburgh, Pennsylvania.

Ebert, James D., Professor of Biology, The Johns Hopkins University, Baltimore, Maryland.

English, Janet, Serrano Intermediate School, Lake Forest, California.

Epstein, Samuel, Division of Geological and Planetary Sciences, California Institute of Technology, Pasadena, California.

Florio, David, Consultant, Washington, District of Columbia.

Goldsmith, Timothy, Department of Biology, Yale University, New Haven, Connecticut.

Goodstein, David, Professor of Physics, California Institute of Technology, Pasadena, California.

Gray, Harry B., Beckman Institute, California Institute of Technology, Pasadena, California.

Hazen, Robert, Carnegie Institute of Washington, Washington, District of Columbia.

Hoffman, Kenneth, Professor of Mathematics, Massachusetts Institute of Technology, Cambridge, Massachusetts.

Holton, Gerald, Professory of Physics, Harvard University, Cambridge, Massachusetts.

Johnson, George B., Department of Biology, Washington University, St. Louis, Missouri.

Kahle, Jane Butler, Condit Professor of Science Education, Miami University, Oxford, Ohio.

Kirschner, Marc W., Department of Cell Biology, Harvard Medical School, Cambridge, Massachusetts.

Labinger, Jay A., Beckman Institute, California Institute of Technology, Pasadena, California.

McInerney, Joseph D., Director, Biological Sciences Curriculum Center, Colorado Springs, Colorado.

Moore, John A., Emeritus Professor of Biology, University of California, Riverside, California.

Pister, Karl S., Chancellor, University of California, Santa Cruz, California.

Pollard, Thomas D., Department of Cell Biology and Anatomy, The Johns Hopkins University School of Medicine, Baltimore, Maryland.

Press, Frank, Cecil and Ida Green Senior Research Fellow, Carnegie Institution of Washington, Washington, District of Columbia.

Raven, Peter H., Director, Missouri Botanical Garden, St. Louis, Missouri.

Rigden, John S., Professor of Physics, University of Missouri, St. Louis, Missouri.

Rubin, Vera, Department of Terrestrial Magnetism, Carnegie Institute of Washington, District of Columbia.

Silver, Leon Theodore, Division of Geological and Planetary Sciences, California Institute of Technology, Pasadena, California.

Singer, Maxine, President, Carnegie Institute of Washington, Washington, District of Columbia.

Smith, Philip M., Executive Officer (former), National Research Council, Washington, District of Columbia

Stolper, Edward M., Professor of Geology, California Institute of Technology, Pasadena, California.

Trefil, James, Robinson Professor, George Mason University, Fairfax, Virginia.

Waldvogel, Jerry, Biology Program, Clemson University, Clemson, South Carolina.

SPECIAL THANKS TO FUNDERS

Bither, Eve, Acting Director, Office of Reform, Assistance, and Dissemination, U.S. Department of Education, Washington, District of Columbia.

Eckstrand, Irene, Acting Director, Office of Science Education, National Institutes of Health, Bethesda, Maryland.

Owens, Frank C., Director, Education Division, Office of Human Resources and Education, National Aeronautics and Space Administration, Washington, District of Columbia.

Williams, Luther, Assistant Director, Education and Human Resources, National Science Foundation, Arlington, Virginia.

Additional thanks for the many efforts of the following people:

Erma Anderson, Cathy Chetney, Janet Coffey, Barbara Cozzens, Doug Disrud, Cynthia Doherty, Megan Fitch, Edith Gummer, Lolita Jackmon, Keith Lutman, Sue McCutchen, Tonya Miller, Darlene Scheib, Maureen Shiflett, Sam Spiegel, Ginny Van Horne, Judy Van Kirk, John Weigers, Yvonne Wise.

Index

criteria for selection of, 109-110

curriculum and, 20, 22-23, 103, 110, 111, 212-214

in development of student goals, 30

diversity of learning experiences and, 20, 221-222

earth and space science, 106
    grades K-4, 130-134
    grades 5-8, 158-161
    grades 9-12, 187-190

examples of implementation, 34-35, 39, 47-49, 64-66, 80-81, 124-125, 131-133, 136, 146-147, 150-153, 162-164, 182-183, 194-196, 202-203, 215-217

grades K-4, 110
    Standard A, 121-123
    Standard B, 123-127
    Standard C, 127-129
    Standard D, 130-134
    Standard E, 135-138
    Standard F, 138-141
    Standard G, 141

grades 5-8, 110
    Standard A, 143-148
    Standard B, 149-155
    Standard C, 155-158
    Standard D, 158-161
    Standard E, 161-166
    Standard F, 166-170
    Standard G, 170-171

grades 9-12, 110
    Standard A, 173-176
    Standard B, 176-181
    Standard C, 181-187
    Standard D, 187-190
    Standard E, 190-193
    Standard F, 193-199
    Standard G, 200-202

history and nature of science, 104, 107
    grades K-4, 141
    grades 5-8, 170-171
    grades 9-12, 200-202

implementation, 7, 103, 110-112

life science, 106
    grades K-4, 127-129
    grades 5-8, 155-158
    grades 9-12, 181-187

local considerations, 231

personal and social perspectives of science
    grades K-4, 138-141
    grades 5-8, 166-170
    grades 9-12, 193-199

physical science, 106
    grades K-4, 123-127
    grades 5-8, 149-155
    grades 9-12, 176-181

presentation format, 108-109

program standards and, 209-210, 212, 213

rationale, 104

scientific inquiry, 104, 105
    grades K-4, 121-123
    grades 5-8, 143-148

    grades 9-12, 173-176

system standards and, 230-231

technology and science, 106-107
    grades K-4, 135-138
    grades 5-8, 161-166
    grades 9-12, 190-193

unifying concepts and processes, 104-105, 115-119

Council of State Science Supervisors, 14

Creative thinking, 46

Critical thinking, 33, 145, 175

Curriculum
    assessment practice and, 87, 211
    college/university preparation of science teachers, 61, 238
    components of, 22, 212
    content standards and, 6-7, 20, 22-23, 103, 110, 111
    coordination across subjects, 214
    defined, 2-3, 22
    developmentally appropriate, 212-214
    development of student goals and, 30
    equity issues in design of, 222
    flexibility, 30, 213
    framework, 211
    mathematics-science coordination, 214-218
    patterns in program design, 212-214
    program standards, 7-8
    research and development process, 213
    selection of units and courses of study, 211
    social considerations, 231
    teaching practice consistent with, 211
    teaching standards for planning of, 30-31

Curriculum and Evaluation Standards for School Mathematics, 13

D

Diet and nutrition, 139, 140, 168, 197

Disabilities and handicaps, 37
    access to learning opportunities, 20, 221
    assessment of students with, 86, 222

District level
    assessment activities, 89-90
    changes in emphases in system standards, 240
    in educational system, 227, 228
    implementation of program standards, 8, 210
    implementation of standards, example of, 234-237
    science program planning, 51-52, 211-212

Duration of class, 37

E

Earth and space science
    developing student understanding
        grades K-4, 130-134
        grades 5-8, 158-159
        grades 9-12, 187-189
    earth system, 159-160, 189
    evolution of earth, 160, 189-190
    fundamental concepts underlying standards for
        grades K-4, 134
        grades 5-8, 159-161
        grades 9-12, 189-190

history and nature of science, content standards for, 200-202

life science content standards, 181-187

personal and social perspectives of science, content standards for understanding, 193-199

physical science content standards, 176-181

science and technology, content standards for understanding, 190-193

science as inquiry in, content standards for, 173-176

unifying concepts and processes in, 104-105, 115-119

Graduation requirements, 231

H

Health science, 138-141, 157, 167, 168, 197-198

History and nature of science, 104, 107

culture and traditions of science, 21

developing student understanding

grades K-4, 141

grades 5-8, 170

grades 9-12, 200

example of classroom activity, 194-196

fundamental concepts underlying standards for

grades K-4, 141

grades 5-8, 170-171

grades 9-12, 200-204

grades K-4, content standards for, 141

grades 5-8, content standards for, 170-171

grades 9-12, content standards for, 200-202

student evaluations of scientific inquiries, 202-203

Human biology, 156-157, 186, 187

natural and human-induced hazards, 168-169, 198-199

I

Implementation of standards, 243-245

activities in, 244-245

challenges, 2, 9

changing emphases in assessment practice, 100

changing emphases in professional development, 72

changing emphases in teaching practice, 52

content standards, 103, 110, 111-112

equity in, 2, 16, 20

example of system functioning in, 234-237

learning environment for, 13

local contexts and policies in, 8, 29

long-term commitment, 13

as ongoing process, 9

professional development standards, 219

program standards, 210

responsibility for, 244

science content standards, 6-7

science program standards, 7-8

science teaching standards, 29, 137

system-wide participation in, 9, 12, 21

Inquiry. *See* Scientific inquiry

L

Laboratories, 220

Lawrence Hall of Science, 14

Leadership

continuity in policy and, 231-232

for reform of education of science teachers, 238

science program, 211-212, 223-224

Life science

cellular studies, 184-185

characteristics of organisms, 129

developing student understanding

grades K-4, 127-129

grades 5-8, 155-156

grades 9-12, 181-184

diversity and adaptation of organisms, 158

environmental studies, 129

evolutionary concepts, 185

fundamental concepts underlying standards for

grades K-4, 129

grades 5-8, 156-158

grades 9-12, 184-187

grades K-4, content standards for, 106, 127-129

grades 5-8, content standards for, 106, 155-158

grades 9-12, content standards for, 106, 181-187

interdependence of organisms, 186

life cycles of organisms, 129

living systems studies, 156-157, 186-187

populations and ecosystems, 157-158

regulation and behavior, 157, 187

reproduction and heredity, 157, 185

M

Mathematics, 116-117, 148, 175, 176

coordination with science program, 214-218

Measurement, as science practice, 118

skills in grades K-4, 126-127

skills in grades 5-8, 149

Musical instruments, 47-49

N

National Association of Biology Teachers, 14

National Committee on Science Education Standards and Assessment (NCSESA), 14-15

National Council of Teachers of Mathematics (NCTM), 13, 15, 218

National Education Goals Panel, 13

National Governors Association, 13

National Research Council (NRC), 13, 14, 15

National Science Education Standards

conceptual basis, 19-21

guide to using, 15-16, 17

historical evolution, 13-15

role of, 12

terminology, 22-24

See also Goals of standards; Implementation of standards; *specific standard*

National Science Foundation, 14

National Science Resources Center, 14

National Science Teachers Association, 14

Nation at Risk, A, 14

relationship to student's lives, 212-213
resources for teaching, 218-221
role of, 209-210
school scheduling, 219
Standard A, 210-212
Standard B, 212-214
Standard C, 214-218
Standard D, 218-221
Standard E, 221-222
Standard F, 222-224
support for teachers and teaching, 211, 219, 222-224
system standards and, 230-231
teaching practice, 211
Public perception and understanding
of assessment practice, 85, 89, 211
of system reform, 238

R

Race/ethnicity, assessment and, 85-86
Research activities for professional development, 58
Resource management in teaching, 43-45, 168
adaptation of externally produced materials, 213
assessment standards, 79
budget planning, 220
materials-support infrastructure, 220
necessities for scientific inquiry, 220
physical space requirements, 220
policy-making and, 232
for professional development of teachers, 70
program standard, 218-221
resources outside the school, 45, 220-221
responsibility for, 218
science program planning, 51-52
to sustain and encourage reform, 223
teachers as resource, 218-219
time as resource, 219
Risk-benefit analysis, as scientific concept, 167, 169

S

Safety, 44
Scheduling of classes, 44, 219
Science for All Americans, 14, 15
Science Olympiad, 39-41
Scientific inquiry, 23-24
abilities for, 145, 148, 175-176
grades K-4, 122-123
grades 5-8, 145-148
grades 9-12, 175-176
adult models of, 37, 50-51
assessment of student achievement, 98-100
characteristics of, 2
classroom environment for, 44
classroom resources for, 220
in college/university preparation of science
teachers, 61
defined, 214
developing student abilities and understanding
grades K-4, 121-122
grades 5-8, 143-145
grades 9-12, 173-175

in development of teaching and learning models, 31
example of implementation in classroom, 34-35,
146-147
forms of, in classroom, 33
fundamental concepts underlying standards for
grades K-4, 123
grades 5-8, 148
grades 9-12, 176
goals for students, 13, 105
grades K-4, content standard for, 105, 121-123
grades 5-8, content standard for, 105, 143-148
grades 9-12, content standard for, 105, 173-176
historical development of, standards for
understanding, 104, 107
meaning of, to students, 173-174
peer review of, 174
personal and social development and, 104, 107
professional development standards for teachers, 59
as program component, 214
responsibilities of system personnel in teaching of,
212
in science learning process, 2, 105
scientific method and, 144-145
skills assessment, 6
student collaboration in, 50
student evaluation of scientific studies and results,
171, 202-203
teacher's management of, 33, 36
technology as design and, 107, 166
See also Scientific literacy
Scientific knowledge and understanding
assessment of, 82
of cause-and-effect, 145
of chemical reactions, 179
college/university education of teachers, 60-61, 238
of constancy and change, 117-118
cultural and traditional elements of, 21
curriculum design for, 213
depth and breadth, 59, 110
of earth and space, 130-134, 158-161, 187-190
of energy, 154, 155, 157, 178, 180-181, 186-187, 189
of environmental and resource issues, 139, 140,
198-199
of evolution and equilibrium, 119
of form and function, 119
goals of standards, 13
of health, 138-140, 141
as human endeavor, 141, 170, 200-201
lifelong learning, 68-69
of living systems and organisms, 127-129, 155-158,
186-187
of measurement, 118, 126-127, 149
of motions and forces, 127, 154, 179-180
of natural selection, 181-184, 185
nature of, 23
pedagogical content knowledge, 62-68
of population issues, 140
of prediction, 116-117, 145, 148
of probability, 116-117

professional development standards for teachers, 59-61

of properties of objects and materials, 123, 126-127, 149-154, 178-179

of risk-benefit analysis, 167, 169

of scientific description, 145, 148, 176

of scientific explanation, 117, 122-123, 145, 148, 174, 175-176, 201

scientific inquiry and, 144-145

sources of, 31

of substance abuse, 140

of systems analysis, 116-117

teacher's, 28

of technological design, 135-138, 161-166, 192-193

unifying concepts and processes in, 104-105, 115-119

use of evidence, 117, 145, 174, 201

use of scientific models, 116, 117, 159, 175

See also Scientific inquiry

Scientific literacy

characteristics of, 21, 22

cultural and traditional elements of, 21

defined, 22

developmental approach, 18

goals of standards, 13

importance of, 1-2, 11-12

See also Scientific inquiry; Scientific knowledge and understanding

Scientists, 233-238, 245

Self-directed learning, 88

Sexual behavior and reproduction, 156, 158, 168, 197-198

Social issues, 138-141

Solar system, 215-217

State government

changes in emphases in system standards, 239

in educational system, 227-228, 229

national standards and, 12

resource allocation, 232

system standards, 230-231

in teacher certification, 229, 230

Students

assessment reports, 43, 88-89

classroom inquiry, 33, 36

classroom organization of, 31-32

classroom participation, 36-37

as community of science learners, 45-46

determinants of learning, 28, 29

development of goals for, 30

encouraging classroom collaboration and discourse, 36, 50

grouping of, 222

in implementation of standards, 244

involvement in design of learning environment, 45, 46-50

program considerations, 212-213

responsibility for learning, 27, 36

self-assessment, 42, 88

social and cultural considerations in teaching strategies, 32, 37

student-teacher relationship, 29

teacher's respect for, 46

Substance abuse, 140, 168, 197

Systems analysis, 116-117

applied to educational systems, 227-228

earth and space science, 158-161, 187-190

interdependence of organisms, 186

living systems, 156-158, 186-187

System standards, 8

changes in emphases in, 239-240

congruence among standards, 230-231

continuity in policy-making, 231-232

coordination of policies, 231

equity considerations, 232-233

examples of implementation, 34-35, 39, 64-66, 124-125, 150-153, 162-164, 234-237

ongoing evaluation of policy, 233

resource considerations in policy-making, 232

responsibility for reform, 8, 233-238

role of, 227

Standard A, 230-231

Standard B, 231

Standard C, 231-232

Standard D, 232

Standard E, 232-233

Standard F, 233

Standard G, 233-238

T

Teacher collaboration

for assessment, 67

in college/university preparation of science teachers, 61

for design of professional development programs, 71

for development of pedagogical content knowledge, 63-68

development of scoring rubrics for assessment, 93

mathematics-science, 214-218

new forms of, 67

with outside institutions, 223

for professional development, 57-58

for research on practice, 223

school environment for, 222-223

for science program planning, 32, 51

with scientists, 233-238

for self-assessment, 69

Teaching practice

as active learning process, 2, 20, 28

assessment of, 6, 42-43

assessment practice consistent with, 211

classroom organization of students, 31-32

consistent with curriculum framework, 211

culture and traditions of science, 21

determinants of student learning, 28, 29

equitable access to opportunities for students, 221-222

flexibility, 213

good qualities, 12, 218-219

grouping of students, 222

Credits

Cover, title page, and p. 16. Students at Glebe Elementary School, Arlington, VA, work on an activity from *Organisms,* a first-grade unit in the Science and Technology for Children (STC) curriculum program. Photographer: Eric Long, courtesy National Science Resources Center (NSRC).

Cover and p. 18. Students at Bailey's Elementary School, Fairfax, VA, work on an activity from *Ecosystems,* a fifth-grade STC unit. Photographer: Dane A. Penland, courtesy NSRC.

Cover and p. 19. Student at Bailey's Elementary School, Fairfax, VA, works on an activity from *Animal Studies,* a fourth-grade STC unit. Photographer: Dane A. Penland, courtesy NSRC.

Cover and p. 81. Student at Watkins Elementary School, Washington, DC, works on an activity from *Chemical Tests,* a third-grade STC unit. Photographer: Dane A. Penland, courtesy NSRC.

Cover and p. 102. Students at Watkins Elementary School, Washington, DC, work on an activity from *Chemical Tests,* a third-grade STC unit. Photographer: Jeff Tinsley, courtesy NSRC.

Cover and p. 173. Fairfax County, VA, high-school student. Photographer: Randy Wyant.

pages iv and 146. Teacher demonstrates pendulum. Photographer: David Powers, courtesy University of California, San Francisco.

facing page 1. Children on statue of Albert Einstein in Washington, DC, at the National Academy of Sciences. Photographer: Barry A. Wilson.